A Talent For War
The Military Biography Of
Lt Gen Sagat Singh

A Talent For War
The Military Biography Of
Lt Gen Sagat Singh

by

Maj Gen (Retd) Randhir Sinh, UYSM, AVSM, SM

Foreword by

Lt Gen (Retd) S K Sinha

(Established 1870)

United Service Institution of India
New Delhi

Vij Books India Pvt Ltd
New Delhi (India)

Published by

Vij Books India Pvt Ltd
(Publishers, Distributors & Importers)
2/19, Ansari Road
Delhi – 110 002
Phones: 91-11-43596460, 91-11-47340674
Fax: 91-11-47340674
e-mail: vijbooks@rediffmail.com

Copyright © 2013, United Service Institution of India, New Delhi

Paperback 2015

All rights reserved.

No part of this book may be reproduced, stored in a retrieval system, transmitted or utilized in any form or by any means, electronic, mechanical, photocopying, recording or otherwise, without the prior permission of the copyright owner. Application for such permission should be addressed to the publisher.

The views expressed in this book are those of the author in his personal capacity. These do not have any official endorsement.

DEDICATION

Dedicated to the Indian Armed Forces
Who stand as tall as their mountains
And
Their families
Who stoically follow the drum

Contents

Dedication	v
Foreword	xi
Acknowledgement	xix
Prologue	1
Denouement	1
Chapter One	15
The Rathore Legacy	15
Chapter Two	29
Command	29
Chapter Three	44
The Liberation Of Goa	44
Chapter Four	70
Toil And Turmoil	70
Chapter Five	97
IV Corps: Setting The Stage	97
Chapter Six	124
IV Corps: Into The Ring	124
Chapter Seven	163
IV Corps: The Hammer	163

Chapter Eight — 191

IV Corps: The Crowded Hour — 191

Chapter Nine — 234

The Final Trumpet — 234

Chapter Ten — 249

The Legacy Of Sagat: Generalship — 249

Bibliography — 269

Index — 287

Maps & Photographs

Maps

1. Liberation of Goa — 293
2. Pak and Indian Force Level — 295
3. Battle of Dhalai — 297
4. Northern Sector — 299
5. Central Sector — 301
6. Southern Sector — 303
7. Capture of Dacca — 305

Photographs

1. Kusumdesar — 13
2. Haveli — 14
3. With HQ Staff in Persia — 23
4. Marriage — 27
5. CO 3/3 GR — 38

Contents

6.	Confrontation at Nathu La	78
7.	With the Chogyal at Nathu La	78
8.	In Mizo Hills with Governor B K Nehru	90
9.	GOC IV Corps	96
10.	With Maj Gen Krishna Rao & Gp Capt Chandan Singh at Shamshernagar	138
11.	With Maj Gen BF Gonsalves and Brig Tom Pande at Dhalai	138
12.	With Brig R N Mishra after Battle of Akhaura	140
13.	Bunkers at Dhalai	169
14.	With Maj Gen Rocky Hira and Maj GS Sihota	169
15.	At Burichang with Brig Tom Pande & Maj OP Kaushik	170
16.	With Brig Anand Swaroop and Brig BS Sandhu. Planning the Operation	170
17.	The Surrender Ceremony	233
18.	After the Surrender with Lt Gen AAK Niazi and Maj Gen Gandharv Nagra	233
19.	With Ranvijay	244
20.	Talking to Digvijay	244

Appendices

A	Organisation Tree - IV Corps	279
B	Main Characters and Units in Chapters on IV Corps	281

FOREWORD

This biography of Lt Gen Sagat Singh written by his erudite and devoted former ADC, Maj Gen Randhir Sinh makes a most interesting reading. It describes in detail how the most distinguished battle field commander of the Indian Army conducted operations during the liberation of Goa, handled insurgency in Mizoram, broke the myth of ten feet tall Chinese soldiers by getting the better of them during a big skirmish in Sikkim and provided dynamic leadership to his Corps against all odds, leading his formation from the front in the Indo-Pak War of 1971. His outstanding leadership was a major factor contributing to the unprecedented victory of Indian arms in over a millennium. It is an unfortunate fact of our history that in the medieval and early modern period, we always succumbed to foreign invasions with disastrous consequences. Field Marshal Montgomery in his magnum opus, 'A History of Warfare' has stated, "The Rajputs were tremendously brave……..they advanced against well prepared artillery like moths in a flame." They repeatedly sacrificed their lives in wars for their country but did not win wars for their country. Lt Gen Sagat Singh showed how a war can be won for his country. He played a stellar role in the 1971 glorious victory. Over 90000 Pakistan soldiers surrendered and were made prisoners of war. A new independent nation of nearly a hundred million people was born.

I had the privilege of interacting with Sagat Singh on various occasions in three decades of our lives. We were good friends. I admired his professionalism even when we were serving together as Majors. I felt that he had a big future ahead of him. I first met him in 1948. He had risen from the ranks in the Bikaner State Army. Notwithstanding this, he was very well educated and better in this regard than most army officers of our generation. He had recently been absorbed in the Indian Army. He was commissioned in the

State Army three years before I got my commission in the Indian Army. His seniority had not then been fixed in the Indian Army. Normally State Force officers joining the Indian Army lost some seniority. He had qualified from Staff College, Quetta. This was then rare for Indian officers of the Indian Army and much rarer for an officer of the State Forces. He had also successfully served alongside the Indian Army in Persia and Iraq during the Second World War.

In 1948 Sagat was posted as GSO-2 at Headquarters Delhi Area in Delhi Cantonment. At that time I was GSO-2 (Operations) in Headquarters Western Command, which was then located in New Delhi. Delhi Area was one of the formations of Western Command. We often interacted officially. Although Delhi Area was not involved with the war in Kashmir, we often discussed the ongoing operations in Kashmir. We at times met at Vaughan Club in Delhi Cantonment. He drank hard and could hold his drinks. This had no adverse effect on him nor in any way affected his working the next morning.

Sagat's seniority was decided in his favour. His was a rare case of a State Force officer getting all his service as a commissioned officer in the State Army to reckon for seniority in the Indian Army. This made him three years senior to me. He soon became a Lt Col, while I continued to remain a Major for sixteen years till I picked up the rank of Lt Col in 1962. In early Fifties I served along with him as Instructor in the Tactical Wing of the then Infantry School at Mhow. He was an Instructor in the rank of Lt Col on the Senior Commander Course while I was an instructor in the rank of Major on the Junior Commander Course. We next served together at Army Headquarters when he was full Colonel, Deputy Director Personal Services in Adjutant General Branch. He made his mark as a competent staff officer. The then Adjutant General, Lt Gen Kumaramanglam was much impressed with him and took the unprecedented step of getting him, then a non paratrooper, appointed Commander of 50 Para Brigade. As a Brigadier, he did the required parachute jumps and qualified as a paratrooper. While he was in AG Branch, I was a Major, staff officer of Quarter Master

Foreword

General, Lt Gen B M Kaul. We crossed swords on an issue where we had different views. Our differences on this issue did not affect our personal relations and we continued to be good friends. He was too large hearted to hold this against me.

I also had an interesting interaction with Sagat after he admirably commanded 50 Para Brigade during operations in Goa. This needs to be put on record. I was in the UK doing a course at the Joint Services Staff College (now National Defence College) during the liberation of Goa. I was the only Indian officer on the course. The British Press was very anti-India and went all out to support Portugal, Britain's oldest ally. A leading newspaper had a headline "Nehru Sanctimonious Bully". I saw on BBC Television, Sagat and another friend Sucha Singh, marching into Goa. The next day as I walked into the lecture hall at the College, my colleagues gave me a standing ovation and said, "Welcome the new Imperialist and the new Aggressor." I went up to the rostrum. There was now pin drop silence. I spoke into the microphone, "This is what comes of keeping bad company". My colleagues had a hearty laugh and enjoyed the joke. I thought the matter had ended on this humorous note. On return to India, I met Sagat and told him about this exchange I had in England. He was most amused and said that I did as well in England as the Army had done in Goa!

Pakistan began its military crackdown in East Pakistan on 25 March 1971. It moved two extra infantry divisions to East Pakistan. The Government tried to ruthlessly crush the opposition of the people. There were reports of horrendous atrocities in East Pakistan. One crore refugees were forced to flee East Pakistan, seeking refuge in India. This imposed a heavy economic burden on us.

There were different views being expressed about the strategy to be adopted for the war in Pakistan. One view was that we should secure a large chunk of territory in the northern part of East Pakistan to rehabilitate the refugees there. This would also provide depth to the narrow Siliguri corridor connecting the North East. This was rightly rejected because it was not feasible to conduct such a large displacement and rehabilitation of population in the proposed lodgment area. Another view was that the main thrust into East Pakistan should be from the North which would entail much lesser crossing of water obstacles. Logistic build up would be easier than in Tripura, which had a 240 kilometre long metre gauge railway line connecting Guwahati to Dharmanagar. Yet another view was that the shortest distance to Dacca was from the East even though this required tremendous build up of logistics and crossing of numerous water obstacles including the formidable Meghna, the widest river in East Pakistan. The choice fell on having the main thrust from the East. Thus the offensive was planned with a Corps comprising two divisions advancing from the West and a division from a Corps in North plus Area units and the main thrust by a Corps of three divisions from the East. Dacca was not spelt out as an objective for the operation. Even the operation instruction issued by 4 Corps tasked the three divisions to advance deep into East Pakistan without any mention of Dacca. This may have been for different reasons. We may not have felt confident of advancing up to Dacca against strong resistance in a short war. Perhaps what happened in the 1965 Indo-Pak War may have influenced our thinking. In 1965 we had to deal with a hostile population in West Punjab while in 1971 we had a friendly population in East Pakistan. Be that as it may, a war rarely goes as planned once the conflict starts. Flexibility is a principle of war. A good commander should always be prepared to exploit opportunities as they arise in battle. Sagat Singh was a Commander with an eagle eye to exploit opportunities in battle. He showed tremendous drive to do so to the hilt. From the very beginning he had set his eyes on Dacca and had made preparations for it. Mobilising obsolescent helicopters, he prepared for heliborne operations in that war. This was the first time such operation was conducted by the Indian Army in battle. The Air Force particularly the helicopter crew responded wonderfully and undertook most hazardous operations facing tremendous risks. Sagat in a helicopter was as they say, "here, there and everywhere" during the war, inspiring his troops and directing the battle. On occasions he was flying over his leading troops and beyond. Once, his helicopter was hit by enemy machine gun fire. This did not deter either Sagat or his young Air Force pilot. Rarely in modern war has a higher commander shown such daring and dash leading his troops from the front.

It is unfortunate that Sagat did not have the best of relations with either the Army Commander Lt Gen Jagjit Singh Aurora, his immediate superior or with the Army Chief, General Sam Manekshaw. He didn't allow this to affect his carrying out his task with utmost vigour. An interesting incident has been mentioned by the author in this book. When his Corps had reached the Meghna River and he was trying to cross the river to advance to Dacca, Aurora tried to restrain him. Sagat told him that he was surprised at his reluctance when he was not only fulfilling the task given to him but achieving task plus. He successfully conducted an ad hoc and impromptu river crossing operation across one of the widest rivers of the world. This became the final blow of that war.

In 1973 I was posted to command 23 Infantry Division in Assam. The Division was still part of 4 Corps under Sagat. It had performed creditably in the Bangladesh War. I heard many stories from officers in the Division of the outstanding leadership of Sagat. He was now a national war hero. I was happy to serve under an old friend whom I had always admired. I found him a little pensive possibly because of the unfair treatment meted out to him. He got the very high award of Padma Bhushan for his contribution in the 1971 War. I had served as Deputy Adjutant General during the war and had dealt with various disciplinary cases involving officers and soldiers. There was no disciplinary case involving Sagat for corruption or any unbecoming behaviour that came to our notice. There were of course widespread rumours of his affairs with the fair sex. Perhaps these were unduly magnified and were mostly baseless. Even a sedate person like General Eisenhower the Supreme Commander in Europe was widely known for his affair with a British woman Sergeant, who was his staff car driver. This did not come in the way of his becoming the President of USA.

I served under Sagat for only a couple of months. He continued to be friendly as ever. We drank together in the evenings when I went to his Headquarters at Tezpur or when he visited my Division at Rangiya. We also played croquet to which he had lately taken. We discussed old days and also the recent war in Bangladesh. There were rumours that he would not be promoted Army Commander and he would be going to the Corps at Mathura from where he would retire after a year. Lt Gen K K Singh, junior to him, was being promoted over him and he would be serving under him. I considered it very unfortunate that the higher ups should treat a war hero who had done so much for the Country in such an unfair and unjust manner. Sagat seemed resigned to this. He never talked about this and I did not raise the matter with him as I felt it was too personal and very sensitive. He seemed to take have taken it stoically. He may have had compelling personal reasons like building a house at Jaipur not far from Mathura, to continue serving and accept an assignment under an erstwhile junior. The latter was an old friend of his. I was reminded of General Patton the best battle field senior commander of the US Army. He was treated very unfairly by his Government. Despite this he agreed to serve under General Bradley his erstwhile subordinate. Perhaps this was because of his patriotic feelings when his country was engaged in a war and needed his services. He rose to the occasion to serve his country in the ongoing war, winning further laurels in battles. India was not involved in a war in 1973 and Sagat had no patriotic compulsion to continue to serve for another year. In his position I would have resigned irrespective of any personal difficulties.

Destiny was unkind to Sagat in his retirement. He suffered personal tragedies which he bore stoically. My heart went out to him when I heard of his tragedies. He passed away in Jaipur when I was Governor of Assam. I felt a sense of personal loss at the demise of a good friend and a great General who had become a legend in his life time. India will not see the like of Sagat Singh again.

The author has most painstakingly put together incidents of the life story of this great General whom he served devotedly as

Foreword

his ADC. He has done so on the basis of extensive research and interaction with a large number of officers who had been with him in war and peace. This must have taken him years of hard work. I congratulate him for his splendid effort in writing on the life and times of a legendary General. I commend this book to every student of military history and to our present and future generations of military officers, aspiring to high command. The saga of Sagat is now a part of India's military lore.

New Delhi,
31 July 2013

Lt Gen (Retd) S K Sinha

ACKNOWLEDGEMENT

I have tried to be as accurate as possible in recording events. To my dismay I found getting timelines pat was not that easy. Several accounts of an event differed in the way people experienced or saw it. This was brought home to me forcefully when I was researching the Bangladesh War. I had maintained a diary and was present with General Sagat during most of the incidents. Nevertheless, some events did not fit into the timelines remembered by others. In the face of overwhelming evidence I had to accept that I had erred. It was a salutary lesson and I made it a point to get the timelines correct by referring to other sources. I must not be the first to realise that the urgency of an event sometimes leads one to lose one's perspective. I have allowed the Biography of Sagat to play out as others saw him and wherever possible in his own words.

There are many people to thank including those who requested anonymity. I first need to thank Mrs Jane Himmeth Singh and Maj Chandrakant Singh who salvaged the interviews conducted by the late Director of USI, Col Pyare Lal, from the archives of the USI. They dusted the cassettes, improved their digital format and even got them converted to print. The interviews conducted of Lt Gen Sagat Singh, Air Marshal Chandan Singh and Lt Gen Himmeth Singh have formed the bedrock of the narrative to the 1971 War. They allowed the main protagonists to speak for themselves. I nevertheless authenticated their timelines and versions through corroborative research.

I am grateful to Ranvijay and Damyanti, Sagat's eldest son and daughter-in-law and their highly competent daughters, Sanyogita and Meghna. They provided essential logistic support and were primary contributors to my research on Sagat's early life. My visits to Bikaner and Kusum Desar, as well as meetings with his relatives, colleagues and friends would not have been possible without their help. All personal papers held by the family were handed over to me. Their house, presided over by a serene Damyanti, was a haven.

I must thank Shri Jeoraj Singh, Sagat's younger brother and Col Mohan Singh, who provided a wealth of information on Sagat's early life. Amongst many others I need to thank Lt Gen Chiman Singh, Brig Jagmal Singh, Dr Ajit Singh and Col Nawal Singh. They filled in important blanks.

There are a host of senior retired officers I must thank who served with Sagat and unhesitatingly shared their memories. On Sagat's regimental life I need to acknowledge my late parents contribution. They knew Sagat and Kamla as friends, from the days he was a Major. Lt Gen Raj Anand and Maj Gen Tirath Verma, served under Sagat when he was a battalion commander and their contribution on the chapter on Command is evident. They were patient and excellent hosts too. Mrs Verma, in particular, provided exceptional insight into Kamla's personality. Of particular mention is the hard boiled war veteran, Havildar Pas Bahadur Rana, who saw warfare to last several lifetimes.

I am particularly grateful to General KV Krishna Rao, who made me welcome at his house in Secunderabad. His memory remains as sharp as his ramrod posture. His insights as well as reminiscences conducted over two days have proved most valuable. I have followed his advice and eschewed cheap controversy as far as possible. I particularly acknowledge my gratitude to Lt Gens OP Kaushik, GS Sihota and SS Mehta. Gen Kaushik had a wide ranging discussion with me over two days at his home in Dehra Dun. He served with Sagat during three tenures and his erudition and comprehension have been of great value and are evident throughout the book. I closely questioned him several times about the critical telephone conversation Sagat had with Lt Gen Aurora on Sagat's intentions of crossing the Meghna. The General was emphatic on the way the discussion evolved. Lt Gen Sihota welcomed me at his Chandigarh home where Mrs Sihota provided a sumptuous lunch. He was perhaps closest to Sagat during the War and his memories proved most valuable. His gallantry remains a benchmark of the War. Lt Gen SS Mehta had a long conversation at the USI which we carried over into lunch. He was an essential and gallant figure during several crucial battles. But what was more important to me was the perspective he brought into the discussion on operational art and

Acknowledgements

generalship. He will recognise his contribution to these aspects in the book.

I also need to thank Lt Gen Gambir Negi and Mrs Negi. Gambir, a second generation officer, knew Sagat when he was a child while Mrs Negi's memories of Sagat have been acknowledged in the book. Their generous lunch is still remembered. Maj Gen OP Sabharwal and his elder brother, Brig LM Sabharwal filled in the blanks during critical periods of Sagat's life. I have known the General since childhood and though I myself am now reaching a venerable old age, he and Mrs Sabharwal still treat me like their own child. This is a good opportunity to acknowledge their many kindnesses. Maj Gen Ian Cardozo provided an insight into his battalion, the outstanding 4/5 GR, as well as their part in the crucial Battle of Sylhet.

My gratitude to Maj Gen VK Singh, who has himself written a biography of Sagat. He introduced me to others who form a part of this narrative. He also provided me with much essential information on Sagat as well as his tenure in Sikkim. I interviewed late Brig MMS Bakshi the defender of Nathula, who retained his decided views on that bloody engagement. Brig Rai Singh and Lt Col Attar Singh provided essential inputs. The Brig, by the stoical manner in which he handles his injuries, remains a source of inspiration.

My thanks to my friend Ransher Ranawat, who provided a subaltern's glimpse into the dirty part of the war where it was kill or be killed. His narrative will strike a chord with every young officer. I must thank Lt Gen Karan Yadava. He provided all the papers of his father, Maj Gen Shivdayal Singh Yadava. For the first time one gets a proper perspective on the Battle of Dhalai, one of the bloodiest battles of this or any other war. The savagery and gallantry on both sides lend authenticity to the narrative. My thanks to Col Subhash Kaushik who provided a young staff officer's insight and to Mrs Kaushik for her warmth and hospitality during my stay at Secunderabad.

Amongst the many who have written to me I must especially thank Maj Gen KJS Jamwal and Maj Gen AK Verma. The former, despite personal tragedies has given useful inputs on the aftermath of the War. The latter's perceptions, at times at variance with others, rounded off the essential chapters.

My gratitude to Vijay Kumar of KBK News Graphics and his excellent cartographer Ramneek Singh, who has made some of the finest maps I have seen. I hope they will make the reader see how the Campaign shaped up. Any inaccuracy has to be laid at my door as Ramneek made exactly what I wanted.

Thanks to Brig AS Nirodi, Lt Col AK Sharma, Lt Gen PG Kamath, Brig UK Dhar and Col JP Santhanam, who were foisted parts of the draft to critique. Their suggestions were always wise but I plead guilty to not following all of them.

I must thank the Director USI, Lt Gen PK Singh and the staff of this excellent Institution for making the facilities available to me to carry out my research.

Lastly I thank my family members, including my brothers Yashoraj and Bharat, whose gentle sarcasm spurred me on when I was grappling with writers block. I especially thank my late parents who, despite being ill, patiently bore my neglect as I sat in my secluded corner trying to meet my self imposed deadline. My wife, Gayatri, remained remarkably patient and encouraging throughout these trials. The dedication is also to my son, Abhay and daughter-in-law, Karuna and the 3rd Gorkha Rifles of which he is the third generation. While I have long since passed on my torch to him, he and his men with gallantry and fortitude continue to face the travails, which our armed forces do, with honour and pride. God bless them.

I acknowledge that any errors are solely my own.

LIST OF ABBREVIATIONS AND LOCAL WORDS

ADC	aide-de-camp
AD	air defence
AG	Adjutant General
AHQ	Army Headquarters (India)
AR	Assam Rifles
ARTRAC	Army Training Command
ASC	Army Service Corps
Anda	Egg ie good things in life
Basha	thatched hut
BGS	Brigadier General Staff
Bigha	area of land
BM	Brigade Major
BOP	border outpost
BRO	Border Roads Organization
BSF	Border Security Force
Brig	Brigadier
Capt	Captain
Cmdre	Commodore

COAS or Chief	Chief of the Army Staff
CGS	Chief of General Staff
CI	counter insurgency
COS	Chief of Staff
CO	Commanding Officer
Col	Colonel
CRPF	Central Reserve Police Force
CSO	Chief Signal Officer
DIG	Deputy Inspector General
DMO	Director of Military Operations
Danda	stick ie authoritarianism
EBR	East Bengal Regiment
EME	Electrical & Mechanical Engineers
EPCAF	East Pakistan Civil Armed Force
FF	Frontier Force (Regiment)
Flt Lt	Flight Lieutenant
Gen	General
GHQ	General Headquarters (Pakistan)
Govt	government
GOC	General Officer Commanding
GSO	General Staff Officer (grades 1 to 3)
Hav	Havildar (Sergeant)
Haveli	traditional house
HQ	headquarters

Abbreviations

IA	Indian Army
Jagir	traditional land grant
JCO	Junior Commissioned Officer
Jhanda	flag ie trappings
Jhoom	periodic clearing of forest patches for cultivation
Jonga	Nissan Jonga 4WD Army Vehicle
Khud	canyon
Khichdi	meal of mixed rice and lentils (indicate a mish mash)
Kms	kilometres
Kukhri	Gorkha fighting knife
Lt	Lieutenant
Maj	Major
Maru	desert
Machan	platform generally atop a tree
MES	Military Engineering Service
MOD	Ministry of Defence
Mtr	metre
Mukti Bahini	Bangladesh freedom fighters
NCO	Non Commissioned Officer
NEFA	North East Frontier Agency
Nk	Naik (corporal)
OP	observation post

Para	parachute
Parathas	oily pancakes
POK	Pakistan Occupied Kashmir
AK	Azad Kashmir (Pakistan term)
Pongo	slang to describe the infantry
POW	Prisoner of War
Pt	point
Punjis	sharpened bamboo stakes
Rajrif	Rajputana Rifles
Razakars	irregular paramilitaries recruited by Pakistan Army for policing
Rfn	Rifleman (soldier of a rifle regiment)
Risala	horsed/ camel borne cavalry
Sahib	sir
Satyagraha	non-violent resistance
Sep	Sepoy (soldier of an infantry regiment)
SFF	Special Frontier Force
Sqn Ldr	Squadron Leader
Sub	Subedar
Thikana	chieftenship
2/3 GR	2nd Battalion the 3rd Gorkha Rifles (the units and regiments are named accordingly)
2ic	Second-in-Command

PROLOGUE

DENOUEMENT

Sound, sound the clarion, fill the fife,
Throughout the sensual world proclaim
One crowded hour of glorious life
Is worth an age without a name

— Mordaunt, Thomas Osbert

Sagat woke up early from a dreamless sleep, to the cadence of the battle raging on the Lalmai Hills, now awash with the orange hues of the rising sun. The day before had been long and arduous and he had been on the road well into the night. Regardless of how late he slept or how heavily he drank, he would invariably be up at dawn, making up for any lack of sleep by catnapping during the day. As usual his helicopter was late in landing the previous evening and though Major (Maj) Ganesh Rai, the Military Secretary, had illuminated the helipad with desperate improvisation, the pilot could not locate it in the dark and had flatly refused to hazard a landing so close to the battlefield and the enemy held Maynamati Cantonment. There was no other option but to fly back to Agartala, down a couple of whiskies with Brigadier (Brig) Raja Apte[1] and drive for nearly three hours over strange roads to Comilla where his headquarters had just that day re-located, well within enemy field artillery range. Now, though he had barely slept for four hours, he was fresh enough. It was 16 Dec 71 and Sagat was confident that before the sun set that day, it would finally see the birth of a new country.

---

1 Apte and his 81 Brigade, who had just been moved out of Sylhet, were positioned at the airfield for a heliborne operation on Dacca.

Before climbing into his helicopter Sagat held a quick meeting with the staff to fine tune the push into Dacca. They were asked to ensure three things. 101 Communication Zone Area must take control of 2 Para as they prepared to enter the outskirts of Dacca from the North; Sagat was well aware that the Commanding Officer (CO), Kulwant Singh Pannu[2] would like nothing better than a dash into Dacca and end the war on his own. The communication problems between 101 Communication Zone and 57 Mountain Division had to be resolved as the latter, with three brigades, had ringed Dacca from the North and East and he did not want any casualties due to friendly fire.[3] He asked for helicopters to be kept ready for 81 Mountain Brigade to leapfrog into Dacca if the situation so warranted.

During the rest of the day he intended to be at the decision points to chivvy the final surge of his formations into Dacca. He was well aware that the East Pakistan Government and Army Command were desperately looking for a cessation of hostilities and wanted them to remain off balance. Brig Jagdev Singh, the Chief Engineer, was to accompany him and do what he could to get the chaotic road communications through.

The helicopter did a looping curve as it flew westwards to avoid the battle raging below. The fiery orb of the sun showed Maynamati and the Lalmai Hills in stark relief so that the flowers of dust created by the artillery were clearly visible. Suddenly, silvery flashes on the horizon rapidly grew into the first of the fighter bomber sorties as they swooped down to attack the defences. Sagat was sanguine

---

2 Pannu had served under Sagat in Goa and was known for his recklessness.

3 This never came about. The Corps HQ only got in touch with 101 Communication Zone after the War was over. In a personal communication to the Author, Brig (later Maj Gen) HS Kler, Commander of 95 Brigade, was emphatic in saying that at no stage was he aware that his formation was now under 4 Corps in the chain of command. In addition, owing to some peculiar and perhaps antiquated problems of signal authentication, 301 Infantry Brigade of 23 Mountain Division, which had been put under command 57 Mountain Division for the push to Dacca, could not get in touch with the Formation. Page 245, **Operation Windfall: Emergence of Bangladesh by Brig HS Sodhi, Allied Publishers, New Delhi, 1980.**

that it was just a matter of time before the defenders capitulated and so had other things on his mind. Completely surrounded, the enemy had nowhere to go. As the helicopter flew West he could see the flat plain below, interspersed with glinting ribbons of water. These low lying alluvial plains, crisscrossed by water channels and massive rivers, get completely water logged during the Monsoons and are barely dry by December. The many water bodies had ensured that the troops were forced to march to Dacca, while the engineers constantly battled to get the wherewithal and artillery through on broken, embanked tracks and blown bridges. As the helicopter started crossing the burnished waters of the Meghna River, Sagat reflected ironically on the fact that while he had not seen a river till well into his teens, rivers had been an essential part of his military career. And now he had used the Meghna to confound his adversary who, despite the way these rivers created a ring around Dacca, failed to make them the cornerstone of his defences.

The helicopter landed at Narsingdi, the hub for the advance to Dacca. It was not far from here that 4 Guards had landed, in a daring heliborne operation on 9 Dec, under the baffled eyes of an entire Pakistan brigade, now cooped up at Bhairab Bazaar. Sagat knew that if Major General (Maj Gen) Majid, the Pak 14 Division Commander, had reacted the first day, the tenuous airhead would easily have been pushed back into the River. After that it was too late as Group Captain Chandan Singh, with his aging fleet of MI–4 helicopters, rapidly built up 57 Mountain Division. Simultaneously the engineers, through ingenuity and sheer hard work, constructed the rafts and collected an assortment of steamers and boats to get the troops, medium artillery guns and supplies across.

Leaving Jagdev to coordinate and direct the progress of his engineers,[4] Sagat moved ahead to reconnoitre the battlefield.

---

4 The engineers were required to establish crossings over two more rivers, get the ferry operations across the Meghna moving smoothly as well as construct an advance landing ground for Caribou Aircraft at Narsingdi (it was never used). Pp 216-217, **Dismemberment of Pakistan: 1971 Indo-Pak War by Brig Jagdev Singh, AVSM, Lancers,**

He was followed by a gaggle of press people eagerly waiting to know the fate of Dacca. The previous day there was a near riot as members of the Press Corps fiercely vied with each other to get scoops.[5] A hiatus had set in on the Battlefield as the opposing forces adhered to an informal cease fire awaiting the results of negotiations going on between the two armies. Radio intercepts were clearly indicating the frantic efforts being made by Lieutenant General (Lt Gen) AAK Niazi, the Army Commander of Pak Eastern Command, and his aides to parley some kind of an armistice before the Indian Army entered Dacca.[6] Meanwhile, Lieutenant General (Lt Gen) JFR Jacob, the Chief of Staff, Eastern Command, was on his way to Dacca to organize the modalities of the surrender.

Sagat was led to the roof of one of the buildings overlooking the Lakhya River, the last obstacle before Dacca. By now the River was securely in Indian hands and the troops were already on the outskirts of the City, being welcomed by a deliriously happy populace. In the midst of a briefing he suddenly received instructions from Calcutta to proceed to Agartala. Lt Gen JS Aurora, the Eastern Army Commander, wanted Sagat to accompany him to Dacca when he took the surrender of the Pakistan Army. Dogged by the press on his way to the helicopter, Sagat, with thankful pleasure, absorbed the fact that the War was over. As he flew back over the Meghna, with an elated and relieved Jagdev sitting behind him, he could not help but look back on his achievements. Though Dacca was not even an objective given to him, he had known with

---

New Delhi, 1988.

5 The embedded press moving with the advancing troops, hungry, dirty and tired, were resentful of their colleagues living at the Intercontinental Dacca, filing reports, in between the proverbial scented sheets. The latter had moved out of Dacca on 15 Dec and contacted the advancing troops. **From the recorded conversation between Lieutenant (Lt) General (Gen) Sagat Singh and the late Editor and Director USI Journal, Colonel Pyare Lal, 1973.**

6 101 Communication Zone had adroitly bypassed 73 Mountain Brigade, which were engaging the enemy at Tungi, and were on the outskirts of Kurmitola Cantonment. Perhaps this was one of the reasons why they persistently remained out of communication.

unerring strategic foresight that without it the Indian Army would achieve a pyrrhic victory and the dreams of millions of Bengalis of East Pakistan would have been lost in a limbo of diplomatic conundrums. He had kept his options close to his chest, focused his aim and resources towards Dacca and with ruthless energy directed his forces towards it. If there were no roads his men walked; if there was a river it was bounced either by helicopters or crossed by all kinds of river crafts; if the enemy stood in his way he was deceived, bottled, demoralised and bypassed. In the end he had Dacca nearly enveloped and within his grasp. It was all over bar the shouting.

When the Corps Commander landed at Comilla, he was met with much jubilation by the Staff. Sagat however, had very little time for back slapping. On speaking to the Command Headquarters, he was vaguely informed that he had to stay on at Dacca after the surrender and handle the situation. With barely an hour up his sleeve he gave rapid instructions to his staff to ensure that a skeleton Corps tactical headquarters was in place at Dacca by 17 Dec. Last minute instructions were given to pass on to his Divisional Commanders to take charge of their areas firmly, organize the surrender of Pakistani troops, prevent any reprisals or looting and administer the new country before the Civil Affairs people got their act together. It was obvious that the toughest task would fall on Major General BF 'Ben' Gonsalves of 57 Mountain Division, who had to ensure Dacca remained peaceful and incident free. The Brigadier in Charge Administration, Brig KG Pitre and the Chief Signal Officer, Brig GS Sidhu, were asked to accompany him as logistics and communications would prove vital in the days ahead. His division commanders were to meet him at the Surrender Ceremony at Dacca.[7]

The Air Force was asked to organize a fleet of helicopters at Agartala and await the Army Commander and other VIPs, who

---

[7] Maj Gen KV Krishna Rao, commanding 8 Mountain Division and overseeing the Battle of Sylhet, was to rendezvous at Agartala while the other Divisional Commanders, Maj Gen RD 'Rocky' Hira and Maj Gen BF 'Ben' Gonsalves, were already on the outskirts of Dacca and were instructed to meet Sagat there.

were coming in two planeloads with a slew of reporters. As Sagat hurriedly departed, Colonel Osmani, the C-in-C Armed Forces of the Interim Government of Bangladesh, arrived at Comilla on his way to Agartala. For unforeseen reasons he could not make it to the Surrender Ceremony. This led to much heart burning subsequently.

The Army Commander, accompanied by his wife, dressed in an elegant silk sari, arrived at Agartala by plane from Calcutta at approximately 2 PM.[8] In addition to his staff and senior officers of the nascent Bangladesh Armed Forces, the Air Officer Commanding in Chief Eastern Air Command, Air Marshal Dewan, the Flag Officer Commanding in Chief Eastern Fleet, Vice Admiral Krishnan, were also with him. Group Captain Chandan Singh had laid on five MI-4 and five Allouette Helicopters. He was also bent on ensuring that his gallant band of pilots would be present at Dacca to witness the surrender.[9] Shortly, two plane loads of Press arrived. Gen Aurora had left Calcutta in anticipation that Gen Jacob would have negotiated the terms of surrender of the Pakistan Army by the time he had landed at Agartala. Since nothing was heard from him, they had to wait until confirmation was received. This gave Sagat an opportunity to clarify his role in Dacca and ask for his charter of duties. However, Aurora was of little help here and told him that since events had moved rapidly he had very little time to work this out. Sagat would have to play it by the ear. He was required to remain at Dacca and take charge of the situation and manage the modalities of transfer of authority from the Pakistan Army to India and thereafter to the representatives of the Government of the new nation of Bangladesh.

It was well after 3.30 PM that information was received from Command Headquarters that Niazi was prepared to sign

---

8 It seemed strange that Aurora had to take a circuitous route to enter Dacca but that was the safest course as the direct route would have had him fly over territory still being fought over.

9 "I made sure that the pilots witnessed the actual signing of the surrender." **Taped conversation between Air Marshal Chandan Singh and Director USI, Col Pyare Lal, 1973.**

the Instrument of Surrender. With congratulations again being exchanged all around, the senior officers got into helicopters and took off for Dacca. Wanting to land with the sun behind their backs they flew over Dacca Airfield in a symmetrical formation. Visible below were the menacing barrels of antiaircraft guns and a row of Pakistan Sabre Jets. The latter had been unable to fly after 6 December once the IAF had repeatedly bombed and made the Tezgaon Air Field unserviceable.[10] The scene below was one of exuberant chaos. Rooftops were flying the Bangladesh Flag, a country which had not yet come into existence. The helicopters landed under a brilliant early evening sky amidst roistering masses, while a sea of frantically cheering faces lined the route from the Airfield to the Ramna Race Course, five kms away, where the surrender was to take place.

Lt Gen Jacob and Lt Gen Niazi were present to receive Gen Aurora but whatever solemnity the occasion demanded was thrown overboard by the wild cheering and enthusiasm of the people. In the scramble for transport it nearly became everyone to himself as people struggled for any type of vehicle to convey them to the Surrender Ceremony. Scruffy Indian troops lined the road to provide some form of route protection but looked somewhat nonplussed as the celebrating masses surrounded them, some of whom even put flowers in the barrels of their rifles and hugged them. It was the first time in many months that young girls and women moved freely on the streets welcoming the troops and spontaneously throwing their homes open to them. All those who were present on that momentous day will never forget the occasion. It rarely happens in a person's lifetime that he is instrumental and present during the birth of a nation. As Sagat drove through the streets, being cheered and waved to by the masses, he could not help but experience a sense of déjà vu. It was exactly a decade ago, nearly to the day, on 19 Dec 1961, when driving through cheering crowds he

---

10 The fighter pilots were considered a most valuable asset. Once the writing was on the wall they were all evacuated to West Pakistan on 8 and 9 Dec. P. 132; **Witness to Surrender by Sadiq Salik. Lancers, New Delhi; 2000**

had reached the residence of the Portuguese Governor General in Panjim and liberated Goa! It is a very rare person in history who can be credited for the liberation of two nations in his lifetime.

A guard of honour was laid out at the Race Course composed of troops from the two belligerents. While the spruced up Pakistani contingent, comprising mostly of their Military Police, was commanded by the strapping ADC to Lt Gen Niazi, the Indian contingent, consisting of troops of 2 Para and 4 Guards, looked decidedly scruffy, down at heel and weary.[11] 4 Guards had fought and marched the entire distance, more than 100 kms, from the Indian border to Dacca without a suitable bath or a change of clothes. Nevertheless a few days later, this same Battalion, in white gloves and knife creased Guard regalia, gave a spanking Guard of Honour to the Indian Army Chief, Gen SHFJ Manekshaw. An immaculate performance sufficient to bring tears of pride into the eyes of those who knew what the Battalion had gone through in the past month.

The senior officers proceeded to the venue of the Ceremony surrounded by the press and flinty eyed paratroopers trying to keep some order. An open ground, on which stood a table and two chairs, had been cleared by the soldiers who kept the cheering crowd at bay. Generals Aurora and Niazi occupied a chair each while behind them stood the Air Force and Naval Regional C-in-Cs flanked by Gen Sagat.[12] Lt Gen Jacob stood on his left. They were ringed by a crowd of reporters, like modern day paparazzi, all desperately trying to find the most advantageous perch while those behind elbowed for position marring the solemnity of the Ceremony.

---

11 "I looked down the lines of the Indian and Pakistani troops; the Pakistani troops were immaculately turned out while the Indian troops were the scruffiest looking crowd you can find anywhere. And that basically, is to my mind the history of the performance of the two forces.......The Pakistanis had chosen not to soil their clothes therefore had not fought, certainly not fought in the manner desired of them. The Indian soldier had forgotten the business of turnout and had dedicated himself to the business of fighting...." **Taped conversation between Lt Gen (then Lt Col) Himmeth Singh and Director USI, Col Pyare Lal, 1973.**

12 Sagat met his three Divisional Commanders together for the first time at Dacca that day after the War had started. It was a happy and emotional reunion for them.

Prologue

Gen Aurora produced the surrender document asking Gen Niazi to read it. Since Niazi had already seen the draft document he did not waste much time and after perfunctorily glancing through the single page confirmed his assent to Aurora. Five copies of the Instrument of Surrender were produced for Niazi's signature, one by one. For a moment he looked disconcerted as he had no fountain pen. One was promptly produced by Surojit Sen of All India Radio, who was seated with a tape recorder and mike, adjacent to him on the ground. The five copies were thereafter signed by Niazi, palpably keeping his emotions in check, followed by Aurora. With that the Indian Army had inflicted the greatest defeat on an enemy in its History and 93000 Pakistanis marched into captivity.

While this momentous event was taking place, there was cacophony all around. The young Air Force helicopter pilots, so much instrumental in creating this history had left only one of their colleagues behind to guard the helicopters[13] and had all converged at the Race Course. Not too bothered by protocol they wanted to be a part of the historic event and were pushing their way to an advantageous position. And so it came about that at that precise historical moment, which produced the most famous photograph of India's post independence military history, Flight Lieutenant Krishnamurthy was snapped clutching an outraged Gen Jacob and peering over his left shoulder. And that's how it should be because he epitomized all the young officers, who careless of life and rules but full of determination, led their troops to victory.

Immediately after the signing of the documents was completed, the two generals got up to go. Gen Aurora then asked Niazi to hand over his revolver. Reluctantly and with whatever dignity he could muster, Niazi removed his epaulette buttons and with the lanyard attached, took out his revolver from the holster and handed it over to Aurora. As mentioned by Jacob in his book,[14] the weapon

---

13 The crowd at the Airport wanted to converge on the helicopters. The Officer showed characteristic presence of mind by going to the ATC and putting on the air raid siren.

14 P 148. **Surrender at Dacca: Birth of a Nation by Lt Gen JFR Jacob, Manohar Publishers, New Delhi 1997.**

obviously did not belong to Niazi. His ADC had commandeered it for him from one of the military policemen. Before he left Dacca for a prisoner of war camp in India, Niazi handed over his weapon, a pearl handled chrome plated revolver, to a well known Bangladesh family, which had been much harassed by the Pakistan Army.[15] Perhaps it was a measure of atonement by him.

The focus of attention now shifted to the immediate environment, which definitely had become hostile towards Niazi and his soldiers. The crowd had started getting restive and was keen to mingle with the Indian officers. Contrarily they were aggressive towards Niazi in particular and were calling him names like 'butcher' and 'murderer'. The clarion cry of 'Joi Bangla' was reverberating around the grounds. This had Sagat worried about Niazi's safety. As an immediate measure, the Indian Generals and Sagat's personal staff surrounded Niazi and manoeuvred him to where the vehicles were parked. They however, could not prevent an odd missile from striking him and them. No one had doubted Niazi's personal courage. Under such a trying situation, including the Surrender Ceremony, he carried himself with dignity; only losing his cool when a stone struck him as he was about to get into his car. With adequate protection he was whisked off to the safety of Dacca Cantonment. Much later in the evening, when Sagat met him, he found him sentimental and maudlin.

Sagat accompanied Aurora to the Airport and saw him off. He also had a few quick words with Jacob, to clarify issues on the administration of Dacca, before the helicopters took off. Just before flying off, Aurora handed him a copy of the Instrument of Surrender and asked him to hand it over to Niazi. As the helicopters winged their way into the sunset, Sagat found himself alone at the airfield with only his staff officers and wireless operators.

Dacca was in a state of ferment. The people were out in the streets celebrating; the Mukti Bahini were exuberantly establishing

---

15 One prominent academician had been murdered while another influential member had been apprehended and tortured in a cage.

their hegemony and wildly firing weapons in the air looking to settle scores with 'traitors'; the Biharis and local Razakars,[16] with their families, were either desperately trying to find sanctuary or were barricading themselves in their ghettos.[17] Pakistani units were abandoning their positions and warily retreating into the Cantonment knowing that the fate of stragglers would be unpleasant, while Indian Army units were fanning out to designated areas trying to establish order. On its first night of freedom, Dacca was a crucible of competing emotions and interests. If not handled properly the situation could well deteriorate in a manner that would wipe off the sheen of victory, especially as it was the cynosure of attention of the world press. Sagat felt lassitude creeping in but he had a long night ahead of him, part of which he would spend celebrating with his subordinates. For now he started issuing his orders crisply and got into the rickety car to find Niazi.

Through sheer force of will and determination Sagat had kept his campaign going, not sharing his vision with his superiors as he was unsure of their support and not burdening his subordinates with what were perhaps dangerous expectations. He had run his War the way he wanted, carrying that load on his giant craggy frame and looking towards an objective only he foresaw in the beginning with his 'thousand mile grey eyes'.[18] He had won, as he knew he would, overwhelmingly and with certitude. He had made powerful enemies and was unsure of his fate but there was no doubt what his place would be in the eyes of history. Born to minor nobility in the Thar Desert, an Other Rank in the Bikaner State Forces, he indeed had come a long way. Through sheer hard work and professionalism he had risen to such heights that in thirteen days he, his peers and their soldiers had transformed a miserable

---

16 Local paramilitary home guards set up by the Pakistan Army to maintain order.

17 A couple of days later, the Author, on urgent instructions from devotees and family members, went looking for the Ashram of Ma Anandmayee. He found it peaceful as ever in serene surroundings.

18 Observation of Brigadier KP 'Tom' Pande, MVC, Commander of 61 Infantry Brigade during the War.

province like East Pakistan into the joyous independent Republic of Bangladesh.

Haveli

CHAPTER ONE

THE RATHORE LEGACY

'Ran Banka Rathore'
(The Warrior Rathore)
- The Motto on the Rathore Coat of Arms

In 1465, after years of turmoil, Rao Jodha had finally consolidated his kingdom in the lands of *Maru* (present day Jodhpur). He looked with pride and satisfaction at his sons and kinsmen and wondered, half in jest, whether there were no other lands to conquer. Thus challenged, the proud Bika, his second born, unsheathed his sword and decided to seek his destiny elsewhere. Accompanied by his brother Bida, Uncle Kandhal, and a faithful band of warriors he set forth westward into the desert wastes. It took him thirty years but blessed by *Karni Mata*[1] of Deshnoke, he succeeded in carving out his own kingdom in the arid sands of the Thar, displacing the Bhatis and establishing his suzerainty over the local Jat[2] principalities and ethnic tribes. When India became independent in 1947, the state of Bikaner comprised the modern districts of Bikaner, Churu, Hanumangarh and Ganganagar. This vast tract mostly covered in sand, waterless and harsh, bred people of a frugal nature with fierce pride and attachment to their land. Poor they may be but they would not bow their heads to anyone except to their suzerain.

---

1. The Mystic was alive then and was a great influence in enabling Bikaji to establish his Kingdom. Her Temple now attracts vast multitudes, which have to tread carefully while stepping amongst the hordes of holy rats that throng and breed in the Temple.

2. It remains the right of the Chief of the Godara Jats to anoint the forehead of the new ruler when he ascends the throne.

In the Churu Region, Bika's brother Bida, after displacing the Mohil Chauhans, established the stronghold of his own sub clan, the Bidawats. As the Maharajas of Bikaner consolidated their hold over the Kingdom, the Bidawats too spread their influence over the neighbouring territories. One of the offshoots from the main branch, known as the Khangarot Bidawat, carved out their own *thikanas*[3] at Khuri and other places and held sway over the routes leading from the West and North into Bikaner. The rights of primogeniture required that the younger brothers seek their fortune elsewhere or be allotted a lesser grant of land. It thus came about that in 1776 an ancestor of Sagat, Guman Singh, was given a grant of 600 *bighas*[4] and the Village of Kusumdesar to establish his own *thikana* in the fringes of the area governed by Khuri. In due course the younger son of the Thakur, Brijlal Singh, was given a grant of 200 bighas and the wherewithal to construct his own *Haveli*. The *Haveli* still stands strong, built in the traditional manner, double storied, with a central courtyard.

A visit to Kusumdesar, even today, will starkly bring home the harsh environment in which the people must have lived. The summer heat is unbearable in its intensity and the hot and arid desert wind *Loo,* sucks the moisture out of your body. The ground, sandy and stony in places, is loath to yield even the single crop that is harvested. Trees stand stunted, prickly and give poor shade. Domestic animals are scrawny and have to be hardy like the people to survive. The land, then as now, is merciless and unforgiving. What astonishes those who have not understood the character of the people is the fanatical love they have for this land though they barely eke out a living.

---

3   The Thikanas were principalities comprising lands and villages given in grant by the Ruler to his kinsmen and faithfuls. Elaborate ceremonial rituals developed between the King and his Thakurs, which at times were the bane of the Kingdom. A perceived slight could result in a blood feud if honour was at stake. For more details on the Thikanas of Bikaner, the reader may consult the website http://www.rajputsamaj.net/history/Bikaner/bikaner-thikana.htm

4   1.75 bighas approximate to an acre

The Rathore Legacy

The history of Rajasthan is replete with tales of forlorn hopes and sacrifice as its people desperately fought off invaders. It is thus important to understand the Rajput character and the interplay between the ruler and his subject. Though a feudal ethos prevailed, no Rajput would consider himself inferior to another, however high that person's status may be. He took pride in what he owned and considered it perfectly natural for his ruler to show his loyalty to him in order to deserve his fealty. The basic courtesies they maintained amongst each other even now remain in place and during ceremonial occasions, elaborate rituals continue to be observed. Thus Brijlal Singh, serving as an Other Rank in the Army,[5] never considered he was in any way inferior to those who occupied higher stations in life. He felt it was his natural right to socially converse with even the greatest noble when the occasion so demanded.

Brijlal Singh joined the Bikaner Ganga Risala of the Bikaner State Forces, saw service in World War I in Mesopotamia, Palestine and France and retired as Company Quarter Master Havildar (Sergeant) just prior to World War 2. Recalled to the Colours at the outbreak of War, he again served in the Battalion in various capacities before finally coming home as an Honorary Captain. A man with an ascetic bent of mind, he devoted his retirement to prayer and meditation, though he ensured that his daughters were settled and his sons so educated that they aspired to do well. It was however his wife, a Bhati lady from Hadla, who was more remarkable amongst the two. Jarao Kunvar was a known beauty and Sagat inherited his grey eyes from her. She ran her Family with an iron hand and over the years developed a reputation for piety and faith healing.

Sagat, the eldest of nine siblings,[6] was born on 14 Jul 1919. When he was a toddler a local saint, much revered by his mother, seeing his disproportionately long hands predicted a career of renown as a

---

5   'He carried a certain aura around him and though he was a non commissioned officer, he had an imposing personality and all ranks used to address him as *Sahib*'. **In conversation with Brig (retd) Jagmal Singh, VrC, VSM on 29 May 2009 at Bikaner.**

6   They were three brothers and six sisters

warrior. Sagat grew up in the other rank lines of The Bikaner Ganga Risala and received his early education in the nearest vernacular school. As a boy, he was easily identifiable by his gangly figure and light eyes. In his early teens he was noticed by one of the great personalities of Bikaner State, Colonel Rao Bahadur Thakur Jeoraj Singh of Sarothia, who later became the Home and War Minister of Bikaner. Granted the *Jagir* of Harasar, he was a trusted noble at the Court. The serious and studious Sagat, who nevertheless had a touch of impish mischief about him, piqued enough of his interest to get him admitted to the Walter Nobles[7] High School.

Bikaner at that time was being ruled by one of its greatest rulers, Maharaja Ganga Singh.[8] Educated at Mayo College, he desired a similar education for the children of all his noblemen and thus established the Walter Nobles High School on the same lines as his Alma Mater. The Principal at that time was an Englishman named Scott Dale, who insisted that all the boys speak in Hindi and not the vernacular Marwari. Though the medium of instruction was English, picking up Hindi was a struggle and a great deal of effort was required to even learn a smattering of English. Sagat stood out by his earnest desire to learn. He displayed no particular outstanding trait at this stage in his life though he had an excellent grasp of mimicry and could play the most difficult shots in volleyball with relative ease. All his energies were channelised towards educating himself. Even then, it seemed that he yearned for a horizon beyond his ken. His confidence, ease of conversation and loyalty towards his friends remained a hallmark of his character. Rarely punished, if he did undergo punishment for some truancy, he handled it with contemptuous detachment.

Bikaner in the thirties, though steeped in feudalism, was at the cusp of change. The long reign of Maharaja Ganga Singh was drawing to a close. A grand reformer but an absolute monarch,

---

7   Walter was the AGG of the Governor General at the Court of Bikaner.

8   General Maharaja Sir Ganga Singhji, GCSI, GCIE, GCVO, GBE, KCB, KIH (1880 – 1943). One of the greatest and certainly the most enlightened of rulers. His benevolent rule made Bikaner into a model kingdom.

he had initiated many changes to improve the lives of his people and modernize the State. For youth looking beyond their narrow prospects he opened new vistas. With his sharp intelligence, Sagat understood all this and always strove to rise beyond the environment that confined him. Sagat's younger brother Jeoraj Singh was no mean achiever himself. He attained great distinction in learning and sports; for three years being the Cox Gold Medallist at the Rajasthan University. He subsequently joined the police force and served out his career.[9] Sagat finished his schooling in 1936 and joined Dungar College to do his graduation. However, fate decreeing otherwise, he had barely completed his intermediate exam in 1938 when the second-in-command of Bikaner Ganga Risala, Maj (later Brig) Khem Singh, who always had an eye on him, produced him before the Commanding Officer, Lt Col Balu Singh Shekhawat, for enrolment. One look at him and Balu Singh dismissed him as a *'Lil Paro Bokro'*. A semi contemptuous term for someone considered too lanky. Khem Singh was not one to take no for an answer and replied *'Lil Paro Lal Paro Padeyado to Hai!*[10]*'* He succeeded in convincing Col Balu Singh that educated soldiers were hard to come by and they were lucky to get one. It now seems ironic but Sagat was enrolled into the Army purely because he had succeeded in educating himself.

Enrolled as a Naik (corporal) in the Bikaner Ganga Risala he immediately underwent recruit training. His father still served but was due to retire. Sagat had barely cleared the recruit training when war broke out and the Bikaner State Forces commenced preparation for service overseas. Sagat, who had excelled in training, was made a Jemadar (now known as naib subedar)[11] and platoon commander in the Battalion. The exigencies of war required that units be made

---

9 As an acquaintance put it that though Sagat benefited many who came to him, his personality was too overpowering for those closest to him. 'He was like a banyan tree under whose shade only the hardiest plants can grow'. When questioned, his brother Jeoraj vehemently denied this.

10 **In conversation with Col Mohan Singh on 29 May 2009, near Ratangarh.**

11 The naib subedar is a junior commissioned officer (JCO) in the Army. The JCO is unique to the armies of the sub-continent.

up to strength and fresh units be raised. All officer vacancies had to be filled immediately. The Brigade Major of the State Forces, Major (later Brig) Bhag Singh, prepared a merit-based list of potential officer candidates amongst the Junior Commissioned Officers (JCOs) and put it up to the C-in-C State Forces, Gen Hari Singh Bhati. The General selected five to six JCOs who had the potential to become officers. Sagat's name figured in the list and he received an immediate commission as 2/Lt into the Bikaner Ganga Risala, which by then had received mobilization orders for Aden. It was 1940 and Sagat got hands on training in preparing a subunit and moving it overseas for war, no doubt under the eagle eyes of Maj Khem Singh and his Father. Sagat's career however took another turn when the Ganga Risala was diverted to Sindh in 1941 to put down the Hoor Agitation. They were replaced by The Sadul Light Infantry. It was axiomatic that it be made up to full officer strength and Sagat was immediately transferred to the Battalion.

The Middle East was now an area of great strategic significance. The Vichy French had taken over the League of Nations Mandate in Lebanon and Syria while the Iraqis themselves were none too friendly to the British. Persia under Reza Shah was developing its own independent policies and either consorting with the Russians or encouraging Nazi Germany. Turkey was maintaining dangerous neutrality while the Mediterranean and North Africa were battlegrounds with fluctuating fortunes for the British Empire. The Middle East was now the strategic pivot of the Empire. Though the Indian Army could ill spare units to secure this frontier, Iraq force under Lt Gen Sir Edward Quinan was formed as a corps sized formation. It landed in Basra in April 1941 and established control over rebellious elements in Iraq.[12] Thereafter, in a bloody campaign lasting over two months, it defeated the Vichy French in Lebanon.

With the western flank secured, Iraq force turned its attention eastwards. In August, it occupied parts of Persia, subsequently deposing the monarch. Meanwhile, stirring things were happening

---

12 10 Indian Division under Maj Gen William Slim (later Commander 14 Army) was a part of Iraqforce.

in the Caucasus and the North African Desert. Hitler violated his treaty with Russia and had his juggernaut rolling towards Crimea and beyond. In what looked like a giant pincer, Rommel was threatening Egypt. Iraqforce, undergoing several transformations, was designated Paiforce in September and became the 10th Army in February 1942. It came under the newly created Persia and Iraq Command based at Baghdad in August 1942. By then the situation had partially stabilized. The main task of the Command was now to secure the lines of communication for dispatching the massive American Lend Lease aid to Russia through the Caucasus.

Sadul Light Infantry moved to Iraq in Jan 1942 and was located at Jubair, near Basra, under command of Headquarters 7 Lines of Communication Sub Area. Jubair was a major logistical hub and the Battalion deployed to secure it as well as protect the lines of communications. The Battalion was a fixed class unit with two Rajput, one Jat and one Kayamkhani Muslim company. Sagat, after obtaining an Instructor grading on the Military Transport Course, was appointed the Unit Military Transport Officer. He became the Adjutant for some time and was then given command of D Company, the Muslim company, by end July 1942. The heat and swampy conditions (so well narrated by all those who have served in Iraq) took a steady toll of personnel who required hospitalization and even evacuation to India. There was thus a constant trickle of reinforcements moving in. One of them was 2/Lt Mohan Singh,[13] who developed a warm friendship with Sagat, which continued to last well into their retirements. What Mohan Singh noticed then was the hold Sagat had over his men and his calm demeanour regardless of how volatile the situation was. Sagat made no bones about either his desire to learn his profession or improve his social graces. He never hesitated in applying for all courses on offer, even if they were physically challenging and found it relatively easy to obtain an instructor grading. Mohan Singh remembers him

---

13 Later Colonel. One of his sons, Karni, joined 17 RAJRIF (the Battalion in which Col Mohan Singh also served) and went on to win the Kirti Chakra in counter insurgency operations in Manipur.

volunteering for the 'Tough Tactics Course',[14] despite efforts by his colleagues to dissuade him. He would sometimes come to the tents bruised, covered in swamp mud and hollow eyed but never without good cheer. In addition, whenever there was a visit he was often nominated to conduct the visitor. He would closely observe that person's behaviour, speech and bearing and put his talent for mimicry to good use. It was soon noticed that his English speech and accent had improved considerably.

In November 1942, the Battalion, less a company, was moved to Basra where the Sub Area made a request for a 'Staff Learner'.[15] Sagat was nominated and Mohan Singh took over the Company from him. Being on the staff enabled Sagat to develop a wider social circle, which obviously included ladies with whom he became quite popular. A state force unit like the Sadul Light Infantry was usually very insular and conservative as all officers and men came from one region and had a similar outlook. Most of the officers, except those of the higher nobility, would rarely have had the advantage of an egalitarian upbringing. This was particularly true of the Bikaner State Forces, steeped in traditional feudalism. The staff attachment followed by a posting gave Sagat an opportunity to interact with a wide cross section of officers and men from the Indian and the British Army. While most officers under similar circumstances may have retreated into their shell and kept their colleagues at a social arms length, Sagat, because of his innate confidence, welcomed this opportunity to improve his social graces. Mohan Singh remembers pulling his leg about this and warning him about getting too westernised but Sagat's answer, so prescient that it still remains embedded in his memory was, "Come on Mohan, the world is changing and we need to change with it if we want to make our mark." Col Bill Sykes, the officer overseeing the functioning of the Battalion, was especially fond of him and mentored him

---

14 A local version of the Commando Course.

15 This obviously was a coy term to extract officers from a battalion for attachment to the formation headquarter, something which our Army can well emulate to sugar coat the same thing they do now.

whenever he could. Sagat's dynamism and loyalty made him stand out amongst his peers. Mohan distinctly remembers how all ranks looked up to him to resolve staff and administrative problems.

He was earmarked for professional advancement and at a

With HQ Staff in Persia

relatively junior rank was sent to do the Middle East Staff Course[16] in Apr 1943. He was the only state forces officer nominated along with an Indian Army Officer, Major Har Kishan Sibal.[17] Immediately after the Course, Sagat was posted as General Grade Staff Officer 3 (GSO3) at Headquarter 40 Indian Infantry Brigade, located at Ahwaz, Persia. The Brigade was under command 6 Indian Division, which was responsible for securing Iran against any restive elements. After Reza Shah was deposed, there was a great deal of ferment and it became necessary to move additional troops to secure the countryside, especially the lines of communication. The Sadul Light Infantry also moved to Ahwaz and came under 40 Brigade. Sagat, because of his background in command of Muslim troops, proved

---

16 As the Army reorganized itself in the Middle East, it established an elaborate training infrastructure, which included a staff college at Haifa with a wing at Sarafand.

17 Sagat took over 4 Corps from Sibal in Nov 1970.

invaluable to the Brigade in smoothening religious sensibilities.[18] Unfortunately, all was not well with the Battalion, which had got embroiled in parochial internal dissensions. Maharaja Ganga Singh had died after a long battle with cancer and his iron hand was lacking while his son and successor, Maharaja Sadul Singh, was trying to find his feet. The atmosphere had considerably vitiated and even the more balanced officers like Sagat and the overseeing British Officers were unable to resolve matters easily.[19] Alarmed at the situation, Maharaja Sadul Singh made a trip to Ahwaz to investigate the matter himself. He wielded the stick ruthlessly and the Commanding Officer and other senior officers were removed and returned to Bikaner. Only Sagat, temporarily with the Battalion, and Mohan Singh, amongst those with some experience, remained. While other officers were in the process of being posted in, the Battalion received officers on attachment from the Indian Army. Lt Col Prem Singh took over the Battalion and was conducted around the area by Sagat. In one instance a couple of Russian officers got into the front seat of the vehicle in which Sagat was to escort his commanding officer and brusquely ordered them to sit behind. Sagat was the last man to stand for this kind of behaviour and roughly pulled the Russians out and with elaborate courtesy requested his commanding officer to get in. The nonplussed Russians meekly got into the rear of the vehicle.[20] Despite overtures from State Forces Headquarters, the Brigade Commander of 40 Brigade, Brigadier JW Hinchcliffe, was loath to let Sagat go back to the Battalion. He however, could not withstand the royal pressure and eventually released him, recommending him for the Staff Course at Quetta. This was ironic as a month earlier, while

---

18 The turbulence in Persia was evident as a little known cleric named Khomeini published his *Kashf Al Asrar* ("The Discovery of Secrets") and two parties, which subsequently played a major role in the Iranian political scene ie the *Tudeh* and the *Fedayin-e-Islam*, were born.

19 Mohan Singh himself had written to the Maharaja, despairing of anyone else resolving the matter.

20 **As narrated by Col Nawal Singh, son of Lt Col Prem Singh, at Bikaner on 30 May 2009.**

Sagat was doing a sub unit tactical course, Hinchcliffe had stood the argument on its head and rejected Sagat's nomination for Quetta on the grounds of inexperience and age.

Sagat reported back to the Battalion, now under command a Lt Col Hurley, by September 1944 and was appointed Adjutant. He became a close confidante of the Colonel and got immediately involved in sorting out the many administrative issues as an aftermath of the review by the Maharaja. By the beginning of 1945, HQ State Forces had come to know that Sagat was a serious contender for entry to the Staff College, Quetta. He was recalled to Bikaner and made the Brigade Major of the State Forces. It was a rare honour for a state force officer to be nominated for this prestigious course purely on merit and the Commander-in-Chief wanted him to come under his personal tutelage. The War itself was winding down and it was apparent that the Indian Army might have to look eastward for driving out the Japanese from South East Asia. Maharaja Sadul Singh, who had travelled extensively immediately on accession to the throne, seemed to have realized that post war dispensations would be different and subtly started preparing his kingdom for the future.

Sagat came home, not yet 26 years old, a different man to the one who had left the State in 1942. The impact of Mahatma Gandhi's agitations was apparent all over the sub continent and had permeated down to the simple households of urban Bikaner. Sagat had interacted and made friends with a wide cross section of officers, both British and Indian, and like them, realized that the halcyon days of the Empire were over. In addition, the Americans involved in the Lend Lease operations going on through the Caucasus also influenced him. It was inherent in his nature to develop an independent world view different from what was seen through the tinted prism of Imperial India. The personal decisions he took, based on his convictions, would have far-reaching impact on his life and career. One may also imagine the impression he must have made on his family and friends. They had seen him depart as an awkward lanky youth comfortable only while speaking Marwari and on his return found him, a tall, tough sophisticate with firm opinions and cool confidence.

Sagat's nomination for the 12th War Staff Course at Quetta was received in April 1945 and he did the Course from May to November that year. On termination of the Course, he was appointed Brigade Major of the State Army and posted to Bikaner. From a line boy living in the barracks he had moved much higher in life. The War had wound down and the State Force units were returning, either to be disbanded or reduced. Sagat's Father had finally retired and returned to his village to devote himself to deep prayer and meditation. In 1946 it became apparent that India would become independent. While the State officials got involved in matters of accession, Sagat was responsible for the staff work required in absorbing the State Force units into the Indian Army. This was by no means easy as the Indian Army itself was being cut back and many a battalion, some with hoary traditions, were being disbanded or transferred to Pakistan. Maharaja Sadul Singh's hard work and the staff work done to build up the reputation of his units seemed to have carried the day. The Bikaner Ganga Risala merged with the Jaisalmer Risala to remain the Indian Camel Corps and was designated as 13 GRENADIERS (Jaisalmer Ganga Risala).[21] The Sadul Light Infantry was absorbed by the Rajput Regiment as 19 RAJPUT (Bikaner) and today continues to serve with élan and pride.

These were trying times for state force officers as they sought to get themselves absorbed into the Indian Army. The selection committee, comprising of senior officers of the Army and bureaucrats was quite stringent and a number of officers were rejected. Sagat, because of his qualifications, was quite sure of getting absorbed; he was however, more concerned with his seniority as that would ultimately affect his career. Frequent trips to Delhi followed by correspondence with various branches at Army

---

21 The Unit distinguished itself in the desert during the 1965 War with Pakistan. The camels had outlived their utility and were taken over by the BSF shortly thereafter and a 500-year-old tradition came to an end. 13 GRENADIERS remains an infantry unit serving with distinction wherever it is deployed

HQ found him confronting the unfeeling behemoth of the famed Indian bureaucracy with whom he continued to tilt for nearly two years.

Meanwhile, he also had other things to do. His sisters had to be settled and he had to look for a bride for himself. Realizing that service in the Indian Army would require a fair amount of travel all over the Country and meeting with all types of people, Sagat decided to find a bride with a more cosmopolitan and sophisticated background. He well knew that the rigid orthodoxy of his parents might saddle

him with a wife steeped in an unbending rural background who may find it difficult to live a harmonious life in the career he planned to chart for himself. Knowing well the consequences of his actions, he put a matrimonial ad in a newspaper. Sure enough, a fair number of excellent proposals were received out of which he decided to respond to the reply received from the family of the late Chief Justice Richhpal Singh of the J&K High Court.[22] A meeting was fixed at Dehra Dun and Sagat presented himself, spruced up and cool as ever, at the late Justice's household. One look at this tall, rugged man with the mocking grey eyes and Kamala's heart was won. Sagat found this petite, pretty girl with curly hair and a sunny temperament, most beguiling. The contrast was apparent. He was a soldier from an arid desert kingdom brought up in a strict, rajput conservative household with a military background. Kamala was a girl brought up on modern ideals of equality and with a liberal outlook. Meeting and conversing with people in a sophisticated environment was second nature to her. Something in each other's nature appealed to what they looked for in a life partner. Justice Richhpal's household was impressed by Sagat's bold, confident nature and ease in conversation. The courtship was short and the wedding sanctified on 27 Jan 1947. As Kamala journeyed to her new home, little did the couple know that six months later India would emerge independent and their lives would be intertwined with their new Country's turbulent journey.

---

22 Richhpal Singh's father Umrao Singh was a rich landlord with vast properties in Punjab. A gate in Lahore is named after him.

CHAPTER TWO

COMMAND

'Tis not in mortals to command success,
But we'll do more Sempronius; we will deserve it.

- Joseph Addison

Sagat served more than three years as the Brigade Major of the Bikaner State Forces. There was no proper accommodation available and he was living in a tent on a major's salary,[1] when one day Maharaja Sadul Singh asked him as to why he had not gotten married. Sagat boldly replied that it would be criminal on his part if he brought a bride into tented accommodation. The Maharaja immediately ordered a bungalow, the present 'Gun House', to be built[2] and that was where Kamla started her married life.

Kamla refused to put on the veil in the highly conservative Bikaner society. She led a lonely life until the Maharani took a liking to her and started inviting her to the palace, where she developed a close friendship with some of the ladies.[3] Jeoraj was studying in Bikaner and he came to live with Sagat. Kamla's simple and affectionate nature won him over and he remained devoted to her throughout her life. Jeoraj recollects that Sagat was a voracious reader and scoured the State Library for military classics.[4]

Bikaner was one of the first states that acceded to the Indian

---

1 The Bikaner State Forces gave a salary of Rupees 250 a month to a major. The Maharaja subsequently increased Sagat's salary and made it at par with the Indian Army.

2 **Personal correspondence of Shri Jeoraj Singh dated 06 Jun 2009.**

3 Ibid.

4 **In conversation with Shri Jeoraj Singh at Bikaner on 29 May 2009.**

Union and Sagat did most of the staff work that ensured a smooth transition of the units of the State Forces into the Indian Army. He also helped a fair number of his colleagues in getting absorbed into the Army.

In Feb 1949, Sagat was transferred to the Indian Army and put on the panel of 3 Gorkha Rifles.[5] He was posted as General Staff Officer Grade 2 (GSO2), responsible both for operations and intelligence, to HQ Delhi Area, then commanded by Maj Gen Tara Singh Bal. As a parting gift, Maharaja Sadul Singh presented him with the complete four volume set of the Biography of General Robert E Lee. Sagat had to leave Kamla behind as Ranvijay, his eldest son, was born that very month at the Government Hospital, Ratangarh. Kamla spent a forlorn few months, including an extended stay at the Village, where she and her mother-in-law developed a healthy respect for each other.

Delhi was a hotbed of military and diplomatic activity as HQ Western Command, which was fighting the War in J&K, was also located there. Sagat held a crucial appointment and was kept extremely busy. During this period he also made a sustained effort to get his seniority from the state forces restored in the Indian Army. Lt Col Duleep Sinh, who was the Military Secretary to Lt Gen KM Cariappa, then Army Commander, Western Command, recalls that he and Sagat became good friends. 'He was flamboyant, a thorough professional, very hard working and extremely cheerful. I was instrumental to some extent in getting his state service recognised, which catapulted Sagat in seniority. He never forgot this and right till I retired, without my asking, endeavoured to help me. This strong feeling of gratitude, loyalty and friendship was one of his greatest qualities.'[6] Knowing his helpful nature most former state

---

5 Sagat had given his first choice as 5 GR, second as 3 GR and third as Rajputana Rifles.

6 **In conversation with Lt Col Duleep Sinh at Rajpipla on 16 Mar 2009.** Being a part of the Military Secretary's Committee for absorbing and posting state forces officers, he recollects that Sagat stood head and shoulders above others. It was coincidence that both of them joined the Third Gorkha Rifles.

forces officers would gravitate to him with their problems.[7] GSO2 Delhi Area was a high pressure job and though Sagat carried an air of insouciance about him he had to work very hard. The frenetic social life of those days established a habit and he developed a hard head for alcohol.

Once Sagat's seniority was restored, he was posted as the Brigade Major (BM) of the Samba Brigade in J&K in Oct 1950. Coincidentally, his second son, Digvijay, was born the same month that he moved to Samba, putting Kamla again under strain. Sagat was very regimental minded and he made it a point that all officers of 3 GR, who passed through Samba, availed his hospitality.[8] Typical of him, when a vacancy on a pilot Command Mountain Warfare Course was allotted to the Brigade, Sagat managed to wheedle the Brigade Commander to allow him to attend it. In June 1951, he was also short listed for the command of the President's Bodyguard. Fortuitously nothing came of it as then his career may have digressed on a different path. He ran the Western Command Pre-Staff Course in his usual competent manner and was especially thanked by the Army Commander. It was obvious that Sagat's military ability was bringing him into the limelight. Lt Gen (then Capt) K Chiman Singh remembers staying with him in Samba, where he had come for his promotion exam. Sagat used to play a daily game of either basketball or volleyball with his troops and was very popular with them.[9] Samba was on the neck that joined J&K with the rest of India. It was barely two years since the war over the state had come to an uneasy halt and Sagat's Brigade was always on alert on account of frequent posturing by Pakistan armoured forces along the border.

After spending three years as BM, Sagat received his posting to 3/3 GR, located at Bharatpur, which he joined as a company

---

7 **In conversation with Brig Jagmal Singh, VrC, VSM, at Bikaner on 29 May 2009.**

8 **In conversation with Lt Gen (retd) Raj Anand at New Delhi on 16 Sep 2009.** In addition Mrs Duleep Sinh recollects that when the family was moving to J&K, Kamla and Sagat overwhelmed them with their hospitality. "Kamla was gentle, soft spoken, very helpful and very simple." **In conversation with Mrs Duleep Sinh at Rajpipla on 16 Mar 2009.**

9 **Lt Gen K Chiman Singh.** In correspondence with the Author.

commander in Oct 1953. There was something about his personality, the strong aura of strength and competence as well his ready ability to laugh and maintain his serenity, which established a strong bond between him and these simple hill people. The bond remained strong right through his service and beyond. This was a crucial period in the absorption of Gorkha troops into the Indian Army. They were elite amongst the imperial soldiery of the British Empire and though most had volunteered to remain in the Indian Army after Partition, they remained wary of the Indian Officer, who had never commanded them till Independence. Even now a large number of their officers were former Viceroy Commissioned Officers (now called JCOs), who had been commissioned as officers from their ranks. Trust, then as now, has always been an issue, which the officer had to work hard at; once given, the Gorkha soldier was his to command. Sagat had a natural talent for command and the men took to him willingly. He took over as the second in command (2ic) in Jun 1954 and his third son, Veervijay was born that Aug. These were some of the happiest and earliest memories of Ranvijay and he remembers his father taking him to his native village, where he was put under the tutelage of an old *risala* veteran to learn the desert lore.

The Maharaja of Bharatpur used to visit the Battalion often and he and Sagat became good friends. It was a friendship which remained till Sagat retired, despite the latter's occasional volatile and eccentric behaviour. Once Sagat invited the Maharaja as the chief guest to a unit function and declared that he had been gracious enough to agree to present a gift to the Battalion. Sure enough when the Battalion received orders to move to Dharamsala in Nov 1954, the Maharaja presented some beautiful silver trophies to the Unit.[10] Sagat moved the Battalion to Dharamsala, where their Brigade Commander was Brigadier (later Lt Gen and Colonel of the Regiment) PO Dunn, formerly of 1/3 GR. He had barely settled

---

10 '....... which are objects d'art and are preserved till today.' P 66. **Flash of the Kukhri: History of the 3rd Gorkha Rifles by CL Proudfoot. Vision Books, New Delhi. 1984.** Also recollected by **Lt Gen GS Negi (in conversation at Dehra Dun on 27 Sep 2009)** who remembered this incident as told to him by Maj NB Chand.

down with his family when he received his promotion orders, with instructions to take over command of 2/3 GR in Feb 1955, at Ferozepur.

The Commanding Officer of 2/3 GR, Lt Col (later Brig) NL Kapoor, MC, had gone on posting to the Defence Services Staff College. He left the Battalion to Sagat with a strong base in ceremonial functions.[11] Sagat, more down to earth, took that as an opportunity to focus his attention on training and sports. One of the first acts of Sagat was to appoint Capt (later Major General and Colonel of the Regiment) Tirath Singh Verma as his Adjutant and Capt AS Thapa as his Quartermaster. The Battalion was on collective training and Sagat immediately put his stamp on the Unit by refusing to accept any shoddy work. The men and sub units had to adhere to standards set by him. He initially focussed on the training of his non commissioned officers even going to the extent of taking classes himself. Special emphasis was given to section and platoon tactics. 'He was very strict in promoting people and put on the brakes at the first NCO promotion cadre ie Rifleman to Lance Naik (lance corporal). He repeatedly said that if you make the correct selection at the Ummedwar (Rifleman to Lance Naik promotion cadre) level, you will never go wrong.'[12] On the other hand he insisted that the officers treat the men as individuals and were never to be brusque with them, especially where their promotion and career prospects were concerned.[13]

To get the Battalion habituated he emphasised on drills and procedures to the point of laboriousness. However irksome to the officers, he closely monitored their implementation so that no

---

11 The Battalion had hit a nadir in its performance when it was at Mhow and was sneered at as 'labourers dressed in uniform.' Brig Kapoor thus had concentrated on improving its profile and the confidence of the rank and file. **In conversation with Maj Gen Tirath Singh Verma at Dehra Dun on 27 Sep 2009.**

12 Ibid.

13 **In conversation with Lt Gen Raj Anand.** "He emphasized that it was an important function of command and leadership that the soldier was convinced as to the reasons why he failed."

shortcuts were taken. His successors, like Lt Col (later Lt Gen and Colonel of the Regiment) Abhimanyu Vohra, strictly followed his example in adhering to procedures. Because of that even now the Battalion still retains its reputation as one of the finest in the Indian Army. Lt Gen (then 2/Lt) Raj Anand recollects that the priority Sagat gave to training 'never left my mind...... as I watched him hone up a unit; and I must confess that I used those techniques throughout my career.'[14] Sagat also laid stress on the training of his young officers. He had an easy way about him and was always supportive of his officers though he abhorred slipshod work or flouting of norms. 'He laid down in detail what an officer had to do and insisted that they set an example in implementing unit regulations. He was pretty strict in the conduct of retention examinations and was not willing to put up with failures.'[15] Somewhat reluctantly and then with enthusiasm, the officers started to trust and respect him. This had a positive impact on the Battalion, which set exceptional standards in performance.

Sagat's next focus was on creating a healthy fund position for the Battalion. Though highly principled and open, he did cut some corners. As Tirath Verma recollects, 'Sagat said, put a line on what you take over and put another line when you leave. If you have not put your unit on a sounder financial footing, you haven't done one of your primary jobs.'[16] 'He considered himself a trustee of the Regimental Funds and ensured they were used for the good of the troops. When he left, the Battalion was on a sounder financial footing from the precarious stage at which he had inherited it.'[17]

Another revelation in the Battalion was Kamla. Her open friendly nature endeared her to all the ladies. She had no inhibitions about being a Commanding Officer's wife and was regarded by all more as a first amongst equal rather than a superior. Mrs Tirath

---

14 Ibid.

15 Ibid.

16 Verma op cit.

17 Anand op cit.

Verma recollects that there was no activity which she considered below her and involved all her ladies in it. 'There were frequent trips to Ferozepur on bicycles, which we all learnt to ride, however precariously. There was one instance when we all returned from a shopping trip laughing and chatting and Mrs Negi, mother of Gambir Negi (later Lt Gen and Colonel of the Regiment), took a toss right at her front gate much to our amusement.'[18] There was another instance when the Vermas were celebrating their son Vicky's (later Lt Col Vikram Singh Verma) birthday. Kamla spent the whole morning helping out at the Verma's home and in the evening Sagat arrived there to get the party going with the Battalion Band in attendance. Gambir, then studying in Class 4, recalls that he and other children constantly frequented her company.[19]

There were two major events which took place at Ferozepur. The first was the visit of the Minister of Defence, Shri VN Katju. The Unit learnt about Sagat's attention to detail when he ensured that every aspect and program was meticulously rehearsed and prepared. The brigade commander had specifically selected 2/3rd and was not disappointed. The Minister left highly pleased and praised the Battalion in Delhi. The next major event was the first celebration of Pirkanthi Day, the Battle Honour awarded to the Battalion for capturing the tactically important feature of Pirkanthi on 26 Jun 1948 at the height of the Kashmir Campaign. The event was planned on a grand scale, to the extent that slabs of ice were used to depict the snow line on a model prepared of the 10386 feet high massif on the Pir Panjal Range. There was not a single aspect of this occasion, which Sagat had not scrupulously planned and it showed in the conduct. Sagat was at his aggravating best in these events but as the days went by his officers noticed that once he was satisfied he began to delegate and became more easy going.

Sagat's next emphasis was on sports and his competitive spirit manifested itself in ensuring that every competition was

---

18 **In conversation with Mrs Tirath Singh Verma in Dehra Dun on 27 Sep 2009.**
19 Negi. Op cit.

fiercely fought over. He established a regimen of company level competitions, which were enthusiastically played with lots of cheering amongst the troops. Any failure in performance was analysed with some bantering and fresh preparations begun for the next round.

The Battalion completed its tenure at Ferozepur and left for J&K by train in Oct 1955. The Battalion came under command 268 Infantry Brigade, which was a part of 26 Infantry Division. It was allotted most ramshackle accommodation at Bandowali Rakh but Sagat, renowned for his liaison, immediately got about getting facilities for his troops with the neighbouring battalions, especially 17 Rajputana Rifles, chipping in generously. As Raj Anand admits, 'No other CO could have managed this change with the dynamism and felicity which Sagat exhibited.' Sagat had a relative short stay in the Battalion while it was in field and he moved out on Senior Officers Course in Dec 1955. This short stay was enough for him to ensure that the unit won the Division Skill at Arms Competition by a wide margin. Sagat also came to know that Brig SHFJ 'Sam' Manekshaw was likely to take over the Division. He anticipated the type of person he was and started gearing up the Battalion, going so much as to procure the pamphlets Sam had prepared at the Infantry School and making his officers study them. As Raj Anand points out, 'He had an iron will to get what he wanted. He had personal ambitions of a very high level but he would not compromise his professional ethos. He ensured that his accomplishments were on account of professional competence and not by bluster. His achievements were there on the ground and remained as a legacy for the Battalion to emulate.'[20]

It is fitting that the impact he made in the Battalion be related in the words of an NCO who served under him. Havildar Pas Bahadur Gurung joined 3/3 GR in 1940 and went through the Manipur Battles of the Battalion during World War 2. While on a stint of well earned leave in 1944, he was shanghaied and sent to Italy, with a draft of

---

20 Raj Anand. Op cit.

180 recruits, to 2/3 GR. After landing at Taranto, he fought with the Battalion up the boot of Italy. After Independence he fought in J&K under Maj Kaptan Singh Rana up the slopes of Pirkanthi. By the time he retired in 1961, he was a hardened veteran, having served with British and Indian officers. He vividly recollects the command of Sagat. 'He was very good to the men but uncompromising in his orders. We all used to be wary of his tall and broad frame as he refused to accept any slipshod activity from us. He would not accept no for an answer or cancel an order. Work given by him had to be carried out. His orders had to be implemented like a bullet that without deviation reaches its destination.'[21]

While on Senior Officers Course, where he received an Instructor grading, Sagat got his posting orders to command 3/3 GR, which had been without a CO for some time. In an uncanny piece of coincidence for the luckless Kamla, his youngest son Chandravijay was born the same month that he moved to take over command of the Battalion. 3/3 GR was still at Dharamsala and he immediately began focussing on training and sports. He found the atmosphere somewhat vitiated as his predecessor had issued a fair number of warnings to the officers. Sagat summoned his 2ic, opened the CO's safe and without even reading the letters burnt them. He told him to tell the officers that they all would start with a clean slate under him. He would work them hard but expected them to do their duty. He had no problems thereafter.[22] Sagat set about working on the Battalion Standing Orders and as one of the officer's recollects, 'his practical approach to standards, procedures and drills, which he implemented with unbending zeal, ensured that the Standing Orders were being implemented in the day to day running of the Unit.'[23] These Standing Orders stood the test of time and were only

---

21 In conversation with **Havildar Pas Bahadur Rana at Dehra Dun on 29 Sep 2009.**

22 In conversation with **Col Ranvijay Singh at Jaipur on 27 May 2009.**

23 As told to the Author by **Lt Col (later Lt Gen and Colonel of 3 GR) MK (Mike) Lahiri** while making him work on the Standing Orders of 4/3 GR at Lohitpur in 1970. Mike had come from 3/3 GR to command 4/3 GR and frequently commented on the examples set by Sagat. It is perhaps ironic that when 3/3 GR was reviewing its Standing Orders in 2000, it borrowed the Standing Orders of 4/3 GR. In the same manner when Abhimanyu

CO 3/3 GR

upgraded after 1989.[24]

Immediately after Sagat had taken over the Battalion, the Unit took part in a test exercise being conducted for 5 Infantry Division. Sagat knew exactly what had to be done and the Battalion did so well that it was especially commended by the Corps Commander, Lt Gen JN Chaudhury.[25]

As usual, Sagat also immediately started focussing on sports and professional excellence. The Battalion moved to Amritsar for six months but that made no difference to Sagat as far as the procedures and drills were concerned. It came as no surprise that the Unit won most of the competitions and was adjudged the best battalion in maintenance of arms and technical equipment. While attending a party in 3 Sikh, during that Unit's Centenary Celebrations, the two commanding officers got into a combative mood on the issue of which was the best battalion in the Brigade. It all boiled down to a *Khud Race* (cross country hill race) competition between the two. The Brigade Commander, Brig Dunn, raised the ante by terming it a hill race to test the toughness of Gorkhas and Sikhs. The Maharaja of Nabha, who was present, got into the spirit of the challenge and agreed to present a silver trophy. The Race was conducted at Yol, and required the competitors to run cross country for over four miles up and down hill with an altitude variation of nearly 4,500 ft. To all those who know the Gorkhas, the outcome was a foregone conclusion and the Battalion won by a huge margin. The event was considered important enough to have the Corps Commander witnessing it along with Justice GD Khosla.

As he did in 2/3 GR, Sagat also set about putting the Battalion

---

Vohra set about writing the Standing Orders of 2/3 GR in 1959, he incorporated the notes and instructions left by Sagat. Thus Sagat's legacy was being followed by three battalions of the Regiment in some way or the other.

24 Negi in conversation. op cit

25 P 67. **Flash of the Kukhri**. The General wrote, '......the rate of advance by the Advance Guard was so rapid that they cannot accept it as normal for planning purposes.' In addition the defences were so well camouflaged that the exercise enemy was completely misled in the direction of attack. Op cit.

finances on a sound footing. He equipped the messes with crockery and cutlery, some imported from Sheffield, UK. The band was refurbished and a number of silver pieces were procured. As Gambir recalls, by the time Sagat left, the precarious financial state of the Battalion had improved considerably.[26] Mrs Rajni Negi remembered that years later when Sagat came for a visit he took her around the mess with obvious pride. 'I was a young bride and it was remarkable in the way he knew the history of every silver piece in the Mess'.[27]

Sagat moved the Battalion to Punch in Aug 1957 and immediately set them to renovating the defences. Western Command had decided to institutionalise the Mountain Warfare Course. Brig Jagjit Singh Aurora was put in charge and Sagat along with Lt Col (later Gen and Governor) KVK Rao were made responsible to prepare the syllabus and exercises. As Krishna Rao reminisces, 'Though we had entirely different personalities, we got along very well. I realised I could do business with him as he was professionally very sound and most competent. Our mutual regard stood us in good stead over the years.'[28] By Nov, Sagat received his posting order to report as a Senior Instructor to the Tactical Wing at the Infantry School, Mhow. Years later, while in conversation with a retired Subedar Major of the Battalion, Gambir recalls him mentioning nostalgically that 3/3 GR really came up during the time of Sagat and thereafter never looked back.[29]

One of the first things that Sagat did on his posting to Mhow was to withdraw Ranvijay and Digvijay from Mayo College for two years as he could not afford their education owing to family commitments. He had developed a close friendship with Jack Gibson, the Principal, which he maintained even after Jack retired. The Commandant of the Infantry School was Brig PO Dunn, his

---

26 Negi in conversation. Op cit. 'I learnt a valuable lesson from him to always leave the financial state of an institution in a better shape than when you inherit it.'

27 **In conversation with Mrs Rajni Negi in Dehra Dun on 27 Sep 2009.**

28 **In conversation with Gen KV Krishna Rao at Secunderabad on 03 Jan 2011.**

29 Negi in conversation. Op cit.

former brigade commander. Since he knew Sagat well he got him involved in all facets of activities being carried out by the School. As an instructor Sagat brought his sharp mind to tactical problems in a lucid and logical style. All major exercises were reviewed by him and new concepts incorporated in a methodical professional manner. Maj Gen (then Capt) OP Sabharwal, who was posted in Mhow at the same time, recollects that all major discussions were invariably conducted by Sagat. Dunn made Sagat responsible for many regimental matters as he had become the Colonel of the Regiment on 9 Sep 1958. That year a Battle Honours Committee had been appointed, which asked all regiments to submit their claims of World War 2 and beyond. Sagat and a team of officers of the Regiment did a thorough research into the battles fought by the Regiment. The Research was so consummate and intellectually sound that Brig AK Sanyal, Colonel 3 GR, in 1998 had the research and recommendations printed, bound and distributed within the Regiment as he considered the Paper 'of great value to professionals.'[30]

Lt Gen Chiman Singh, who was also an instructor at the Infantry School, recalls that Sagat lived 400 metres away from his house and visits to each other's home became a regular affair. Kamla used to walk down frequently and more or less adopted them as her family. When a baby was in the offing, Sagat unreservedly gave his car for them to use. Socially Sagat enjoyed the atmosphere of the Central India Club (later the Defence Services Officers Institute) and his head for alcohol stood him in good stead. He was popular with students and was in the middle of all social activities. Dr Ajit Singh, whose father Lt Col Jai Singh was posted in Mhow, remembers meeting him in 1960. He was at the heart of all social events being conducted.[31] During the last six months of Sagat's tenure, he was appointed the head of the School Training Team. Dunn had already

---

30 **Forward written by Brig AK Sanyal to 'Claims of Battle Honours of 3 GR during World War 2' on 28 Feb 1998.**

31 **In conversation with Dr Ajit Singh on 29 Feb 2009 at Jaipur.** 'I remember he used to dress immaculately while Mrs Sagat Singh kept a very good house where I once had an elaborate continental meal.'

kept him longer than the scheduled tenure and reluctantly let him go when he received his promotion to Colonel along with a posting to Army HQ as Deputy Director Personnel Services, in May 1960.

On posting to Delhi, Sagat realised that he had to create an income for Kamla, independent of his salary as his career would likely keep them separated from time to time. His contacts enabled him to make a down payment on a petrol pump in Kotah, the rent of which was thereafter paid into Kamla's account.

Sagat's meticulous work and professional acumen brought him to the notice of Lt Gen (later Gen and COAS) PP Kumaramangalam, the Adjutant General. It was a crucial relationship as Kumaramangalam's confidence in Sagat's abilities would subsequently get him command of the elite Para Brigade. Kumaramangalam disliked long winded summaries and would insist on an issue being explained to him on one page, something Sagat was adept at. While on tour, Kumaramangalam had a pointed habit of paying for his drink and the newspaper. The latter he would share with no one. On one occasion, in Kumaramangalam's absence, Sagat entertained a guest of the General and they spent a very convivial evening in which several drinks were consumed. Sagat paid for them, which Kumaramangalam was informed of when he asked for the bill. When queried, Sagat innocently replied that as the General paid only for his drinks, Sagat had no choice but to pay for the guest. This once Kumaramangalam paid all the bills including Sagat's considerable whiskey expenses.[32]

As Sagat got familiar with his job he realised that there were several knotty issues which had been brushed under the carpet by his predecessors. In typical style he selected the most difficult. There were 5000 accounts which had become redundant over the years and were required to be closed. In painstaking manner Sagat traced out the fund trail, convinced his counterpart at the MOD as to where the funds should be transferred and then closed all the accounts. Ranvijay recollects that another case, the issue of

---

32 Jeoraj Singh op cit.

enhancing the pay of the Military Nursing Service (MNS) came up before the Second Pay Commission. Knowing full well the hardheartedness of the bureaucrat, Sagat convinced the somewhat outraged head of the MNS to pretend to cry pathetically when the issue of pay came up. The lady handled the detailed questioning competently but during a crucial moment, at an imperceptible nod from Sagat, broke out into uncontrollable sobs. The hapless Committee, much pained by this display of raw emotion, quickly acceded to the point.[33] The posting to Delhi proved crucial to Sagat's career as it got him command of the elite Para Brigade. It also taught him to navigate the convoluted corridors of military civil relations. The civil servants he came in contact with remained his friends thereafter and greatly assisted him in getting matters processed rapidly, much to the envy of his other colleagues. Sagat was never shy about networking and though it helped him in his career, the number of people he was able to assist throughout his life is legion. It also established his reputation of getting the job done, however difficult or complicated it may be.

---

33 Ranvijay ibid.

CHAPTER THREE

THE LIBERATION OF GOA

De l'audace, et encore de l'audace,
et toujours de l'audace.

- Georges Jacques Danton

Located on the western coast of India, Goa's status was an anachronism in the latter half of the 20th Century. Post World War 2, while other regions achieved independence, Goa remained a Portuguese Colony. Oliviera Salazar, the Portuguese President, in an etymological sleight of hand had named it an Overseas Province of Portugal.[1] In addition, Portugal had two other small enclaves, Daman and Diu, on the Gujarat Coast.[2] An independence movement, encouraged by India, was active and creating disturbance in the Colony. A *satyagraha* movement launched by the Praja Socialist Party, under Dr Ram Manohar Lohia, was brutally suppressed by the police on 15 Aug 1955, when it fired on the agitators killing 22 and injuring over 225. Throughout 1960 and 1961, public opinion, orchestrated by local leaders and politicians[3] hardened, while

---

1 In a speech to the National Assembly at Lisbon on 20 Oct 1949, Salazar had firmly reiterated that 'Goa is integrated in the Portuguese sovereignty for many centuries.' P. 21. This was further reinforced when on 01 July 1955 the Portuguese possessions in India were legally incorporated as part of Portugal. **Operation Vijay: The Ultimate Solution by Shrikant Y Ramani; Broadway Book Centre, Panjim, 2008.**

2 The smaller enclaves of Dadra and Nagar Haveli, adjacent to Daman, had wrested themselves free in 1954 through a local movement and were integrated into India in Aug 1961.

3 Some of these politicians wanted to be seen leading the advance into Goa and importuned the Army to take them along. They were politely rebuffed. P 113. **War in the High Himalayas: The Indian Army in Crisis by Major General DK Palit, VrC; Lancer International, New Delhi, 1991.**

Nehru and his foreign minister tried to explore the diplomatic route for a peaceful transfer of power.[4]

By mid 1961 the Government of India had turned round to the view that there was no alternative except for the use of force. Some intelligence inputs also indicated that the Portuguese Government was planning to make the harbour facilities of Goa available to Pakistan. The flashpoint was the Anjidiv Incident when an Indian steamship and subsequently some fishing vessels were allegedly fired upon by the Portuguese garrison on Anjidiv Island, resulting in casualties. The Indian Navy thereafter initiated a linear patrol off the coast of Goa with two warships.[5]

Goa is located just south of Maharashtra, separated from that State by the Terekhol River. To the east it is bounded by the Sahayadri Range of the Western Ghats, adjacent to the Belgaum and North Kanara Districts of Karnataka. It has an extent of 100 kms by 64 kms with an area of 3635 sq kms. Offshoots from the Sahayadri form numerous hills and valleys with fast flowing rivers. These rivers widen and flow westwards through Goa and ultimately have a junction with either the Mandovi or the Zuari Rivers. These two rivers, which are linked by a creek, encircle the island of Goa and form a major obstacle to any approach to the capital at Panjim. While any movement from east to west is through hilly and forested countryside it nevertheless is along the grain of the country. Movement from either North or South, being against the grain, would involve frequent river crossings, delayed by blown bridges.

Sagat was posted as Commander of 50 Para Brigade at Agra, on

---

4 Lt Gen BM Kaul, who was the Chief of the General Staff during that period, brings out the ambivalence felt by Nehru as he contemplated armed action. **The Untold Story by Lt Gen BM Kaul; Allied Publishers, New Delhi, 1967.** Pp 290 – 301.

5 "I am not certain how much……..reported about Goa was true Intelligence and how much tendentious fabrication. It is even possible………that the whole scheme was cooked up between Krishna Menon, Bijji Kaul and the Intelligence Bureau to make out a feasible *casus belli*……..". p 420 **Memories and Musings Vol II by Maj Gen DK Palit, VrC; Palit and Palit, New Delhi, 2004.** The Author was the Director of Military Operations during this period.

promotion from Army HQ, in Sep 1961. Lt Gen PP Kumaramangalam, the Adjutant General, who was on the lookout for a dynamic officer to take over this elite formation, had no hesitation in posting him to the Para Brigade, despite Sagat being a non para officer. Though this was not a precedent, it was viewed with some apprehension by the insular minded Brigade. Sagat, always ready for fresh challenges, was delighted with his posting. In his own words, what struck him most was the 'outstanding comradeship, zeal and esprit de corps prevailing in all ranks of the Brigade.'[6] As Sagat said, his 'more immediate concern was......... to earn his wings'[7] in order to make himself acceptable. This he did in 'record time,' at times making two jumps in a day. Though he never revealed this to anyone, he injured his back in the process. This caused him a fair amount of pain and discomfort though he bore this stoically, even going to the extent of carrying out his mandatory jumps every year. At that time the Brigade was one battalion short but Sagat set to the training of the Formation with a will, conducting exercises for 1 and 2 Para and bringing them to a sharp state of readiness. Sagat's arrival was like a breath of fresh air and he soon endeared himself to all ranks.[8] Professionally and socially he could outdo anyone. It is here that his reputation for hard drinking got firmly established. Much to the admiration of the officers, it never interfered with his work. Even after a prolonged bout of drinking at night, Sagat would be found the next day, at the crack of dawn, cool and collected as ever.[9]

By the end of August the Indian Government had reluctantly come to the view that force may have to be used for the liberation of Goa. The Army Chief asked the Army Commander of Southern Command, Lt Gen JN Chaudhury, to carry out a reconnaissance and

---

6 P. 151. **The Story of the Indian Airborne Troops by Major General (retd) Afsir Karim, AVSM; Lancer International, New Delhi, 1993.**

7 ibid.

8 **In conversation with Maj Gen Afsir Karim at NOIDA on 17 Sep 2009.**

9 This is one tradition of the Brigade which seems to be firmly established. To be known as hard bitten and tough as nails one had to have a hard head. What set these elite troops apart are a unique panache and the 'characters' among the officers who, luckily for the Indian Army, regularly rise to higher ranks.

submit a report with options for the liberation of Goa. Chaudhury submitted a military appreciation[10] by 11 Nov. A few things stand out in the Report, which had implications in the conduct of operations:-

- The poor state of roads on the Indian side and few kms either side of the Border, especially on the Northern Axis. The approach from Karwar along the existing coastal highway (present NH17A) was the best maintained but, for obvious though erroneous reasons, Chaudhury did not consider it as a major thrust line.

- The grain of the country and the problems likely to be faced in moving from north or south across the river obstacles. It was felt that the Portuguese would demolish all the bridges over the rivers, thus severely inhibiting any movement.

- It was estimated that there were three infantry battalions of the enemy in Goa.

The conclusions of the Report obviously affected the planning process. Firstly, the poor condition of the roads did not seem have been given adequate consideration when the selection of the main axis of advance was done. The roads through the Sahayadris were in no state to take on sustained and heavy traffic, especially the large bridging trains which were expected to move on them.[11] Secondly, the problem of moving against the grain and the impact of blown bridges on the momentum of the advance seems to have been over emphasised.[12] Thirdly, the estimated strength of the Portuguese armed forces and their capability seems to have been misinterpreted. Either this was a deliberate ploy to garner additional

---

10 The full appreciation is available for reading in the book by Ramani. Op cit. '...... Muchu..... sent us a text- book solution for a formal set-piece operation – whereas what we wanted was a quick smash-and-grab attack....' P. 420. Palit in Musing .Op cit.

11 The main road through the Ghats has heavy traffic. Even today in case of breakdown of a heavy vehicle traffic can get backed up for miles.

12 Kaul, with his trademark dynamism, moved large quantities of bridging equipment from all over India with which 17 Division (even the Para Brigade) was burdened with as it struggled through the Sahayadris.

resources or the Indian intelligence agencies may not have been aware that Portugal had cut down its military strength in Goa in 1960. The Appreciation gave a ballpark figure of three Portuguese infantry battalions and additional 3000 local levies and police. In actual fact there were three mixed groups (with a fourth group to be created once Indian intentions were known) composed out of four reconnaissance companies and eight infantry companies; 1/3rd of them comprised indigenous troops.

It may be apposite to give a comment here on the tactics planned to be followed by the Portuguese forces in Goa. The Governor General was Maj Gen Vassalo De'Silva, who was also the Commander-in Chief of Portuguese Forces in Goa. Being an engineer officer, he had personally planned the demolitions and denials on the ingress routes, which were executed fairly efficiently. All these routes had troops earmarked. They were required to take all police and custom personnel under command and fight a systematic delaying action in consonance with the demolitions being carried out. Thereafter withdrawal was to be along successive delay lines to the inner fortresses of the Marmugao Peninsula and the Island of Goa. In a letter to the President, De'Silva, ever sceptical, had written that it would be a miracle if they could resist for even eight days.[13] The Portuguese leadership in Goa did not seem to have any illusions about their powers of resistance, regardless of the fiery exhortations from the Mother Country. Their best troops had been withdrawn for service in more critical colonies and the remnants were an 'ill organised and undisciplined force........with no central logistical system.'[14] In addition, their leadership, in an attempt at reverse motivation, had painted the Indian Army as a ferocious bunch of hooligans, which only spread apprehension. These ad hoc sub units were required to carry out a disciplined and orderly withdrawal, the most difficult operation of war. No wonder Chaudhury was sanguine about victory but even he did not anticipate the speed of advance and how Sagat would turn the

---

13 P. 102. Ramani op cit.

14 P. 157. Afsir Karim op cit.

Campaign on its head.

In his outline plan, Chaudhury had planned for two infantry brigades plus a battalion being allotted to him.[15] The Para Brigade was slotted to advance on what he thought was the easier approach, the direct route across the Sahayadris, while another infantry brigade was to advance from the North. Obviously, his efforts to garner additional resources seem to have worked better than expected,[16] as along with the Para Brigade, 17 Mountain Division less a brigade was allotted to him. He thereafter switched the axes of advance and allotted the Northern Axis to the Para Brigade. 17 Mountain Division, with its two brigades, was allotted the Central Axis and was to advance directly from Belgaum.[17] As a deception, one company of 20 Rajput, designated 20 Infantry Brigade, was to move on the Southern Axis from Karwar.

Sagat was on leave and driving to Jaipur from Agra in his battered old Standard Vanguard when a 'Flash' signal was received at the Para Brigade that he was to contact the Director of Military Operation immediately. Though Palit in his book claims that he kept the planning for the whole operation under wraps, it was obvious that the Para Brigade had inkling that something was afoot. The Brigade Major tried desperately to contact Sagat the whole day and finally succeeded in getting through by the evening. Sagat was back in Agra the next morning and took charge of things in his usual unruffled way after having a word with Palit. There was a 'visible calming of nerves'[18] as he set things in motion. The next day, on

---

15 Initially Gen Chaudhury had requested for 1 Armoured Division to be allotted to him. P 117 Palit. Op cit.

16 He played upon the fear of the politician that own forces may suffer a local reverse at the hand of a European country, that too a member of the NATO Alliance.

17 Chaudhury, ever on the lookout for some personal glory, was keen to put the Para Brigade under his command. However, GOC 17 Infantry Division firmly rejected the idea. P 147, Palit. Op cit. This had a petty implication subsequently on the conduct of the Campaign.

18 **In conversation with Col (retd) RR Chatterjee at New Delhi on 22 Sep 2009.** Col Chatterjee was the Brigade Signal Officer during this period.

29 Nov, Sagat was called at the Operations Directorate at Army Headquarters, which he reached within 50 minutes as the Air Force Station Commander, who was a good friend of his, made an Air Force Dakota available to him. Palit and Sagat were old friends since their Staff College days and as Palit says, 'I had known Sagat for some years. He was an unorthodox, rough cut and practical soldier, always happier with troops than behind a desk and with a field operative's disdain for the systematist....' Palit was keen that Goa be captured before international opinion could sway Nehru and asked Sagat to have 'alternative plans to have a part of his force in the Goan capital within 24 hours.'[19]

He and Sagat were both keen on a paradrop. This created vigorous discussion at Army Headquarters as the Air Force barely had a two company lift capability. In addition, they flatly refused to do a night drop. 'I finally suggested that one company be dropped at dawn, another at first light and the rest of the Battalion by day.'[20] Thereafter, 2 Para was moved to Begumpet (Hyderabad) for airborne training. The operation was subsequently called off; it seemed, at the behest of the Air Force, though Palit felt that it was rejected by Chaudhury as he did not want the Para Brigade to get to Panjim before the main body.[21]

That same day the General Officer Commanding (GOC) of 17 Mountain Division, Maj Gen MM Khanna, MVC, was summoned to Army Headquarters for briefing. He was most irate as he had just been nominated for a course at the Imperial Defence College (now the Royal College of Defence Studies) and was apprehensive that the Goa Operation would prevent him from going. Despite reassurance by Palit that the operation would be of short duration, he remained unwilling. Not wanting to have a reluctant GOC at the helm, the CGS asked for a replacement. Brig 'Unni' Candeth, posted

---

19 P 136. Palit op cit.

20 P 152. Sagat in Afsir Karim. Op cit.

21 P 138. Palit. Op cit. Palit is somewhat uncharitable enough to suggest that Chaudhury even denied Para Brigade the use of a mule company.

at Army Headquarters, was catapulted in command, promoted and briefed by Palit on 30 Nov.[22]

Sagat now was in the mood for war and did not allow petty distractions from affecting his preparations. On 30 Nov he gave out his warning orders for operations. The Brigade was ordered to be ready to move by 2 Dec. There was hardly any time to get the units prepared and battle worthy. However, since para units are always slotted for sudden moves the Para Brigade's battle procedure, under the efficient Brigade Major, Madan Chadha, switched smoothly into high gear. While the Air Force flew down 2 Para[23] to Begumpet, the other units got down to the more humdrum ritual of carrying out a rail move. All those who observed Sagat during that period noted his absolute confidence and hands on approach. He used his contacts to make up deficiencies in officers and material. He also began acquiring information about Goa from all possible sources, including the IB, who helped in contacting local politicians and influential people.

The Brigade moved in several stages and in different modes of transport. While the Brigade Harbour Parties moved on night 2 Dec, the main body moved by rail after midday on 3 Dec. Some important personnel were moved by air to Poona and thereafter by rail to Belgaum. Sagat, with his Brigade Major and intelligence staff officer, along with a jeep, moved in a Fairchild Packet Aircraft directly to Belgaum on 5 Dec. The Brigade Headquarter and the unit concentration areas were established north of Belgaum on the road to Sawantwadi. Meanwhile, the main body had to trans-ship onto a metre gauge line from Poona and reached Belgaum on 6 Dec. Guns and heavy vehicles had to move by road and reached somewhat later. Despite lack of vehicles and other hurdles, the move had been carried out fairly smoothly and received the compliments of

---

22 It adds to Candeth's status that he retained his equanimity throughout these bewildering turn of events even to the extent of standing up to the over powering personality of Muchu Chaudhury.

23 It is to Palit's credit that he ensured 2 Para moved to Begumpet by 1 Dec, despite reservations from several quarters.

the Army Commander.[24] Meanwhile 17 Division, which had moved from Ambala on 2 Dec, concentrated at Belgaum by 12 Dec.

To make up the deficiency of the third battalion, 2 Sikh LI was allotted to the Brigade and moved from Madras. At that stage it was discovered, much to the disappointment of all, that the airborne operation had been called off and 2 Para also rejoined the Brigade. Sagat was astonished to discover the deficiencies[25] existing in 2 Sikh LI and set about urgently to rectify them. He also had to get the Unit organised for operations. As he mentions, '..... (it) was performing garrison duties and had done no collective training for a considerable period.' He also did his best to imbue them 'with the enthusiasm and culture of the *esprit de corps* of the paratroopers'.[26] In the short time available the Brigade did some essential training. Weapons were zeroed, some field firing was carried out and battle drills were practiced. Troops were also trained in fabricating improvised river crossing expedients. It had become clear to Sagat that rivers would be a major obstacle to the rapid advance he was contemplating.

On 9 Dec, Candeth gave out his orders for OP VIJAY, as the operation was now called. Sagat issued his preliminary orders on 11 Dec. To use the subsidiary Northern Axis the Brigade had to move across the Western Ghats to an Advance Concentration Area at Sawantwadi, approximately 70 kms away. Despite transport constraints the Brigade concentrated there by 13 Dec. Units left all their heavy equipment at the Sambre Airfield of Belgaum and had shaken out for war. At Sawantwadi, the Maharaja called on Sagat and generously agreed to help in setting up a 40 bedded

---

24 Gen Chaudhury was sceptical that a concentration of such a large body of troops could be completed in the time contemplated. It thus became a prestige issue for the General Staff Branch, which approached the Railways, who responded magnificently to the challenge. 17 Division itself had to entrain from six different railway stations. Both Palit and Kaul have testified to the Railways efficiency. P 297, Kaul. Op cit.

25 The infantry battalions are fairly low down the order as far as deficiencies are concerned. In 1961, when no major conflict had taken place for more than a decade, the lack of urgency in making up shortfalls was understandable, if not forgivable.

26 P.152. Sagat in Afsir Karim. Op cit.

hospital for casualties. The Brigade engineers immediately started constructing separate airstrips for Auster and Dakota aircrafts and also a helipad. Meanwhile Sagat, after a great deal of wheedling, managed to secure a transport company consisting of the new 1 ton Nissan trucks. These proved invaluable during the advance. By some convoluted logic, higher headquarters allotted 7 Cavalry and a squadron of 8 Cavalry to the Brigade despite fears that it would get bogged down while moving against the grain of the country and attempting to cross at least four rivers![27]

On the evening of 14 Dec, Sagat gave out his final orders. All that was left was setting the final date for entering Goa which, everyone was told was likely to be 16 Dec. There was a bit of a hiatus here as Nehru, loath to go to war, tried some last minute diplomatic efforts. After some inner turmoil and persuasion, he finally gave the go ahead and the date for the offensive was fixed for 18 Dec.[28]

The Division advance was to be mainly on two axes.[29] The Red Route i.e. the axis of the Para Brigade was the northern one and was basically meant to tie down Portuguese troops. In his orders, Candeth had laid down the following tasks for the Para Brigade:-

- To secure Assonora and Bicholim and Usgao Bridge *with a view to advance on Ponda* (italics by Author).

- Secure Mapuca (after which the force nominated was to come under direct command of 17 Division).

The Yellow Route was the Divisional main axis across the Sahayadris and was to be led by 63 Infantry Brigade up to Mollem. Thereafter the advance was to be taken over by 48 Infantry Brigade.

---

[27] It is also likely that the prospect of trundling down the Ghats with 17 Division and its bridging equipment did not appeal to the Armoured Corps.

[28] The Portuguese thought that the Para Brigade was located at Poona for carrying out airborne operations, until well after the offensive was launched.

[29] Palit comments that in his briefing Candeth planned a copy book advance. '…… needlessly cautious and deliberate, he planned to move in formal stages'. P 146. Palit. Op cit.

The advance of the company of 20 Rajput from Karwar was directly under HQ Southern Command, which established a tactical headquarters at Belgaum on 13 Dec.

Sagat worked out a plan which allowed his units adequate flexibility and elbow room with reserves in hand to exploit any opportunity that came his way. Knowing the potential of his troops he was unwilling to relegate them to a sideshow. The fact that he had at least four rivers to cross and was abysmally short of transport does not seem to have fazed him. Three days prior to the Operation, Sagat was visited by the Chief, Gen PN Thapar and the Army Commander. Chaudhury was most sceptical of Sagat's plan, especially his timings, but his confidence was so infectious that he was allowed to carry on.[30] So confident was he of his abilities that he had pledged a drink at Mandovi Hotel with Palit that he would be the first to enter Panjim.[31]

As the hour for the offensive approached, Kaul, the CGS, decided to participate in the advance with the leading elements[32] and reached the Division Headquarters, located West of Belgaum. Then, with the Commander of 63 Brigade he, 'moved forward to the headquarters of a Sikh battalion in the advance guard'.[33] He gives a colourful account of a dangerous but speedy advance, which is somewhat belied by the actual happenings on the ground. His invitation to Chaudhury, to accompany him on this high adventure, was rather brusquely declined. Palit comments that he and the CGS 'held different views' and Kaul would not 'countenance my opinion that Brigadier Sagat Singh's Para Brigade, operating from Sawantwadi from the North, would beat the main column and get

---

30 P 303. **Leadership in the Indian Army by Maj Gen VK Singh; Sage Publications, Delhi, Fifth Printing, 2008.** Sagat was lucky in having supportive officers holding important posts at Delhi and Poona. Palit was at Army HQ and Brig Dunn at HQ Southern Command.

31 Palit flew down to Goa for the drink as promised to Sagat. '.....if the Para Brigade succeeded in beating the main column to Panjim'. P 154. Palit. Op cit

32 '...a peacockery I could not dissuade him from'. P 420. Palit in Musings. Op cit.

33 P 302. Kaul. Op cit.

to Panjim first.'[34]

Sagat's plan envisaged an advance on two axes, with self supporting armour and artillery, in order to speedily secure the Sanquelim and Usgao Bridges and the ferry crossing at Betim.

- 2 Para was to advance on the route Dodamarg – Bicholim – Sanquelim – Usgao – Pilliem.
- 2 Sikh LI was to advance on the route Dodamarg – Assonara – Tivim – Mapuca – Betim.

1 Para was in reserve to take over the advance from 2 Para, once the situation crystallised, and capture Ponda (though Candeth had given this job to 63 Brigade). The Battalion was also required to secure the firm base by capturing the villages of Ibrampur, Dodamarg and Maulinquem well before the start time, at 5.30 AM on 18 Dec.

On the night of 17 Dec, the Brigade, by moving along a carefully reconnoitred circuitous route, occupied an assembly area approximately 30 miles from Sawantwadi opposite Dodamarg. The first move in the offensive was carried out by C Company, 2 Para, which was tasked to capture the Sanquelim Bridge through a *coup de main*. The Company, taking two local guides, infiltrated into Goa along the 'smugglers route' just north of Curchirem at approximately 10.30 PM on 17 Dec and by 4.30 AM on 18 Dec, had arrived on the heights overlooking Sanquelim without the enemy coming to know. However, at that stage village dogs set up a cacophony of barking and soon after a loud bang was heard from the direction of the Bridge. Realising the implications, Maj Uthaya, the company commander, rushed forward with a platoon. It was too late and the Portuguese succeeded in firing off a second demolition.[35] Both the ends had been fired and the 110 foot single span fell into the river. Since the Portuguese had fled, the Company quickly secured both the banks and cleared Sanquelim by early morning 18 Dec.

---

34 P 420 Palit in Musings. Op cit.

35 The Portuguese came to know of the Indian advance by a broadcast on All India Radio.

The Brigade engineers subsequently raised the span with the help of hydraulic jacks and the bridge was again put in place and used. Sagat describes meeting Uthaya at Sanquelim. He had 'tears rolling down his eyes and in a choked voice telling me, "Sorry I have failed you."[36] Sagat was however, well pleased by Uthaya's action and complimented him.

1 Para saw more action in its preliminary operations than what it did during the rest of the Campaign. The Commanding Officer of the Battalion, Lt Col (later Brig) Sucha Singh, was a prickly character, short tempered and did not always get along with Sagat. However, there was no doubting his fighting qualities. He had got a Military Cross during World War 2 and a Vir Chakra in the bitter fighting of the '47 Kashmir Campaign. He was the right man to lead a daring advance into Goa.[37] The Battalion had been tasked to secure the Brigade firm base and had nominated C and D Companies to capture the three villages required, on night 17/18 Dec. A platoon of C Company secured Ibrampur without incident. However, when the balance of C Company under Maj (later Maj Gen) IR Kumar went to secure Dodamarg, they encountered opposition. The Portuguese had occupied a fortified building and opened heavy fire in which one other rank lost his life. A determined assault drove them out with heavy casualties and 24 of them surrendered. Meanwhile, D Company under Maj (later Lt Gen) Sushil Kumar had no trouble in securing Maulinquem. In the subsequent aggressive patrolling six Portuguese were killed and three wounded.

2 Para commenced its advance into Goa at 5.15 AM on 18 Dec. The initial movement proved a bit difficult and the armour element had to be left behind. At Bicholim, finding the bridge demolished, the Battalion crossed over at a ford and soon had its momentum going. It linked up with its C Company at Sanquelim by 10.30 AM. No time was wasted here as the Battalion quickly crossed over at a ford secured by the Company and commenced its advance towards

---

36 P. 142 Afsir Karim. Op cit.

37 P.166. Ibid.

Usgao. By 11.30 AM the vanguard was 'barely 300 yards away' from the Madei River when the Portuguese blew up the Usgao Bridge. As Sagat points out, 'The Madei is a major river containing the back flow of the high tide sea water.'[38] It is nearly 500 feet wide with high banks. The Battalion however, had the bit between its teeth and without further ado effected a crossing with the help of improvised rafts constructed out of coconut trees cut and piled nearby. Mortars and other heavy weapons were also ferried across. A company led by Capt (later Maj Gen) Kulwant Pannu commenced a dash towards Candepar River, the last river before Ponda. Here Sagat was in a bit of a dilemma. Though he knew that 63 Brigade had been tasked by Gen Candeth to capture Ponda from the direction of Mollem, he was not aware as to the progress of its advance as the Division had gone out of communication. Also Sagat had envisaged that at this stage 1 Para would take over the advance and capture Ponda, if Candeth permitted. Pannu however, had already bounced the Candepar River and was straining at the leash. In the absence of any contact from 17 Division, Sagat took an immediate decision to allow 2 Para to maintain its momentum. That was all Pannu required and by 1.45 PM he had entered Ponda amidst scenes of jubilation. The balance of the Battalion caught up with him by evening. This was typical of Sagat. His ability to take the bold and right decision in the fog of war was a priceless talent.

As things stood, the leading elements of 63 Brigade reached the Candepar River, from the direction of Mollem and finding the Bridge demolished, decided to firm in for the night. They were expected to hand over the advance to 48 Brigade, which had got stuck behind the bridging train and had got bogged down on the Ghats. Candeth, though keen on his Division entering Ponda and thereafter advancing to Panjim, was informed that 2 Para was already in Ponda. With no choice but to acquiesce to Sagat's *fait accompli,* he changed his Division's objectives. Since 48 Brigade was nowhere in the firmament, he ordered 63 Brigade to carry on its advance and head for Margao. Sagat still did not get any orders

---

38 P. 155. Ibid.

to exploit his gains. Unfortunately, communications had not been restored and Sagat was unable to persuade Candeth to allow the Para Brigade units to maintain their momentum. As night was setting in the Brigade communications also failed temporarily. Sagat's earlier orders to his units were unequivocally clear; they were not to get involved in a fight in built up areas at night. With no orders to head towards Panjim, the units settled down for the night. While the Para units did not allow this to affect their attitude and devil may care spirit, the lack of communications somewhat inhibited the Commanding Officer of 2 Sikh LI.

2 SIKH LI had been tasked to advance to Betim from the north via Mapuca. The advance was led by A Squadron of 7 Cavalry (AMX tanks) and a troop from 8 Cavalry. Considering the nature of the terrain and the demolitions executed by the Portuguese, the armour made creditable progress. They were followed an hour behind, by 2 Sikh LI, who kept on clearing obstacles in the form of felled trees, mines and demolished bridges which were found en route. Sagat was not satisfied with the initial speed of advance as he found the men 'prone to hug the ground'[39]. His instinct to lead from the front soon had him personally chivvying the troops along and it was not long before the Battalion was pushing forward aggressively. The Armour, after a slight delay at Dodamarg, reached Assonara rapidly. Finding the bridge over the local creek demolished, they had a temporary causeway made and were across by 8.40 AM. In the absence of the expected opposition, they pushed ahead to Tivim, which they reached around 10.30 AM. The bridge over the river was found to be demolished, which stumped Maj SS Sidhu, the Squadron Commander, for a while. He found the locals most cooperative and they guided him onto a subsidiary track going to Colvale, approximately 6 kms north of Tivim. The track proved an impediment and they only reached Colvale at 2 PM. Mindful of Sagat's orders to head hell for leather, Sidhu made up lost time,

---

39 P. 155. Ibid. This tendency to hug the ground amongst troops who have not been bloodied in battle is a universal problem. Firm leadership is required to get the momentum going. Sagat spent a large part of the day on this axis.

despite some hastily laid mines and road blocks en route and reached Mapuca by 3.30 PM. The locals informed the Squadron that further move onwards from Mapuca may not be possible and advised them to move on a parallel track. Except for some ineffective light machine gun fire, no opposition was encountered and the Squadron reached the banks of the over 500 metres wide Mandovi River at Betim by 5 PM. They were the first to get a view of the Portuguese capital and felt a great sense of exhilaration. A quick firm base was made for 2 Sikh LI and boats on the other side were dissuaded from moving away by machine gun fire.

Meanwhile, 2 Sikh LI met some light opposition before Assonara[40] but captured three Portuguese officers. They were held up unduly long at the Assonara creek, which the Armour had already crossed and could only resume their advance around 12 PM. Much to Sagat's frustration, the Battalion got further delayed on the advance to Tivim as they had intelligence of meeting opposition from a half squadron of armoured cars. These were never encountered. Several obstacles were painstakingly removed and the Battalion reached Tivim to find the bridge demolished. The Battalion then diverted on the Pernem – Mapuca Road by approximately 4 PM. Removing obstacles encountered en route, the Battalion got its momentum going and reached Mapuca by 5 PM. Leaving a company behind for security of the Town and the axis of advance, 2 Sikh LI now showed greater adeptness and were in Betim by 6 PM. Lt Col Cherian, the Commanding Officer, was informed by Sidhu that people had seen the Governor General's Secretariat, visible from across the River, flying a white flag. The Battalion, now with its blood up was raring to cross the River and be the first to capture Panjim but at that critical stage they went out of communication with Brigade Headquarters. Cherian was not one to flout orders[41] and despite a letter of surrender being received

---

40 There was desultory opposition at Kansarpale, enough to cause delay.

41 Col Chatterjee, the former Signal Officer of the Brigade, confirmed to the Author that while the Brigade had remained in communication with its Battalions throughout the offensive, it was at this critical juncture that they went out of communications.

through a Padre, who arrived from Panjim by boat, he did not cross the River and the Battalion harboured for the night at Betim.

1 Para was to follow the Brigade Column on foot. Since the column included the slow moving bridging vehicles, Sucha Singh decided to continue marching regardless of the order of march. By 8 AM it had become clear that there was unlikely to be any worthwhile opposition. That was good enough for Sagat who gave orders for the Battalion to head for Bicholim, which they reached by 10.30 AM. Sagat had adapted quickly to the changing situation and realised that such feeble opposition did not require a formal reserve. What was required was an immediate grab for the nerve centre ie Panjim, thereby completely destroying any reaction capability of the enemy. He thus took a calculated risk and gave Sucha Singh his head. Sucha Singh was bent on seizing the initiative and making up for lost time and decided to head for the next objective, Pilgao, throwing caution to the winds and dispensing with any reconnaissance parties. He was met by Lt Col Vievers, the engineer commander who assured him maximum help in crossing the River at Pilgao. Pilgao was reached at 12.45 PM but the promised engineer help was not adequate. The Battalion was warned of mines at the crossing and selected an alternate site at Amona. It managed to scrounge a few boats and crossed over at both places. All this took time but by 4 PM the Battalion was heading for Banastirim, which they reached by 5.45 PM.

While the Portuguese Army seemed to have decamped without putting up much of a fight, their engineers, with monotonous efficiency, carried out a swath of destruction on all the ingress routes. 1 PARA found the bridge at Banastirim destroyed. This was a major obstacle, part of the river network which ringed Panjim. Sucha was contemplating another wet improvised crossing when orders were received that the Battalion was to firm in at Banastirim, build a helipad and await the arrival of the Army Commander at 9.30 AM on 19 Dec. Sucha Singh, who was keen to be the first to reach Panjim, philosophically decided that it was a lost race. Being the canny soldier that he was, he nevertheless passed orders for some boats to be collected and then 'we had a hearty drink, which our devoted wine waiter, Chockha Ram had carried, and after a full meal we retired for the night, to a sound sleep and dreams of Panjim'.[42]

The situation on the evening of 18 Dec was frustrating for all the commanders up the chain despite the Operation going so well. The Para Brigade battalion commanders had their objectives in sight and were raring to go but were held on a leash as they had already exceeded their briefs. Panjim was open from three directions but could not be occupied.[43] Sagat, who had spent most of the day egging on 2 Sikh LI, had reached 2 Para location by evening to get in touch with Gen Candeth. Victory in Goa was in the palm of his hands. Just to make sure that it was the maroon beret that would be seen on the streets of Panjim, he had unleashed 1 Para in a deliberate gamble. However, it was 17 Division that had been delegated the task of capturing the Capital. Sagat, being what he was, had stretched his orders and had boldly positioned his units to surround Panjim and create a near *fait accompli* but he dare not flout his orders. He was hopeful of persuading Candeth to allow him his head and tried to get in touch with him but 17 Division was out of communications, not only with the Para Brigade but with Southern Command also. For Candeth, who had tried to carry out a text book advance, it was more frustrating. Though he had restrained the Para Brigade, his own troops were not available to maintain the momentum. Ponda, the objective of 63 Brigade had already been occupied by 2 Para. He had thereafter diverted the Brigade to Margao to capture Panjim from the south. To his chagrin he found that the feint ordered by Southern Command from Karwar, which consisted of only a company of 4 Rajput, seemed to have exceeded its brief. The Company had reached Margao just before the arrival of troops from 63 Brigade.

For Chaudhury it must have been more bewildering than

---

42 P.170. Afsir Karim. Op cit.

43 A more apt word at this stage as Portuguese resistance had collapsed.

frustrating. The main advance had slowed down considerably and he found that the slack had been taken up by the Para Brigade. Since he was out of communication with 17 Division he was unwilling to take a decision on 18 Dec evening and decided to make up his mind the next day. Thus the fog of war had enveloped the offensive and created a hiatus that night.

Before we go onto the happenings of 19 Dec, two events which occurred on 18 Dec that affected and even cast a pall on the Campaign are worth mentioning. The first one is the breakdown in communications during a critical period on 18 Dec. As per Col Chatterjee, 17 Div had probably anticipated a likely communication disturbance and had borrowed the powerful 399 sets of the Para Brigade. However, the sets did not seem to have worked[44] and the Division went out of communication by late afternoon 18 Dec after explicitly prohibiting the Brigade from advancing any further.[45] Sagat, being astute as ever, had over insured his communications by using his contacts and the good offices of Maj Gen RN Batra, the Signal Officer in Chief. He had managed to get a radio relay detachment, which remained in communications with the Advance Headquarters of Southern Command at Belgaum, throughout the Campaign.[46] This proved critical as subsequent events were to show. The Brigade Signal Company, displaying initiative, typical of all units of the Brigade, also succeeded in tapping the local telephone line and got through from Dodamarg, much to the astonishment of the Chief Signal Officer.[47]

The second issue was of a tragic nature and resulted in the only major casualty which occurred during the Operation. Major

---

44 'They took away my 399 sets and burnt them out.' Chatterjee. Op cit.

45 'Confusion was perhaps inevitable in view of temporary interruption of wireless communication between different HQs and units; also due to the unexpected advance of various units.' P. 80. **Liberation of Goa and other Portuguese Colonies in India (1961) by PN Khera; Historical Section, MOD. Govt of India Press, Nasik, 1974.**

46 P 305, VK Singh. Op cit.

47 After the Campaign the P&T Department asked Chatterjee for an explanation as to how a civilian line was used without permission. Chatterjee. Op cit.

Sidhu, the 7 Cavalry Squadron Commander, had kept himself alert and abreast of all that was happening astride the River. Once his Squadron had gone into harbour Sidhu had gone to liaise with 2 Sikh LI. On his return at 8 PM, his troops informed him that they had captured two prisoners, who claimed to be demobbed local soldiers going back to their village. With the heady scent of victory and restless to be about, Sidhu led a team of six officers and three men and went to the village to verify the antecedents of the prisoners. There the locals informed them that a Portuguese Army section was holding a large number of political prisoners at Fort Aguada. The night was still young and the officers, with the same cavalier, reckless impulse, decided to go to Fort Aguada, 11 kms away, to rescue the prisoners. They assumed that the Portuguese, as was expected of them, would surrender sensibly. Fort Aguada is a formidable structure and was held by a full platoon of Portuguese troops who had received no orders to surrender by their superiors. Sidhu stopped his team's 15 cwt truck short of the gate, nonchalantly strolled up and demanded the surrender of the Garrison, waving a surrender document sent by the Portuguese from across the River. There was no response for some time and then all hell broke loose as the garrison opened up with machine guns, mortars and even rocket launchers. Surprised and caught in the open, there were inevitable casualties and the truck was destroyed. The firing started around midnight; by the time tanks and reinforcements arrived at 6 AM on 19 Dec, Sidhu and Capt VK Sehgal, of the same squadron, had died. By all accounts, Sidhu, true to his character, sought to bring some coherence in the response of his troops before he succumbed to his injuries.[48]

Sagat was most unhappy at what had happened. The needless loss of the brilliant Sidhu rankled him for years. War is never a game however easy it may look. The enemy is not beaten unless he lays down his arms and marches to the stockades. Sagat emphasised on this lesson when the Bangladesh Conflict was winding down.

---

48 The entire incident is covered in the Official History and brought out in detail by Ramani in his book. Pp 186 – 193. Ramani. Op cit.

Under estimating the enemy is as bad as over estimating him. At times the thin line between boldness and recklessness is difficult to measure, especially if one is new in the business of war. Sagat may occasionally have been arrogant about his abilities but he never allowed hubris to cloud his judgement.[49]

Meanwhile, on night 18 Dec, Chaudhury started having second thoughts about the way the Campaign was shaping up. He had received reports that the Portuguese had more or less thrown in the towel and the Governor General had called a meeting at 8 AM on 19 Dec to consider surrender. Since 17 Division was out of communication and its units were in no position to make a dash for Panjim, Chaudhury spoke to the Brigade Major (Sagat was with 2 Para, trying to establish contact with Candeth) around 10 PM and informed him that he wanted 50 Para Brigade to enter Panjim with the utmost speed the next day. He intended to visit the Brigade Headquarters the next morning instead of going to 1 Para. Around the same time Candeth reached Mollem and issued contradictory orders to 17 Division, including ordering 50 Para Brigade, to hold fast. Since he was out of communication, the confusion could only be clarified to him the next day when he met Sagat. This confusion prevailed for some time but by early morning 19 Dec, 1 Para and 2 Sikh LI had both been informed that they were to head for Panjim.

2 Sikh LI, just across the Mandovi River from Panjim, had the easier time of it. When their communications were restored by early morning on 19 Dec, they were ordered to cross the River, occupy the military installations in Panjim and take the surrender of Portuguese troops. At 7.35 AM, two companies crossed over in commandeered river craft and amidst wildly cheering crowds entered Panjim. They were met with desultory fire which stopped as soon as they marched into the town.

Sucha Singh had given up hope of being the first to enter

---

[49] The classic example is the iconic MacArthur and his subordinates during the Korean War, when they blithely decided to chase the beaten North Korean Army across the 38th Parallel, despite clear warnings of Chinese intervention.

The Liberation of Goa

Panjim, when he received orders to move at 6.55 AM on 19 Dec. He had all reasons to be indignant as he was on the wrong side of the Banastirim River, without much engineer help and with hardly any boats. Still burning with zeal to win the race to Panjim, he ordered his men to swim across the River rather than wait for boats. This they did cheered on by civilians on the other side.[50] Thereafter he immediately commandeered whatever civilian transport that was available and raced for Panjim, still 10 miles away.

The race to Panjim, if one could call it that, seems to have been won by 2 Sikh LI by a short head though 1 Para rightly claims that they were the ones who reached the seat of government first! The Indian troops were welcomed enthusiastically and had very little problem in rounding up the demoralised Portuguese, though the Governor General escaped to Marmugao, where he surrendered to Commander 63 Brigade.

Lt Gen Chaudhury landed at Banastirim, where he was received by the Brigade Major and drove down to Panjim amidst the cheering crowd. Sucha Singh mentions that in his typical flamboyant style, he desired to have a drink at the Mandovi Hotel. However, while going there, some Portuguese troops in the nearby Custom House opened fire.[51] He ordered 1 Para to clear them off, forgot about his drink and proceeded to other business, including a visit to the hospital, where he assured the apprehensive Portuguese inmates of good treatment by their captors.

Sagat met Candeth at Mollem the next morning, where he apprised him of the contretemps which had occurred on account of the orders received by the Army Commander. Both of them then proceeded to Panjim around noon, where Candeth asked the Para Brigade to manage the situation in the City till troops from the Division relieved them on 22 Dec. Sagat had passed orders on 19th morning that as soon as the troops entered Panjim they were to put on the distinctive maroon beret. The paratroopers endeared

---

50 P.171 Afsir Karim. Op cit.

51 P. 172. Ibid.

themselves so greatly to the populace that when they were moved out there were representations made to the Prime Minister to retain them.

No one expected Sagat and the Para Brigade to conduct such a swift operation. Palit has already recorded the scepticism of the Army Commander and the CGS in his book. In addition, there were bets laid amongst the senior officers as to how the Operation would progress. All assessments with regards the Para Brigade proved wrong and it seems Chaudhury lost three bets on that account.[52] In the eyes of the Portuguese, Sagat's 'notoriety' seems to have piqued Salazar considerably as he put a price of $ 10,000/- on his head.[53]

The Para Brigade was the Army Strategic Reserve but because of the popularity of the Red Berets they got to stay in Goa a little while longer[54] and enjoyed its heady atmosphere. As a postscript to the Campaign there was one uncorroborated story which went the rounds during that period. It seems one day an old man sought to meet the officers of the Brigade while they were in the Mess prior to dinner. He informed them that a group of Portuguese were trying to smuggle the embalmed body of St Francis Xavier onto an innocuous civilian vessel through one of the jetties in Panjim. A team of officers rushed to the jetty and foiled this attempt at the nick of time. Since no eye witness has come forward with an account of this incident, it was assumed to be a rumour with only an anecdotal value.[55]

The Goa Operation, despite its lack of military relevance, had its own lessons and should have given a serious student some conclusions about the state of the Indian Army. The lack of

---

[52] P. 306 VK Singh. Op cit.

[53] P 162. Afsir Karim. Op cit.

[54] 'The problems were so multifarious and pressing that we felt it was much easier to fight an action than to organize, control and run a capital.' P. 191.Khera. Op cit

[55] Sagat's brother Jeoraj Singh recollects this story being circulated during the aftermath of the Liberation.

momentum and other inadequacies of 17 Division should have raised the hackles of our top leadership. Unfortunately, everyone seems to have been more than willing to bask in the swift victory over a demoralised Portuguese soldiery achieved by the Para Brigade. The heady feeling blinkered the vision of the politician and bureaucrat and affected the senior officers too. A certain amount of overweening arrogance appears to have crept into our attitude. That balloon was well and truly pricked by the disaster of 1962.

The Para Brigade is an elite formation of the Indian Army. Its units were inheritors of a great warlike tradition so that all ranks had this great urge to prove themselves. Sagat, by his personality and professionalism had welded the Brigade into a confident, cohesive military machine which grasped opportunity by the scruff of the neck and propelled the Army offensive to victory. Goa was in many ways a cake walk and should not be considered a major feat of arms. Nevertheless, even under such easy circumstances the main thrust line got bogged down, enabling the secondary thrust of the Para Brigade to go beyond the objectives set for it. If someone had studied these operations, even in hindsight, two things would have been clear to him.

First was the orthodoxy in concepts that permeated the Indian military system. Its institutions, the bedrock of its military tradition, trained its officers to follow a rigid line of thinking. A mindset was created which prevented a large number of officers to grasp the full potential of a changing battlefield. The lessons of Goa were clear but they don't seem to have done much to shake up our restricted thought processes. Palit, a renowned military thinker of his times, had no doubt that we allowed ourselves to falsely bask in the reflected glory of the Campaign.[56] The CGS, who so enthusiastically took part in the advance with the leading troops, went on to lead a corps into ignominy against the Chinese. 'Muchu' Chaudhury

---

56 'Rather than being alarmed by the military inadequacies displayed by the Operation………the powers that be preened themselves as though they had struck a stunning blow at a major enemy; that in turn led to false confidence in our military dynamics'. P. 113. Palit. Op cit.

became the Chief and led the Army without much distinction during the 1965 War.[57]

It reflects poorly on the Organisation that on the eve of a military operation it permitted the GOC of 17 Division to go abroad on a course because of his hysterical behaviour on the prospect of being denied this lollipop. It is to the credit of 'Unni' Candeth that he made the best of a situation, saddled with an operational plan where his input must have been minimal.[58] This subsequently reflected in the performance of his Division. It was obvious that from the Army Commander to the CGS and sundry staff officers, they had created a 'khichdi', which Candeth inherited and tried his best to put his stamp on. Regardless of that his conservative thinking became evident as the plan was put into effect. The overall poor performance of his Division was luckily not laid at his door and he rose to command the Western Army during the 1971 War, which he led without much merit.[59]

We now come to Sagat. This was his first operational command. However, by the way he conducted himself anyone would have guessed otherwise. In a short time he had got the hang of commanding the most elite formation of the Indian Army, whose men and officers were unforgiving of any kind of lack of leadership. His unshakable confidence, which sat easy on his giant craggy frame, enveloped his subordinates in his aura. The Para Brigade had outstanding junior leaders, who over time and in their own turn, rose to the highest levels of command. Sagat well realised

---

57 Palit has some harsh things to say of Gen Chaudhury who covered his inadequacies under a veneer of urbanity. Perhaps the harshest comments are, '[he] was shallow of purpose, unable to put his undoubted intelligence to proper use or to keep in touch with the real world. He allowed himself to be propelled by his personal concerns, taking snap decisions divorced from reality.' P. 410. Ibid.

58 Lt Gen TN Raina was faced with the same situation when he took over command of 2 Corps just prior to the 1971 War.

59 '[His] rise in the Army may be attributed to his being non controversial and perhaps more pliable than more deserving contemporaries............displayed a slow, deliberate and rather cautious approach to military problems.' Pp 1 – 2; **Defence of the Western Borders by Maj Gen Sukhwant Singh; Lancer Publishers, Delhi, 1998.**

their potential and made a plan which allowed them to use their inherent intrepidity. He seemingly possessed inexhaustible energy and would always be found at the point of decision.[60] Sagat was nothing if not a bold military opportunist. Though well aware that his role was on the sideline of the main advance he was fully prepared to exploit the situation and allow his units to seize the initiative.

In the pre-62 Indian Army, where conventional thinking strait jacketed the military thought process, Sagat's approach was so exceptional and 'out of the box' that his boldness and *savoir faire* were considered more of an aberration.[61] Sagat's superiors, perhaps in an effort to bring him down a notch, tried to restrain his potential but on the battlefield, Sagat was a warrior and marched to his own beat. As he was to show later on a larger stage, it seemed he instinctively knew what the right course of action was. Those who knew him better, realised the sheer professionalism and hard work that always went into any plan he made. Sagat was a leader who had this natural gift of command, which through ambition, hard work and a sharp focus on the job in hand, he developed into a rock solid personality. It is a rare gift and it goes to the credit of the Army, that despite certain peccadilloes, they nurtured his career so that when the time came he proved his worth many times over.

---

60 'He was always very mobile wherever he was. He was right in front and then came back and then was elsewhere. He was always a dynamic kind of person and went where the action was......' Afsir Karim in conversation. Op cit.

61 It bears retelling that Brig Gurbax Singh, Commander 48 Infantry Brigade in Goa, was either singularly unlucky or worse, because as commander of the same brigade in Bomdila he was soundly beaten by the Chinese.

CHAPTER FOUR

TOIL AND TURMOIL

Be bloody, bold and resolute;
laugh to scorn the power of man

- Shakespeare

The Para Brigade was not deployed during the crisis of 1962 though, much against Sagat's wishes, units and sub units were sent forward to shore up the crumbling defences of the Army. Sub units of 17 Para Field Regiment were para dropped at Walong to provide a pathetic artillery backbone to the Indian defences there. They were swept away in the crumbling front as the Chinese advanced. Sagat had some harsh things to say but nobody was listening at that stage. His formation was kept on standby throughout 1963 as the Indians slowly crept forward cautiously onto the watershed. The Para Brigade was slotted to take on an operational role on the Himalayan Watershed but as Palit alleges in his memoirs, timidity and tentativeness, characterised the efforts of the senior leadership[1] and the Brigade remained in Agra. However, the developing confrontation with Pakistan took most people by surprise. The large scale troop movement which had taken place to the East had unbalanced the Western Theatre and required a strategic and tactical review. Sagat, amongst others, was asked to carry this out. Accompanying the GOC of 1 Armoured Division, Maj Gen Zorawar

---

1 Op cit. Pp 457-459 Musings; Palit. He has cast serious allegations against both Chaudhury and Sam. However, Neville Maxwell in a review of the still unpublished Henderson Brooks Report, in the **Apr 14-20 issue 2001 of the Economic and Political Weekly**, has severely excoriated Palit for being one of the 'Kaul Boys' and being partly instrumental in implementing the disastrous strategy which led to India's defeat. The truth lies somewhere in between.

Singh and with Capt Bhawani Singh (later Brig and the Maharaja of Jaipur) in tow, Sagat spent three days at Gurdaspur with Lt Col Duleep Sinh, who was commanding 4/3 GR there. While the day was spent in serious reconnaissance, which subsequently proved of immense value to Sagat, the evenings were spent in carousing late into the night. Duleep recollects that Sagat seemed to have two distinct personalities. During the day he was deadly serious, not leaving a stone unturned to get a proper insight into the terrain and thought processes of commanders. In the evening, after a hot bath and with a glass of whiskey in hand, he did not seem to have a care in the world.

In Jan 1964, Sagat was selected to attend the course at the National Defence College, Delhi. An apex course, it groomed selected brigadiers for the highest ranks. This was a good break for Sagat and his family. The students of the Course received a close insight into the strategic review and re-deployment being carried out by the Army post 1962 and were involved in discussions with several senior officers, including theatre commanders.

On termination of the Course, in Jan 65, Sagat was posted to Jullunder as the Brigadier General Staff (BGS) at HQ 11 Corps. He was appalled at the shortage in units, equipment and war material faced by this vital Corps deployed to defend against any direct enemy threat into the heart of the hinterland. It seemed that the Chinese debacle had altered the focus of the Government and the Army. This became obvious when Sam Manekshaw, the Western Army Commander, was shifted to Eastern Command and Lt Gen Harbaksh Singh replaced him in Nov 1964. Harbaksh' distant personality and style of functioning, without taking his staff into confidence, created a sense of drift in the Command, not helped by the fact that his subordinate commanders, especially Lt Gen JS Dhillon, GOC 11 Corps, was authoritarian and did not seem to inspire confidence with his tactical reasoning.[2]

---

2 The dismal performance of the Corps in 1965, however, did not seem to have affected the General's chances for promotion. He went on to become an Army Commander.

OP Kaushik was a young Capt and General Staff Officer Grade 3 at the Corps HQ when he first met Sagat. He found him constantly on the phone using his contacts and considerable influence in getting equipment and weapons released to make up deficiencies. He would not hesitate to go as high up the chain as he felt warranted and speak 'anywhere in India' to get some critical item for the Corps. On one occasion, he summoned Kaushik and informed him that 1200 three ton vehicles were expected and asked him as to where they should be consigned. The inexperienced Kaushik incautiously told him to have them consigned at the Ordnance Depot at Suranasi. Now an ordnance depot does not handle vehicles. This became evident when the ordnance staff indignantly protested to Sagat. Kaushik remembers going to him with much trepidation, well realising his monumental blunder and the likely resultant chaos. There were nearly a dozen trains on the way. 'Complete chaos and melee was expected at Jullunder.' Unperturbed, Sagat asked him if he could resolve the issue. Not feeling the confidence he displayed, Kaushik told him that he would do the paperwork at the siding itself and issue the vehicles to the collection parties from there only. Sagat told him to get on with it and promptly got on with the next issue at hand. Kaushik faced neither recrimination nor fallout of his mistake, which he was left to resolve.[3]

It should be remembered that Sagat came as the BGS when a fair amount of sabre rattling was going on. The Kutch Incident during Mar – Apr 1965 had the whole Corps mobilising. It set the stage for a long series of discussions and war games, culminating in the most important one held at Jullunder on 15 May. The General Staff was labouring on the sand model the evening before and were visited by the Corps Commander and his BGS. Things were still chaotic and seeing this, Dhillon completely lost his cool and started a flood of recriminations. Sagat remained unperturbed and mildly told him, 'Sir please don't worry, I'm sure these boys will

---

3 **In conversation with Lt Gen OP Kaushik at Dehra Dun on 25 Sep 2009.** 'Any other person would have been so flabbergasted that he would have made an example of the staff officer.'

deliver.' Harrumphing and hinting that his neck would be on the block, Dhillon stalked off. Sagat said not a word and did not even visit the model room until the next morning. His staff laboured the whole night and had things up to the mark the next day. As Kaushik says, 'the credit for building and preparing 11 Corps for war goes to Sagat Singh.' It was at this War Game that Maj Gen Jogindar Singh, Chief of Staff Western Command, noticed differences in operational perceptions between Sagat and his Corps Commander. He goes on to regret that Sagat had to leave before the War. 'I knew that his professional outlook was at variance with GOC 11 Corps and he would have advised against wrong operational decisions.'[4] That very month, anticipating a conflict, Western Command mobilised. By then Sagat was posted out on Jun 1965 to take over command of 17 Mountain Division in Sikkim but not before he had another run in with Dhillon. The matter concerned the user trials of punched tapes which were to replace barbed wires. Dhillon had specifically directed that he would ultimately sign off on the trial report. While he was on leave the trials were carried out. The Trial Report was then prepared and despatched. When Dhillon returned he was furious and demanded to know why his directions had been flouted. On a minute sheet Sagat wrote, 'The Trial Report was cleared by Brig Sagat Singh, BGS. Lt Gen JS Dhillon was on annual leave and during that period ceased to command the Corps. The Corps, however, did not cease to function.' That was the end of the matter.[5]

Sagat officiated as the GOC 17 Mountain Division for nearly a month and a half before he was promoted on 16 Aug 1965. The Division was under an operational transition as his predecessor, Maj Gen Har Prasad (later Lt Gen and Vice Chief of Army Staff), had ordered a redeployment. 112 Mountain Brigade, commanded by Brig (later Maj Gen) Eustace DeSouza, had been moved forward to Changgu in the middle of winter 1964. They had been given no

---

4 P 90. **Behind the Scenes: An analysis of India's Military Operations, 1947 – 1971. By Maj Gen Jogindar Singh, PVSM. Lancer International, New Delhi, 1993.** He is particularly scathing of both Harbaksh and Dhillon in this book.

5 Kaushik. Op cit.

stores and told to manage through local resources. A company held a screen position to the rear of the watershed on the Thegu Ridge while the Watershed itself was held by observation posts. There was no presence of the Chinese at that time. The other two brigades were deployed linearly along the axis at Kyangnosla and Gangtok respectively. 27 Mountain Division was deployed on the eastern flank and was responsible for the defence of the other axis from Jelep La. The extreme high altitude of North Sikkim was the responsibility of 17 Assam Rifles. One of the first actions of Sagat was to carry out a personal reconnaissance of the watershed, including walking up to the 16000 feet high Chola Pass. He noticed the poor habitat and defences made by the troops out of local resources and immediately sanctioned more than 10 tons of defence stores.[6]

The tranquillity on the watershed was broken by the 1965 War. As a token of solidarity with Pakistan, the Chinese started moving their troops forward. In case of hostilities breaking out the division commanders were given the authority to withdraw to the main defences which were on the next ridge line well in depth. While the defences of 17 Division were based at Changgu, those of 27 Division were on the Lungthu Ridge Line. Sagat had serious reservations regarding the defensive posture and had made them known to his Corps Commander, Lt Gen (later Gen and COAS) GG Bewoor. Once the Watershed was vacated it was but a matter of time before the Chinese occupied it and looked right down into Sikkim. Sagat was adamant that he would not surrender the Watershed to the Chinese regardless of provocation. Relationships were decidedly prickly and the matter had filtered down to Sam, the Army Commander. Once the Chinese decided to patrol the Watershed, provocations were a plenty. There were four skirmishes of a major nature which occurred during this period, involving exchange of mortar and small arms fire. Sagat was obdurate that regardless of any aggravation the troops would hold fast and not an inch of ground was to be

---

6 **Personal communication by Maj Gen (retd) Eustace DeSouza.** As DeSouza further authenticates, while Sagat was a hard task master as far as operational matters were concerned, he created many facilities for officers and men alike.

surrendered.[7] In the neighbouring division, Jelep La was vacated, and defences at Lungthu, nine kms to the rear were occupied. On one particular day the escalating Chinese provocations created a high level of anxiety at the Corps HQ. Anticipating it, Sagat had moved out of his HQ, telling his General Staff Officer Grade 1, Lt Col (later Brig) Lakhpat Singh that he was to ensure that he was not made available on the phone. By now the entire watershed in 17 Division Sector had become alive with heavy firing. Bewoor tried repeatedly to contact Sagat but was fobbed off by Lakhpat, much to his annoyance. The Chinese made a noisy demonstration opposite Nathu La, indicating that an attack was imminent. Sagat's instructions to stand fast were known to every soldier and they refused to budge. When the Chinese were barely 50 metres from the Pass, heralding their approach through noisy propaganda broadcast by loudspeakers, they stopped and ultimately withdrew.[8] 33 Corps was now faced with a quaint situation. While 17 Division retained control of the Watershed, its right flank stood exposed by the withdrawal of 27 Division nine kms to the rear. The Division ultimately re-occupied the watershed in its area but was unable to occupy Jelep La Pass, which the Chinese continue to hold till today.

In Dec 1965, an incident of firing between a patrol of 17 Assam Rifles and the Chinese on the Giagong Plateau of North Sikkim highlighted Sagat's qualities admirably. Despite not being acclimatised, Sagat insisted on going and checking himself. A helicopter was arranged and Sagat personally verified the incident. At that stage Eastern Air Command refused to provide a helicopter to bring Sagat back. Sagat walked all the way down from 18000 feet up to the road head and drove back to Gangtok none the worse for wear. The eyeball to eyeball confrontation with the Chinese attracted the attention of the foreign militaries and the media. They

---

7 Ibid.

8 **Article by Brig Lakhpat Singh in possession of the Author.** The Brig strongly felt that Bewoor displayed extreme caution and had lost touch with what was happening on the ground.

descended on Gangtok and were handled by Sagat with aplomb.[9]

During his tenure Sagat developed a close personal relationship with the Chogyal and Gyalmo of Sikkim, which stood the test of time. When Sagat visited Sikkim in 1972, during a visit to 2/3 GR, where his son Digvijay was serving, he was made a guest of the Royal Family and stayed at the Palace with his aide. Every morning the Chogyal himself would lead the band of the Sikkim Guards, which would play below Sagat's window to wake him up.[10] Sagat also had friendly relations with all the civil officials, which enabled him to create facilities for the Army at Gangtok. An officers institute was established where officers coming down from the defences had a place to relax and let their hair down. He even organised an other rank R&R area in Gangtok where basic relaxation facilities, including movies, a club and hot water baths were established. He insisted that units send troops down every couple of months for two to three days to unwind.[11] Sagat also shifted the Division HQ to a more conducive location. Lt (later Maj Gen) VK Singh of the Division Signal Regiment was sent to the General's residence to install and check his telephones. He installed the main connection in the bedroom and one in parallel in the office. Seeing this Sagat asked him to reverse the installation. VK grinned and told him that it was all the same at which Sagat pointed out that the parallel phone would have a three decibel loss and he wanted the office phone to be the main one. VK was flabbergasted. He never expected an infantry general to be aware of such technical intricacies but that was Sagat for you.[12] Shri Bajrang Lal, IPS, who was posted as the Police Commissioner in Sikkim on deputation from 1961 to 1967, recollects that whenever Sagat was in Gangtok, he would make it a

---

9 A team of Military Attaches from various embassies in Delhi were conducted by Duleep Sinh to Sikkim. They were taken to Nathu La and briefed by Sagat. To a man they were impressed with his clear exposition, head for figures and sharp memory. Duleep Sinh. Op cit.

10 Recollections of the Author

11 Op cit. DeSouza.

12 **In conversation with Maj Gen (retd) VK Singh at New Delhi on 23 Sep 2009.**

point to take the police horses and go riding. He was now regarded with awe and people had become aware that here was a general who led from the front, was not afraid of the Chinese and would give as good as he got.[13] The actor Dev Anand, who spent a lengthy period in Sikkim shooting for one of his films, mentions meeting Sagat '.....looking majestic and tall with a look of a commander who knew where all his men were at any time of the day.'[14]

The situation on the Watershed continued to aggravate throughout 1966 and the beginning of 1967. The Indian and Chinese troops were now eyeball to eyeball. Any patrol sent to the watershed was immediately paralleled by a Chinese patrol moving in close proximity. At Nathu La the Chinese had installed loudspeakers which constantly blared communist propaganda, telling on the nerves of troops.[15] In one instance the young officers of a para unit danced naked in front of the Chinese resulting in a strongly worded diplomatic protest to New Delhi. When the fallout reached Sagat he just laughed it off.[16] Sagat had become a dyed in the wool paratrooper and his headquarter was staffed with them. He identified with their joie de vivre and liked having them around him.[17]

In early 1967, fed up of continuous Chinese provocation and their attempts to occupy the Watershed, Sagat decided to demarcate the boundary at Nathu La with a barbed wire fence and

---

13 In conversation at Jaipur with Shri Bajrang Lal (retd), IPS, on 02 Jun 2009.

14 Pp210 – 212. **Romancing with Life by Dev Anand; Viking, New Delhi, First Edition, 2007.**

15 The Chinese had 21 speakers deployed at Nathula and added eight more on 13 Aug. The sound could be heard several kms to the rear up to Changgu. The Indian response was no match. Only six speakers were installed and the tapes sent by Public Relation people from Delhi were insipid and no help in countering Chinese propaganda. **History of the Corps of Signals -Vol 3 (unpublished) by Maj Gen VK Singh.**

16 Ranvijay. Op cit.

17 He was keen to become the Colonel of the Parachute Regiment, but the Paras selected Brig (later Lt Gen and Army Commander) IS Gill as their new Colonel. Sagat was bitterly disappointed.

Confrontation at Nathu la

With the Chogyal at Nathu la

obtained clearance from his superiors. Bewoor had been replaced by Lt Gen JS Aurora as the Corps Commander, while Sam remained the Army Commander. Brig (then Lt Col) Rai Singh recollects that when he moved into the Division Sector in May 1967, en route to Nathu La with his battalion, he was met by Sagat who told him to train his unit to lay a barbed wire fence along the watershed regardless of any interference by the Chinese.[18] Brig MMS Bakshi, MVC, had taken over 112 Brigade in Mar 1967 as DeSouza had already proceeded to the National Defence College. Bakshi, an Armoured Corps officer, had never served in the mountains before. The implications of a major confrontation with the Chinese, well ahead of the main defences were nevertheless clear to him.[19]

Sagat had physically walked the watershed without any violent reaction from the Chinese and it was assumed that during the process of laying the fence, the maximum they would do is intimidate and attempt to prevent the troops from laying it. Rai Singh and his men were hardy six footers and they had no doubt as to who would emerge on top in case the confrontation got physical. As Bakshi clarified, there was 'no intention of changing the status of the border, only to demarcate it.' It is now obvious that the Chinese did not see it that way. The first step in this bloody episode was started by the Chinese as a riposte to the Indian Independence Day Celebrations at Nathu La. On 17 Aug, the Chinese intruded and occupied areas around North Shoulder and Sebula ie to the west and north of Nathu La. A structure was constructed by them and a physical confrontation with the Grenadiers took place with the Commanding Officer in the middle of it. Orders were then received to lay a single strand of wire approximately 300 metres from Nathu La to North Shoulder on 18 Aug. This was laid after much pushing, jostling and loud objection by the Chinese. On 20 Aug, a second strand was laid and on 21 Aug, 400 metres of wire was laid at Sebula. On 23 Aug the Chinese again responded by intimidation

---

18 In conversation with Brig (retd) Rai Singh, MVC, at New Delhi on 18 and 21 Sep 2009.

19 In conversation with Brig (retd) MMS Bakshi, MVC, at Vadodara on 04 Nov 2009. The watershed was held by flimsily constructed observation posts.

and slogan shouting. When that had limited impact they started further strengthening their defences and carrying out additional construction at South Shoulder.

This should have caused the Indians to sit back and think but by now the troops had got the upper hand and such was their confidence that there was no dearth of volunteers. A single strand of wire was laid at South Shoulder on 29 Aug despite a physical encounter which lasted for nearly two hours. Chinese attempts at coercion, including poking bayonets through the soldiers' clothing, had little effect. The Corps and Division Commanders visited Nathula on 1 Sep and decided to go ahead with the fence. On 2 Sep, with Sagat watching, a second strand was laid. On 04 Sep, Sagat visited South Shoulder and pronounced himself well satisfied with the actions of 2 Grenadiers even though he could see the Chinese constructing defence works there. Lt Col (then 2/Lt) Attar Singh was sent by him with a patrol north eastwards along the watershed to reconnoitre a location for defences on the approaches to the heights of Camel's Back, a dominating feature, which would play a vital role as the situation escalated. Thereafter on 07 Sep, Maj Bishen Singh was sent with a company to construct a bunker in the area reconnoitred by Attar Singh. Again much physical jostling took place with the Chinese but the bunker was constructed (subsequently demolished by the Chinese).[20] On 09 Sep, a third strand of barbed wire was ordered to be laid at Sebula. Rai Singh, as was his wont, reached there with his Subedar Major. The Chinese again objected and this time committed the sacrilege of laying their hands on the CO. This was too much for the troops who beat up the offending soldier, who in panic fired a shot. This was the first time a weapon had been fired and the Chinese soon apologised.

It looked as though the Indians were gaining the upper hand and the Chinese did not want to escalate the matter. It succeeded in lulling the men and commanders into complacency. By now the confrontation had reverberated internationally and Nathu

---

20 In conversation with Lt Col (retd) Attar Singh at New Delhi on 21 Sep 2009.

La started getting a stream of visitors, including the international media. The photographs taken by the Time-Life Correspondent showed Indian and Chinese troops standing bayonet to bayonet in grim antagonism. Now India upped the ante further. On 10 Sep, Sagat personally briefed all concerned as to the execution of the pending work. 2 Grenadiers were ordered to convert the barbed wire fences into Cat Wire Type One. Two platoons of 18 Rajput were put under Rai Singh's command along with a platoon of pioneers and a company of engineers. Construction was to be carried out simultaneously by 18 Rajput at North Shoulder and 2 Grenadiers at South Shoulder. Brig Bakshi moved up to Nathu La while Sagat moved to Sherathang, the Brigade HQ location. It was obvious that Sagat anticipated some sort of trouble as the medium guns were moved up and artillery observation posts warned. The troops on the ground, including Bakshi, did not anticipate the scope of the trouble, though weapons were prepared to fire from their bunkers. Two platoons, including the commando platoon, were suitably located to provide assistance, if required.

At 4.30 AM on 11 Sep, the troops had moved to their respective locations. By 5.15 AM it became clear that the Chinese were occupying their defensive positions. In the beginning the Chinese troops came out and started arguing with and jostling the soldiers. Regardless of this interference, the work on the fence went on. Rai Singh, though cautioned by Sagat to remain under cover, stood well out in the open to encourage his men. At around 7.45 AM a whistle blew. Some of the Chinese hastily moved into their defences and opened devastating automatic fire on the troops. Rai Singh received three bullets and was dragged to relative safety by his medical officer. He recollects picking up a light machine gun and shooting down the officer, who a moment ago was arguing with him. The ruthlessness of the Chinese was evident by the fact that they opened fire despite some of their troops still being out in the open. Within a matter of minutes the men in the open were mowed down. Maj Harbhajan Singh of 18 Rajput and Capt PS Dagar of 2 Grenadiers, out of desperation, led attacks on the Chinese defences and were killed.

To add to the chaos the Chinese opened up with their artillery. The volume of fire made the troops nearly catatonic and retaliatory small arms fire was desultory at the most. Some troops could not stand the horror and broke. Bakshi remained at his post and ordered all those who remained in communication to stand fast. 2/Lt NC Gupta, who was the Brigade Signal Officer and received a Sena Medal for his actions, was ordered by Bakshi to go to South Shoulder as the position seems to have been vacated. Gupta held on to the place until relieved by Attar Singh and then evacuated the badly injured Maj Bishen Singh in the face of the enemy.[21] The two platoons earmarked to support the troops did not react; some of them even ran and it required Sagat, who snatched a sten gun and stood on the road coming down from Nathu La, along with the Subedar Major of 2 GRENADIERS, to stem the rout. He threatened to shoot anyone he found moving to the rear. They collected whatever men were available and sent them forward.[22] The coolness of the Brigade Commander, some of the junior leaders who remained in the defences and the artillery observation posts succeeded in stabilising the situation somewhat. By then nearly five hours had elapsed. The wounded lay where they were as no troops were available to collect the casualties. It was then that Indian artillery finally opened up. Sagat had no authority to use the artillery and neither did the Corps Commander. The Army Commander was in Delhi officiating in place of the Chief, who was abroad. Sam was not immediately available to give sanction and Sagat on his authority ordered fire to be opened. The complete Chumbi Valley was visible to our OPs and the fire they brought down was devastating. The news of the flap finally reached Delhi and Sam, cool as ever, told the assembled people, 'I am afraid they are enacting Hamlet without the Prince. I will now tell you how I intend to deal with it.'[23] The

---

21 Personal account of **Brig NC Gupta in History of the Corps of Signals**. Ibid. He is less than charitable towards people and units in his first person account.

22 VK Singh in History. Op cit.

23 P 45. **Leadership: Field Marshal Sam Manekshaw by Maj Gen (retd) Shubhi Sood. SDS**

artillery exchanges lasted for four days. Chinese reinforcements coming up from Yatung were targeted and their trucks destroyed.

Sagat was not willing to take this debacle lying down and he ordered Brig Bakshi to plan an attack on the Chinese on 13 Sep. Bakshi had gone around the defences on 12 Sep evening and had seen that the units were quite rattled. He requested for an additional day to carry out a rehearsal. This was granted but thereafter the attack plan was shelved on orders from Delhi.[24] The heavy casualties suffered by 2 Grenadiers had made the Battalion ineffective and the responsibility at Nathu La was taken over by 18 Rajput.[25] The reverberations of this incident were felt in an ever widening circle. Sagat had got fed up of the constant nit picking going on at the Watershed and wanted to end it once and for all. He proved that the Indian Army were no longer the pushovers of 1962 and his soldiers would defend every inch of Indian Territory. There were, however, nearly 200 casualties, a figure not acceptable to his superiors and Sagat was a marked man. The handing over of the Indian dead by the Chinese on 17 Sep was treated as a media victory by them. Rai Singh, who led from the front throughout this period, to the extent of disregarding advice of not exposing himself, got the Mahavir Chakra as did the incredibly brave officers who rushed the Chinese defences in the face of such annihilating fire. He has suffered terribly over the years for his courage and sacrifice. Years later he visited China as part of a military delegation and was feted by his erstwhile enemies as 'The Hero of Nathu La.' He and his officers still feel bitter that posterity has not been kind to his unit, which faced down the Chinese and lost many men in that fateful struggle.

This was not the end of the face-off with the Chinese. They

Publishers, New Delhi, 2006.

24 VK Singh in History. Op cit.

25 'What purpose the Nathu La incident served I cannot comment on. We were only a year old unit and the casualties seemed such a waste to me.' **Maj Gen (retd) AK Verma in personal communication to the Author.** Troops of the Battalion were shaken by the incident and took a few hours to recover.

had suffered more than 300 casualties and seemed unwilling to let the watershed cool down. On 1 Oct, a confrontation ensued between the Chinese and 7/11 GR at Chola, a pass west of Nathu La and under the responsibility of 63 Brigade. The Gorkhas had that very day taken over the post at Pt 15450 from 10 J&K Rifles. A scuffle ensued between the JCO post commander and his Chinese counterpart over a boulder which was on the watershed. The Chinese bayoneted the JCO and his men retaliated with the deadly use of the kukhri. A fierce hand to hand struggle ensued and a neighbouring post came under attack. The Gorkhas were unwilling to start their tenure with a defeat and got clearance from the Brigade Commander to raise the stakes. Pt 15450, which had been taken by the Chinese, was vigorously attacked with close quarter kukhri work and the Chinese were evicted.[26] This was a clear signal to them that the Indians would not surrender an inch of territory and the area around the watershed stabilised, ultimately being designated as the Line of Actual Control.

Sagat was given the impression that he would be going as the Director of Military Training, a post he had hankered for. However, in Dec 67, Sagat was posted to HQ 101 Communication Zone Area, an innocuous posting. He realised that his defiance of the Chinese had not gone down well and assumed he had been sacked. Shillong was considered a backwater and knowing that he would not be able to keep his family there because of the education requirement of his children, Sagat felt disappointed. However, he had no time to wallow in any self-pity, which in any case was against his nature. Sam, annoyed though he was with Sagat, knew his man well. The Mizo Hills were in flames and he expected Sagat to douse them.

The Mizo Hills (subsequently the State of Mizoram) are remotely located on the south eastern extremity of India. To the North they are bordered by the states of Assam, Tripura and Manipur. To the west they had a 300 km boundary with East

---

26 Pp 7-10. **Article by Maj Gen VK Singh. Defence and Security Alert, Nov 2010.** Also VK Singh. Op cit. This is also corroborated by an article written by **Maj Gen (then Capt) Sheru Thapliyal** on the incident.

Pakistan (now Bangladesh). To the south and east the boundary with Myanmar extends for more than 400 kms. The complete area is extremely hilly comprising 21 hill ranges, with the Blue Mountain, at more than 2000 mtrs, being the highest peak. The Hills are thickly forested, mainly with bamboo jungles, which make cross-country movement very difficult. They are drained by numerous rivers that are tributaries of the two main rivers; the Kaladan, which flows southwards into Burma and the Barak which flows through North Tripura into East Pakistan, subsequently becoming the Meghna. The railhead was at Silchar, 110 kms away by road from the capital Aijal (now spelt Aizawl). The State Highway 54 (it was converted to National Highway specifications subsequently) went along the centre spine of the main range from Silchar to Aijal to Lungleh and further south. Flanked by thick forests it was prone to ambush and required extensive road opening resources. The population was divided into numerous homogenous tribes, with distinct identities, who were mainly Presbyterian Christian. The Church exercised and even now continues to exercise, great influence over the Mizo people. The largest and the most warlike amongst the tribes were the Lushais, who were a thorn in the flesh to the British and were organised by them to combat the Japanese during World War 2. The Mizo Hills were declared an 'Excluded Area' by the British and no political activity was encouraged.[27] In the 1960s the area was largely undeveloped and to an extent neglected by the Union Government. It was a primitive agrarian economy, which followed the *jhoom* method of cultivation, where every few years forest patches were cleared, cultivated and then abandoned.

In 1958, the flowering of the bamboo plant increased the

---

27 The British governing officials, post World War 2 deliberately fostered a sense of autonomy amongst the people. Prior to Independence some parties in the Mizo Hills were actively talking of either remaining a Crown Colony, getting independence or joining Myanmar. A Large number were agitating for autonomy and a separate state. In addition, some groups wanted adjacent areas in other states to be incorporated into the Mizo Hills. The foisting of Assamese as the official language in 1960 did not help matters. **Lost Opportunities: 50 Years of Insurgency in the North East and India's Response by Brig (Dr) SP Sinha, VSM. Lancer Publishers, New Delhi, First Edition, 2007.**

rodent population, which decimated 70% of the crops. Famine conditions prevailed and a social organisation called the Mizo National Famine Front, under the leadership of Laldenga, carried out sterling work to alleviate the suffering of the people. The Indian government received little credit. Laldenga converted his organisation into a political party by dropping the word Famine in Oct 1961. He started exploiting the sentiments of people, including the hereditary chiefs who had been deprived of their authority when the Lushai Hills Autonomous District Council was formed in 1952. Laldenga initially followed the democratic path to power. However, his failure to capture the District Council in 1963 drove him towards militancy. He then moved to East Pakistan to seek assistance from the Pakistan Govt. On his return, he was arrested by the Assam Police but the Chief Minister, BP Chaliha, offered an olive branch and released him. Laldenga started an efficient conduit to East Pakistan where he sent youth for military training and smuggled in arms and ammunition.

By mid 1965, Laldenga had created a 'Special Force' of the toughest Mizos fully armed and trained. In 1964, the 2 Assam Regiment of the Army mutinied and was disbanded. Laldenga utilised the Mizo element of this unit to create the leadership of his military organisation which expanded to four battalions and subsequently to eight battalions, each of approximately 200 well trained fighters. These were grouped under two brigades, the 'Dagger' and the 'Lion'. Thanks to the mutineers and extensive help given by East Pakistan, Laldenga had created a formidable force. The civil administration remained clueless.[28] By end 1965, Laldenga felt he was ready to declare independence. A secret operation code named OP JERICHO was planned to be launched on 1 Mar 1966.

---

28 Pp145-149. **Insurgent Crossfire: North East India by Subir Bhaumik. Lancer Publishers, New Delhi, First Edition, 1996.** See also **Mizoram: the Dagger Brigade by Nirmal Nibedon. Lancer Publishers, New Delhi, Second Edition, 1983.** Not all battalions had the same strength. Also the quality of insurgents was not uniformly good and tended to deteriorate as the insurgency progressed. However, the hard core, which comprised the initial recruits of the Military Wing, could be compared in quality with any well known insurgent organization.

Aijal was to be surrounded and the 1 Assam Rifles (AR) troops, which garrisoned it, were to be forced to capitulate. Armouries and petrol pumps were to be taken over. In addition, garrisons in sub divisions like Lungleh, Champhai and Demagiri were to be made to surrender. The only armed units in the Mizo Hills were 1 AR and 5 Border Security Force (BSF). All their major sub units were to be targeted. Laldenga felt that if the MNF flag could be flown proudly all over for 48 hours, the rebellion would gain legitimacy.

The operation proceeded more or less flawlessly, except 1 AR troops at Aijal refused to surrender and Laldenga could not have his victory march though he made a declaration of independence. As Sam was the first to admit, 'We were caught with our pants down.'[29] Retribution inevitably followed. The Indian Government was so rattled that for the first and only time in the Country's history, they authorised an air strike against its own people. On 4 Mar, Aijal and its surrounding area was bombed and strafed for five hours. These bombing runs continued till 13 Mar in other areas also.[30] The effectiveness of these strikes remains a moot point but they succeeded in making the people run away and gave fresh recruits to the insurgent cause. 61 Infantry Brigade with four battalions and commanded by Brig (later Lt Gen) Jaswant Singh, commenced operations to retake the Mizo Hills. Since the road was under MNF ambushes, the advance was considerably slowed but by 6 Apr, the heroic garrison of 1 AR was relieved. By the end of the month the Army had regained control of Mizo Hills. While the rebels, with much booty in arms, explosives and cash, merged with the population, the MNF HQ shifted to the Chittagong Hill Tracts.

Sam was controlling operations directly from Calcutta and visited the Mizo Hills every couple of weeks. During this period the Malayan insurgency had drawn to a successful close and Sam studied it closely. He saw that the British had effectively isolated the population from the insurgents, thus depriving them of their

---

29 Ibid.

30 Pp 89-90. Sinha. Op cit.

wherewithal and exposing them to ruthless operations by the Army. He decided that something of this nature had to be done in order to destroy the MNF.

To better understand how the CI doctrine in Mizoram was implemented, a brief study of the CI strategy in Malaya is essential. The Malayan Insurgency was started by the Malaysian Communist Party (MCP), which was Chinese in origin. The Chinese formed 38% of the population of Malaya and were specifically targeted by Communist China as part of its worldwide crusade to spread communism. The colonial administration, just recovering from World War 2, where it had armed the MCP to fight the Japanese, now found this very organisation rebelling against it. There was widespread corruption and the venality of the administration was particularly galling to the minorities who were subjected to indignities. The military wing of the MCP, the Malayan Races Liberation Army (MRLA) waged a successful insurgency campaign from 1948 to 1952 and the strength of the insurgents grew exponentially. Army units inducted into Malaya also grew accordingly. The initial heavy handed CI strategy was focused on enforcing law and order through coercive methods. It seemed the Army was more at war with the people of Malaya, especially the Chinese, than the insurgents. The police force was poorly trained and had no sympathy for the Chinese, whose villages were burnt and people deported to China before their government put a stop to it in 1949. The civil administration was at its wits end. Lt Gen Sir Harold Briggs was brought in. He revised the strategy and introduced the 'Briggs Plan' in 1950. Its basis was the forced relocation of half a million people, mostly Chinese, from squatter colonies on the fringes of the forests onto 'New Villages,' which were supposed to be given modern facilities and good administration. What it succeeded in doing was to destroy livelihoods and turned the people against the government. The resettlement centres became squalid slums giving further impetus to the MCP, especially as the MLRA infiltrated these villages. There was also no single individual with complete executive authority. A review was carried out by the Secretary of State for the Colonies and Lt Gen (later Field Marshal) Sir Gerald Templar was appointed with full authority in 1952. He evolved a 'hearts and mind strategy' which was later termed the 'Templar Plan.' The plan was a common sense application to fighting insurgency. Templar felt it was wrong to separate the peace time activity of the government from counter insurgency. He felt that if 2/3rd of the population could be won over, the battle would be won. Good governance formed the essence of his strategy. The Templar Plan was an enlightened refinement of the Briggs Plan.[31] What Sam and the Indian civil administration did was to adopt the Briggs Plan without the refinement required to take into account the unique nature of Mizo social and economic life.

Shri Tarlok Singh, Member of the Planning Commission, visited the Mizo Hills in late 1966 and approved Sam's plan for grouping of villages, as long as they were made economically viable. The plan was to group the villages in a 30 km belt along the highways. The process was to be completed in four phases[32] over a period of approximately four years. 764 villages were to be grouped involving nearly 95% of the rural population. On 3 Jan 1967, grouping of the first set of 67 villages commenced along the Silchar-Aijal Road. 18 'Progressive and Protected Villages (PPVs)[33] were established in an operation (OP ACCOMPLISHMENT) which took several months. Maj Gen (then Capt) OP Sabharwal recollects that the first PPV was established by his Battalion 10 kms away from Aijal and he was made responsible. A model self sufficient township incorporating all the basic facilities was constructed. 'Thereafter an outer perimeter, which included barbed wire and *punjis,* was laid to ensure that the people were kept isolated from the insurgent. The Army Commander came and inaugurated the Village and expressed

---

31 Pp 113-129. **Counter Insurgency in Modern Warfare. Ed by Daniel Marston and Carter Malkasian. Osprey Publishing Limited, Oxford, UK, 2008.**

32 The Gauhati High Court put a stop to it at the third phase.

33 There were four distinct categories; Protected and Progressive Villages, New Grouping Centres, Voluntary Grouping Centres and Extended Loop Areas.

In Mizo Hills with Governor B K Nehru

great satisfaction.'[34] Unfortunately, the implementation of the grouping scheme does not seem to have been thought through. It 'shattered the foundation of the economic and social structures of the Mizos, especially where jhoom cultivation was practiced.'[35] All the ills which were let loose by the unbridled use of the Briggs Plan on the people of Malaya were also visited upon the people of Mizo Hills.[36] It ultimately fell upon Sagat to implement Sam's Plan with his customary ruthless efficiency but he did so once he was sure that he had the insurgent on the run.

Counter insurgency operations were stepped up with the induction of additional troops in 1967,[37] which included the Lima

---

34 In conversation with Maj Gen OP Sabharwal at Dehra Dun on 26 Sep 09.

35 P 71. **Human Rights and Insurgency: The North East India. Edited by Ranjan R Dhavala and S Bhattacharjee**

36 The cultivable land was drastically reduced; the jhoom huts were destroyed and hunting became virtually impossible. Requirements of identity cards and implementation of curfew became highly unpopular. Landlessness and migration increased with the villagers becoming increasingly dependent on the government for most things. A lot of young men disillusioned by such ruthlessness joined the MNF.

37 'At one stage 61 Brigade itself had 23 battalions under its ORBAT.' Kaushik. Op cit.

Sector of Assam Rifles comprising of two infantry, two Assam Rifles and one battalion of BSF. The crackdown resulted in a large number of MNF cadres moving into East Pakistan and Burma. With such a large force operating in the Mizo Hills it became difficult for Command HQ to exercise control over operations from Calcutta. Sagat took over responsibility of Mizo Hills with wide ranging powers in Dec 1967. That same month The Counter Insurgency and Jungle Warfare School was established at Vairangte. Sagat ensured that no untrained soldier was hereafter inducted into the Hills. In Dec cracks also developed between the political and military wings of the MNF. Laldenga had realised within the first few months itself that an independent Mizoram was now a chimera and was open to negotiations. He was however hamstrung by Pakistan on one hand and the hard core of the Military Wing on the other. The latter carried out a major raid in the Chin Hills of Burma as part of their dream of Greater Mizoram. They only succeeded in raising the ire of the Burmese Army.

Sagat started extensive reconnaissance into the Mizo Hills, not hesitating to spend nights at remote posts, interacting with the junior leaders and getting a feel of the ground and operations. His impact was immediately felt. 'While before his arrival there was a great deal of caution, fear of sacking and a no mistake syndrome, Sagat liberated his subordinates from this fear as long as they acted in good faith and boldness.'[38] He also made it a point of interacting extensively with the people and the civil administration. His efforts to resolve the insurgency were at several levels. At one end he tried to break the MNF solidarity and even encouraged Reverend Zairema, in Feb 1968, to broker peace but found the MNF leadership hostage to the Pakistan Army. Sagat nevertheless got a reluctant and unsympathetic Chief Minister and the Governor, Shri BK Nehru on board; the latter having unbridled faith in him.

Sabharwal remembers that Sagat had a 'complete can do attitude' and with his contacts within the government would get

---

38 Ibid. Kaushik was the Brigade Major of 61 Brigade.

things organised, which the local administrator would have found impossible to do. He was always open to the people, constantly laughing and mingling with them and carrying gifts when visiting remote villages. He started making extensive use of helicopters, inserting small teams into the jungle and conducting operations from several directions. He remained very open to suggestions even from the junior most officer. Once Sabharwal spent two hours with him at Aijal, planning an operation which he, a young officer, was to lead. The more unconventional an operation the more Sagat liked it.[39] There was unlikely to be a company commander in Mizo Hills with whom Sagat did not interact and use the full force of his authority to assist him in conducting an operation. There was no question of a unit relaxing. Small team operations were the norm and a high tempo was maintained. Sagat was not above picking up a small team in his helicopter and dropping them off in the jungle to operate.[40] Lt Gen (then Lt) Susheel Gupta recollects that once Sagat spent 12 days in his unit while it was in the process of establishing a PPV. He was with a bare minimum staff, played bridge with the officers in his spare time and drank copiously without in any way losing his sharp edge. He created a sense of easy camaraderie and never lost his temper. He was held in awe by everyone and Gupta felt, was primarily responsible for limiting and ultimately destroying the insurgency.[41]

Kaushik, Sabharwal, Gupta and other army officers who served in Mizoram during the insurgency are emphatic in saying that the grouping of villages isolated the insurgent from the people and made him susceptible to the ambushes and raids of the security forces. The Grouping Centres provided better facilities than what was available in far flung areas. The officers point out to the fact that these Centres are now thriving townships. Also, as per Kaushik, only the Lushais, who had revolted had been targeted. The minorities

---

39 Sabharwal. Op cit.

40 Kaushik. Op cit.

41 **In conversation with Lt Gen (retd) Susheel Gupta, PVSM, AVSM, YSM, at Jaipur on 24 Feb 2009.**

like the Hmars, Paites, Reangs, Chakmas etc were disturbed to the minimum. However, as per statistics collected by NGO's, by the end of 1970 nearly 82% of the population had been affected.

One is not sure as to what Sagat's views were on this. Though ruthless in carrying out orders, his innate sympathetic nature must have empathised with the people who were so cruelly uprooted and moved away from their traditional homes, farming areas and hunting grounds. And then the concept was Sam's brainchild and it would have been a foolhardy officer indeed who would have contradicted the intellectual power of the next Chief. The fact remains that though Sagat set about establishing the Grouping Centres from 1968 onwards, he dragged his feet on implementing these measures for nearly a year and a half with the excuse that the troops were being employed in intense counter insurgency operations. He only accelerated the process in 1970 when several stages were made to overlap and 367 villages were required to be grouped.[42] This caused tremendous disruption in the population and was highly unpopular. It is to Sagat's credit that he involved the Church into the scheme and did not allow public antagonism to become a national outcry. In later years he remained ambivalent as to its efficacy though insisting that it was one of the pillars which helped him to crush the insurgency. By the time he got posted out he had realised the gross disruption it had caused in the people's lives and tried his best to alleviate it. Also surprisingly, his personal popularity never waned.

In 1970, Sagat decided to carry his CI campaign across the international border into East Pakistan. Clearance was obtained from higher headquarters and the raid was carried out on 17 Jan 1970. It was a complete success and large numbers of hostiles were

---

42 The New Grouping Centres required 184 villages to be grouped into 40 Grouping Centres and the Voluntary Grouping Centres required 120 villages to be grouped. Simultaneously, the Extended Loop Area required 63 villages being grouped into 17 Grouping Centres. Pp139-145. **India's North East Resurgent: Ethnicity, Insurgency, Governance, Development by BG Verghese. Konark Publishers, New Delhi. Second Revised Edition, 2004.**

killed and weapons captured. Sagat himself exercised operational control. When asked why he did so, he responded by saying that the raid was fraught with international ramifications. If something had gone wrong, he not any of his subordinates, would have assumed responsibility.[43] The raid broke the back of the Mizo Insurgency. There were a large number of surrenders and while Laldenga was moved to Mirpur, where the suspicious Pakistanis could keep a close watch over him, his cohorts moved deep into the Chittagong Hill Tracts, from where they carried out a daring escape to Burma as the Indian Army closed in, in Dec 1971.

---

43 OP Kaushik. Op cit. Sagat's attitude was in mark contrast to what happened in 1972, when a similar raid went dramatically wrong and the Brigade Commander passed on the blame to the raid commander, who was sacked (he luckily managed to obtain transcripts of the conversation he had with the brigade commander and so got himself exonerated. It speaks something about the Indian Army that both rose to become generals).

GOC IV Corps

CHAPTER FIVE

IV CORPS: SETTING THE STAGE

And 'mid this tumult Kubla heard from far
Ancestral voices prophesying war!

— Samuel Taylor Coleridge

By the end of 1970, Sagat was promoted to Lieutenant General and received his posting to Tezpur as General Officer Commanding (GOC) 4 Corps, where he relieved his old friend from Haifa days, Lieutenant General HK Sibal. He was now responsible for the defence of the North East Frontier Agency (NEFA), now Arunachal Pradesh, and again faced his old nemesis the Chinese. On 26 Jan 1971, his services in the Mizo Hills were recognized by the award of the highest medal for distinguished service, the *Param Vishisht Seva Medal* (PVSM).

The entire territory, though sovereign to India, was disputed by the Chinese who had inflicted a severe defeat on India during the 1962 War. Ill prepared and under equipped Indian troops had faced a well prepared, ruthless enemy and had been out generalled and crushed comprehensively. When it seemed that nothing would stop the Chinese juggernaut from descending onto the plains of Assam, it had inscrutably withdrawn to the original borders defined by the McMahon Line.[1] The area held little meaning to the general

---

1 Colonel Henry McMahon, in an exercise designed to secure the nebulous frontier of the British Indian Empire, demarcated the boundary between India and Tibet along a geographical watershed line on the Great Himalayan Range. The boundary as per an internationally established method of demarcation was accepted by India and an autonomous Tibet, during the Simla Accord of 1914. The Chinese, who were not involved in the exercise, rejected it and put forward a counter claim to vast territories south of the McMahon Line. The dispute remains alive and the border between India and China is known as the Line of Actual Control (LAC).

public. To the soldiers who manned these distant heights they still tasted of bitter gall. Enough evidence lay around their bunkers or kept turning up to remind them of their defeat. In the decade since the War, the Indian Army had painstakingly developed its defences forward. The Border Roads Organisation (BRO) had hacked roads through steep gorges full of impenetrable tropical forests right onto snow covered mountain crags. Defences had been blasted and carved out of the mountains in a coordinated effort. The soldiers were now better armed, equipped and supplied. They were also more confident. Chinese attempts of testing the waters by occasional encroachments were contemptuously rebuffed. Unlike Sikkim, where at many places troops stood eyeball to eyeball, in NEFA, large valleys generally separated the antagonists. The scope of an incident, leading to a conflagration, was limited.

NEFA was divided into several frontier divisions out of which Kameng absorbed the resources of nearly 2/3rd of 4 Corps. The approaches on to the adjacent Subansiri[2] Frontier Division were most difficult and thus left for the Assam Rifles to manage. The three eastern most frontier divisions were under the responsibility of only one mountain division. An incipient insurgency, a fallout of the Naga Rebellion, was rearing its head in the eastern most division ie Tirap.[3] The Chinese had improved their road network, especially opposite the Kameng Frontier Division and were capable of posing an even greater threat than they did during the 1962 War. Vast areas of NEFA remained remote and unexplored, inhabited by wild Mishmi Tribes. The Brahmaputra and its many tributaries savagely divided the Region, as they carved a relentless passage through the Himalayas. The deep gorges were filled with impenetrable tropical forests making movement virtually impossible.

Sagat was determined that the large gaps between the antagonists were not misutilised by the Chinese and so set a punishing schedule to foster an aggressive attitude in his

---

2 The capital of Arunachal, Itan Nagar, is now located in this area.

3 It was through this Frontier Division that the famous Ledo Road of World War 2 fame was hacked out by Gen Stilwell and his American engineers during the Burma Campaign.

command. He visited many remote posts and paid particular attention to administrative shortcomings.[4] Well aware that faulty generalship had led to the 1962 debacle, Sagat methodically set about eradicating a defensive mindset by a series of exercises and war games. He also initiated a vigorous regime of long range patrolling which opened up tracts, earlier barely visited. Perhaps two of the last awards of the McGregor Medal for exploration, instituted by the United Services Institution more than a century back, were given during this period.[5] Sagat aggressively lobbied to garner additional funds to improve habitat and infrastructure as far forward as possible.

With limited social distraction, Sagat was deeply immersed in getting to grips with the vast area of his Corps. He was living a single life as Kamla continued to occupy separated family accommodation in Jaipur to take care of the education of the younger children. The separation from his Family was a financial burden to Sagat and a great strain on Kamla that affected her health. Sagat was however, proud of the fact that his two eldest boys were on the threshold of a military career.[6] The Flag Staff House was a large hut with two bedrooms, located inside the Headquarter Complex, barely fifty metres from his office. The personal staff in the house was well trained and functioned under the strict control of a Subedar Major ADC from 3/3 GR, with Havildar Mani Prasad, from the same battalion, as his batman. He had been with the General a long time and knew how to make him comfortable.

Sagat had some friends and relatives within the tea fraternity

---

4 Rohit Rajpal recollects how Sagat, visited his remote platoon post at Lumpo, in Kameng, and chatted with him as if he had all the time in the world. **In communication to the Author.** The Author had a similar experience.

5 Col Narendra 'Bull' Kumar has lately been given the Gold Medal for his exploits in Siachen.

6 Digvijay, his second son, got commissioned into 2/3 GR, the Battalion he had commanded, in Jun 1971, while Ranvijay after trying for a career in the Air Force, subsequently joined the Officers Training Academy and got commissioned into the Garhwal Rifles.

and a limited social circle amongst the elite of Tezpur. Sociable in character, he looked forward to occasions when he could mix with people and the ladies, the prettier the better. Quiet evenings normally found him sitting on his favourite chair, sipping whisky and reading. He had an egalitarian choice in reading material and a thirst for esoteric knowledge which he absorbed with a near photographic memory. Once on a visit to the famous Jalan Family of Dibrugarh, he surprised them with his knowledge of the tea industry. He made sure that the Library subscribed to a large number of professional publications. They were all put up to him and would be returned with annotations or notes attached, drawing the attention of his staff to articles of interest. Youngsters were frequently asked to follow up on a subject that evoked his curiosity. Life was thus moving at a fairly even keel for a person of Sagat's enquiring and restless frame of mind, when his attention was drawn towards the happenings in East Pakistan.

By Mar 1971, the political turmoil in Pakistan came to a head, when its President, General Yahya Khan, decided that Bengali aspirations, as voiced by Sheikh Mujib-ur-Rahman and the Awami League, could not be managed within the existing power nexus.[7] Unwilling to take a statesman's gamble by allowing greater autonomy to the East Wing or making Mujib the PM of Pakistan, he started large scale induction of troops from West Pakistan and ordered a crackdown. He appointed the hard-nosed Lt Gen Tikka Khan as the Chief Martial Law Administrator. Tikka Khan was given a wide charter to destroy any dissent and he came down with a vengeance on the Awami League and its cohorts. There was an indiscriminate onslaught and the ruthlessness of the method adopted, reinforced the mindset of the average citizen that the West Pakistani, whether bureaucrat or soldier, was an alien occupier bent on subjugating

---

7 It seemed Yahya Khan had developed contempt for the Bengali after serving in East Pakistan earlier as GOC Dhaka. 'It was in East Pakistan that Yahya began to think of himself as one who could wield the 'iron rod' better than anyone else. The apparent docility and softness of the Bengalis went to the head of West Pakistani rulers.' P23. **East Pakistan: The Endgame by Brig AR Siddiqi. Oxford University Press, Karachi, Second Impression, 2005.**

Setting The Stage

him. By April, troops started fanning out all over East Pakistan and the measures carried out over the next six months succeeded in temporarily suppressing all dissent. But a price had to be paid. Political activity was either driven underground or it moved across the border. The large scale killings[8] had created a mass exodus of people from East Pakistan into India so that by the end of the year, it was estimated that nearly ten million people had fled East Pakistan, at the height of the monsoons. They were housed in ramshackle refugee camps, suffering from malnutrition and disease. Heroic effort by relief agencies kept epidemics barely under control.

Some form of resistance started in Apr, which rapidly increased to a full-fledged civil war.[9] It was now that one of the first controversies of the Bangladesh struggle occurred. By mid Apr 1971, the resistance movement led by the Mukti Fauz/ Mukti Bahini had succeeded in unbalancing the Pakistan establishment. West Pakistani troops were barely in the process of spreading out towards the rural areas when they were cornered in their cantonments by

---

8 There were atrocities, possibly from both sides, though the West Pakistan establishment was by far more ruthless and indiscriminate. Major General Hakeem Qureshi in his book alleges that in several areas pro Pakistani Biharis, Bengalis and West Pakistanis were massacred. P 33, **The 1971 Indo Pak War: A Soldier's Narrative by Major General Hakeem Arshad Qureshi ; Oxford University Press, Karachi, third impression, 2004.** Brigadier Siddiqi, on the other hand is fairly clear on the atrocities visited upon the Bengali population. Siddiqi, op cit, pp 132, 167. The atrocities were also well documented by the Western Media and helped the Indian Government in making up its mind to change the political set up in East Pakistan. **Col Nadir Ali**, a former SSG Commanding Officer, in an address to the students of BRAC University, Dhaka, was painfully frank on the atrocities perpetrated on the Bengalis. It has been claimed that nearly 200,000 women were raped. In his unpublished narrative **Brig JS Goraya** has given many instances of Pak atrocities told to him by the people, some of which were verified by him.

9 On 27 Mar 1971, troops of 8 East Bengal Regiment (EBR) under Maj Zia-ur-Rahman rebelled, killed their West Pakistani Commanding Officer and colleagues and broke out of Chittagong Cantonment. Zia announced the independence of Bangladesh on Chittagong Radio, the first such announcement. On 17 Apr 1971, the Provisional Government of Bangladesh was proclaimed from an enclave carved out of East Pakistan though it actually functioned from a suburb of Kolkata.

the Resistance and a hostile population.[10] India seems to have been taken by surprise with the turn of events. While it had neither the means nor the inclination to stem the flow of refugees, its border outposts were not even geared to face the turmoil taking place across the Border. At this stage Mr K Rustomji, the Director General of BSF, took charge of trans-border operations, with what seemed undue optimism.[11] During these heady days it did look as if the BSF and the Mukti Bahini would be able to bring about a change as they made some deep forays inside East Pakistan. The Indian Army Chief, Gen 'Sam' Manekshaw, came under some stick for his reluctance to commence military operations. However, he was firm in his refusal to move in unprepared and so the window, if it ever existed, was closed by end April as the Pakistan Army took control of the situation.[12] The BSF was then placed under command of the Army.[13] By June, the Pakistan Army had re-established itself firmly along the border[14] and the monsoons had started.

Military operations were now not possible until the monsoons were over and the ground had dried up. In the interim, the Army got down to giving the Mukti Bahini[15] more teeth, goaded by the under pressure Army Commander, Lt Gen JS Aurora and the abrasive Maj Gen OS Kalkat; appointed by Sam to oversee the Freedom Fighters

---

10 Qureshi. Op cit. Pp 33-60.

11 This episode is well narrated by Lt Gen Jacob. Pp 36-39. Op cit.

12 'A rapid concentration followed by a swift, surgical operation against under equipped and over extended Pakistani forces would have saved the people of Bangladesh nine months of deprivation, terror and misery'. P. 431. Palit. Op cit.

13 There is enough written evidence to indicate that Mrs Indira Gandhi and her political advisors indulged in a fair amount of wishful thinking, perhaps until the beginning of July, after Gen Manekshaw had told her categorically that the Army would only be in a position to launch operations by the end of the Year. They hoped that an energized freedom struggle would succeed in defeating the Pakistan Army in East Pakistan.

14 P 99. Qureshi. Op cit.

15 In the beginning there were several resistance organizations vying for resources. The main ones were the Mukti Bahini from whom the East Bengal Regiments were created, the Mukti Fauj of former para military/ police deserters, the Naval Commandos and the Freedom Fighters (civilians given weapon training). They were all clubbed later as the Mukti Bahini.

operations.[16] However, it soon became evident that if East Pakistan had to be liberated, it would require the Army to go in and do battle with the Pakistan Army. Over time the guerrillas got more confident and did succeed in unbalancing the Pakistan Army troops deployed close to the Border. They also provided invaluable intelligence and guidance to the Indian Army once hostilities commenced.[17]

East Pakistan forms inverse funnel created by the Bay of Bengal. If that was not enough, the funnel is plugged towards the North by the Himalayas. The region is drained by two of the mightiest Himalayan Rivers, the Ganga, the Brahmaputra and their tributaries. The monsoon rains are continuous and intense. In addition, cyclones generated in the Bay of Bengal churn their way northwards creating devastation in their wake. The countryside is low lying and crisscrossed by water channels and the region has only two seasons, the wet, which extends from mid May to beginning October and the dry, which comprises the rest of the year. During the wet season, movement is restricted to roads and tracks constructed on embankments. The major rivers, which can be several kilometres wide, are navigable for fairly long distances by large boats and steamers. Because East Pakistan never got a fair share of development funds, infrastructure in the region was poorly developed. Military tactical movement was impossible during the wet season, as the complete area would get flooded. The roads remained a perpetual bottleneck. The bridges over the rivers, were few and far between and any defender with some tactical acumen could well predict and negate any hostile movement. On the landward side, East Pakistan was surrounded from all directions by India, while towards the South and facing the Bay of Bengal, was one of the largest alluvial deltas of the world.

---

16 Pp 58-75, Sodhi. Op cit. Brig Sodhi, who was deployed with his Brigade opposite the NW border of East Pakistan during this period, is particularly scathing of the Army Commander and the Army's efforts to produce results with the Mukti Bahini.

17 Some freedom fighters were more effective than others. Lt Gen Sagat Singh **(recorded conversation with Col Pyare Lal, 1973)** has especially commended the work done by the Chattra Parishad (the Youth Wing of the Awami League) and the naval commandos, raised from former Bengali naval personnel of the Pak Navy.

The Ganga and the Brahmaputra/ Jamuna Rivers affected a junction at Goalundo Ghat, approximately 60 kms NW of Dacca and became the Padma. The Padma was joined by the Meghna, approximately 50 kms South of Dacca and became the Meghna[18] till it reached the sea. In between were a nightmare of tributaries and distributaries, wide and deep, which were a headache for any planner contemplating an advance into the heartland. Approach to Dacca by land was possible only from the North, either through the rail and road network coming from Mymensingh or the rail bridge over the Meghna, linking Sylhet and Chittagong to Dacca. All other approaches would require a river crossing with its additional hazards. Since there were no natural tactical features[19] to defend, Pakistani planners realized that the river lines and communication hubs would have to be held to prevent ingress inland. The problem faced by the Pak Eastern Army Commander and his strategic team was how to defend a region encircled on three sides by a hostile neighbour.

On hindsight, the countdown for the War started on 25 Jan 1971 when an Indian Airlines plane was hijacked to Lahore. On 27 Jan, after a much publicized visit by Bhutto, who extolled the hijackers as freedom fighters,[20] it was blown up. This was unfortunate for Pakistan as all over flights between the two wings were banned by India. The detour via Sri Lanka tripled the distance and affected all movement. Shortly thereafter, around 27 Feb, the build-up of Pakistani armed forces commenced and two battalions were

---

18 The drainage of the Meghna was not from the Himalayas but the hills of Eastern India. So intense was the downpour, over 500 cms in six months, that the volume of water which flowed down was more than that generated by the Himalayan rivers.

19 There is a stretch of low lying hills just across the Indian border opposite Tripura called the Lalmai Heights. These hills stretched for approx 16 kms North to South and were 4 kms wide. Because of the flat terrain the Heights, with an average elevation of 200 metres, could be well defended and formed an effective observation post for artillery spotters. The small hillocks around Sylhet and the Chittagong Hill Tracts were the only other heights of any importance.

20 Siddiq Salik seems convinced that the hijacking was a conspiracy engineered by India. P 56. Op cit.

inducted by air. Mujib, now getting more strident in his militant attitude, raised an outcry once the news of the military movement broke out. The provincial government persuaded the GHQ to stop all inductions as they were sensitive about every nuance in the mood of the people. They were especially worried about Mujib announcing a unilateral declaration of independence.[21] Induction only re-commenced from 26 Mar, once Tikka Khan had taken control and Yahya had decided to impose a military solution to the boiling cauldron.

At that stage East Pakistan had only one division ie 14 Division of four brigades, spread in cantonments all over East Pakistan. The mutiny of the East Bengal Regiments and the general civil insurrection put the army units under severe stress and in places like Pabna, Kushtia and Chittagong, several sub units were wiped out. However, from 26 Mar to 24 Apr, two divisional headquarters[22], five brigade headquarters, 16 battalions, including a commando battalion, and several mortar batteries were inducted. In addition, approximately two dozen bureaucrats and 5000 policemen were brought in from the Western Wing. Also the strength of the paramilitary forces was raised to nearly 73,000 men. The division headquarters were located at major communication hubs and the Army ruthlessly brought the situation under control. The flood of refugees into India, further aggravated relations between the two countries. The adverse media coverage did the Pakistan cause no good. By mid Nov, another five battalions had been inducted[23]

---

21 Mujib remained double minded, right till the time he was arrested, as to how far he wanted to go with his movement. There are indications that if Yahya or Bhutto had been more accommodating, he may have accepted an arrangement short of independence.

22 The two divisions, 9 and 16, were equipped with Chinese weaponry. Since Chinese ammunition was exclusively being manufactured at the Ordnance Factory at Jeydebpur, 20 kms outside Dacca, it was logical to induct these formations. They came by sea fully equipped, except for transport. **Lt Gen Sagat Singh in conversation**. Op cit.

23 The number of units inducted remains somewhat hazy, though Jacob (op cit, p. 35) felt that by the time war took place the army in East Pakistan consisted of 35 infantry battalions, six field regiments, four to five mortar batteries and an armoured regiment with two additional squadrons of tanks. As per other sources, including Salik, the figure of infantry battalions was closer to 40.

before an Indian blockade became effective.

Lt Gen AAK Niazi (nicknamed 'Tiger' because of his aggressive attitude) took over command of Pakistan's Eastern Command on 11 Apr 1971. He was also the Martial Law Administrator. He had made a name for himself as a commander of troops and was proud of it. A winner of the Military Cross during World War 2, he was also the recipient of one of the highest awards given by the Pakistan Army, the *Hilal-e-Jurat*.[24] Tikka Khan thereafter remained only the Governor of the Province. He watched his powers being eroded by a domineering Niazi, till he was replaced by a civilian, Abdul Malik, on 21 August, and returned to Pakistan. Niazi came to East Pakistan with certain pre-conditioned notions which, given his inclination for pomposity, bawdiness and sentimentalism, aggravated an already complicated situation and led him and his Army to perdition. Niazi had the tendency, common amongst a large number of his peers and colleagues, of under estimating the fighting ability of the Indian Army. He was convinced of the superiority of his soldiers.[25] The second attitude was far more dangerous. He believed the Bengali was an inferior being led astray by not following the strict tenets of Islam and it was his duty to bring him into the fold.[26] For a supreme commander to carry such notions in such dangerous times was a recipe for poor decision making. In addition, it seemed

---

24 Nasrullah Babar and some peers of Niazi had little regard for his character and even claimed that his award was based on a fictitious incident which ostensibly occurred at Zafarwal in 1965. He was favoured by Ayub and belonged to his unit.

25 Unfortunately, despite evidence to the contrary, this is a common failing in the Pakistan Army Officer Corps. Maj Gen Qureshi was a fairly successful battalion commander in the 1971 War. Despite the signal defeat and years in a prisoner of war camp, he still continues to retain that strange arrogance. If it's a façade, he's doing his people a great disservice. Qureshi. Op cit. This point is highlighted in detail by Maj Gen Lachhman Singh in **the 2005 reprinted edition of his book Victory in Bangladesh; Natraj Publishers, Dehra Dun, 1981.** P 35 ie '..... bizarre belief of the superiority of the Pakistan Army vis a vis Indian Army.'

26 In their books, Salik and Siddiqi have both brought out the character flaws of Niazi in some detail. It is not surprising that Niazi justified all his failures in a self serving autobiography; ***The Betrayal of East Pakistan* by Lt Gen AAK Niazi, Manohar Publishers, Delhi, 1998.**

Niazi was morally flawed. After the War he was severely indicted by the Hamooder Rahman Commission of Inquiry for corruption and moral turpitude. This lack of moral probity and his attitude towards the Bengalis led Niazi to turn a blind eye to the depredations carried out by his troops, who felt encouraged in the atrocities they visited upon the people.[27] He was proud of his common touch and frequently indulged in vulgarity much to the distaste of those who did not share his 'earthiness.' His pomposity made him a victim of his reputation and he would bully his subordinates and exercise excessive control[28] over any decision making.

In the early stages Niazi achieved flattering success. His troops managed to bring the Region under control and secure the borders. The Border Outposts (BOPs) were strengthened and Niazi started declaiming about taking the war into enemy territory. At this stage the troop induction had considerably strengthened his forces though he did not seem to have realised that with the insurgency starting to take root, they were still highly inadequate. To compound the problem, the Army was tied down with the contradictory requirements of strengthening the borders and controlling the internal situation.

Once the induction of troops was completed, Niazi divided the Province into four terrain compatible regions, each under one of his general officers. His plan involved creating a five km demilitarised corridor on the borders and securing the lines of communications. Once the BOPs had been strengthened he insisted on an offensive defence, which resulted in several clashes along the border, some involving tanks. Since the Indians had the Mukti Bahini training program well organised by now, Niazi played into their hands and the entire border area came alive. Incidents mounted and the Pakistan Army started moving their troops about in increasing frequency to douse the flames. This type of fire fighting led to indiscipline in the lower ranks as controls got lax and the soldier became tired and

---

27 P 170 Siddiqi op cit.

28 P 149 Siddiqi op cit.

dispirited. To supplement the troop effort the authorities raised several companies of East Pakistan Civil Armed Force (EPCAF)[29] and irregulars like the *Razakars*. With barely a month of training, they did not prove very effective and got quickly demoralised when faced with a reverse. Their behaviour also contributed to the alienation of the local population. Unfortunately, the ruthless attitude of some of the Resistance leaders stiffened their fortitude later as they felt they had no future in an independent Bangladesh.[30]

Once the contours of a likely post monsoon Indian offensive became evident, Niazi was in a dilemma. He had to secure the frontiers, prevent enemy ingress into the hinterland and protect Dacca. By mid October he should have worked out a strategy to contain the Indian Army along internal lines and used the natural obstacles to degrade their offensive plans since it would have been impossible to guard the entire frontier. Political considerations, which included the fear of a Bangladesh government functioning from captured territory, combined with his own delusions of valour, skewed his planning process. It seemed his planners were also hoping for some kind of international intervention which would call a halt to fighting. A last minute desperate effort to garner additional troops succeeded only partially before India chocked all movement into the Province.[31]

Since 1970 the Army in East Pakistan had been conducting a series of exercises and war games designed to ensure an effective defence against major Indian offensives from three directions. There were three options:-

---

29 The EPCAF substituted for the East Pakistan Rifles, which mutinied en masse in Mar and was disbanded. Its rank and file filled the East Bengal Regiments and gave some backbone to the Mukti Bahini.

30 'Niazi's one egregious blunder was that he had turned a purely internal security operation into a fully fledged military one. He was more concerned with a military victory against India than with normalizing the internal situation.' Siddiqi. Op cit. P 149.

31 By this stage Niazi faced a problem of credibility. His counterparts in the West had seen through his bombast and the Chief of General Staff went to the extent of labelling all reports emanating from East Pakistan as a 'bundle of lies'. P 155, ibid.

- Guard the frontier in strength and deny ingress along communication routes; thereafter fall back to 'fortress' Dacca and defend it along the rivers which girdled it.

- Carry out a positional defence along likely ingress routes with strong reserves in hand.

- Occupy nodal points and turn them into fortresses/ strong points with concrete bunkers heavily stocked to withstand a siege. They would require a disproportionate effort by the enemy to reduce. Each sector would have reserves available to harry, delay and defeat the enemy using the strong points as anvils.

Niazi, whose planners anticipated the main offensive coming from the West,[32] decided to adopt the 'fortress' strategy. Jessore, Jhenida, Bogra, Rangpur, Jamalpur, Mymensingh, Sylhet, Bhairab Bazaar, Comilla and Chittagong[33] were nominated as fortresses to be stocked with 45 days rations and 60 days ammunition. Selected nodal points/ communication hubs on the roads leading to the 'fortresses' and from there to Dacca would be made into strong points. Enemy ingress would be 'fixed' between them, as he struggled to open lines of communications. Reserves would then move tactically and defeat the enemy in detail. The Dacca bowl ie the area encircled by the Rivers Jamuna, Padma, Meghna and their distributaries, would be defended to the last, by when, it was hoped, international pressure on India would force a closure to hostilities. At this stage, the Indian Army would be strung out and vulnerable to counter attacks. If the plan had been retained in its essence, it is likely that East Pakistan may have lost territory near the border but its communication hubs may have been intact and Dacca would have been well defended.

In his arrogance, Niazi shot himself in the foot by declaring

---

32 Pakistan Eastern Command later changed its views and decided that the main offensive would likely come from the East.

33 Salik. Op cit. p 125.

that no post would be allowed to fall until it had sustained 75 percent casualties and no outpost would be vacated. This was like ordering everyone to hold out till 'last man last round' with no flexibility given to junior commanders. Surprisingly, his plan was endorsed by the GHQ at Rawalpindi, who even insisted that the Army carry out some form of a limited offensive towards Malda and a raid on the Farakka Barrage.[34] Even as late as 22 Nov, when active hostilities had broken out, Brig Baqar Siddiqui, Niazi's Chief of Staff (COS), who was in Rawalpindi trying to get additional troops, did not paint a grim picture[35] in his meetings at the GHQ. It seemed Niazi's cocksureness had put blinkers around his and his subordinates' eyes. Once hostilities commenced it became evident that Niazi had unbalanced himself. By reacting to Indian Army's offensive actions in November itself, he denuded himself of critical reserves and strategic reaction capability. He even tried a strategic sleight of hand by creating two additional formations from within his resources. Thus from a three division command he suddenly had a five division one. Once the fighting escalated, this impressed neither the Indians nor the cannier among his commanders.[36] Like Hitler, in the closing months of World War 2, Niazi seemed to get dutch courage from his ad hoc forces. The initial deployment ordered by Niazi was as follows:-

- **Jessore Sector.** It was placed under 9 Infantry Division commanded by Major General MH Ansari[37], who had

---

34 To be fair to GHQ Rawalpindi, they had time and again specified that Dacca should remain the lynch pin of the defensive strategy. However, by this stage Niazi's arrogance had got the better of him.

35 Siddiqi. Op cit. P 193. Baqar Siddiqi (no relation) was subsequently severely indicted by Justice Hamooder Rahman.

36 This desperate ploy seems to have worked partially as, in their initial planning; the Indian planning staff included these formations as fully fledged divisions. Once the fighting started in earnest, it did not take long for Sagat to see through their weakness.

37 A sober man, he was already disheartened by the behaviour and attitude of his troops. In late Sep, while meeting Siddiqi, he told him, '...we will have to account for every single rape and killing when back in West Pakistan. Allah never spares the tyrant.' Siddiqi. Op cit. p 167.

replaced Major General Shaukat Riza[38]. It had two brigades, 107 Brigade, based at Jessore and 57 Brigade at Jhenida.

- **North Bengal Sector.** This was placed under 16 Infantry Division commanded by Major General Nazar Hussein Shah located at Nator. It had two brigades and took under command 23 Brigade, which was based at Rangpur. Of its two brigades, 205 Brigade was responsible for Hilli – Bogra and 34 Brigade was based at Rajshahi. The only armoured regiment was allotted to this Sector.

- **Eastern Sector.** This was placed under 14 Infantry Division, commanded by Major General Khadim Hussein Raja. He had serious differences with both Tikka Khan and Niazi and was replaced by the newly promoted Major General M Rahim Khan. On Rahim Khan being appointed the Deputy Chief Martial Law Administrator, Major General Qazi Abdul Majid took over. The Division consisted of the Division Headquarters, located at Dacca, with 117 Brigade at Comilla, 27 Brigade at Mymensingh (subsequently moved to Brahmanbaria) and 202 Brigade at Sylhet.[39]

- **Chittagong Sector.** Being out on a limb the Sector came under 97 Independent Infantry Brigade Group commanded by Brigadier Ataullah, who reported directly to Dacca. Once the threat to the Chittagong axis, through the Belonia Bulge, materialised, an ad hoc 91 Brigade was also created.

As the situation along the borders deteriorated through Oct and early Nov, Niazi created two ad hoc formations and moved headquarters and units around. The ubiquitous Maj Gen M Rahim

---

38 Shaukat Riza was resentful of Niazi's high handedness and had been replaced at his request.

39 This brigade was further broken up into two brigades. 202 Brigade was located at Sylhet with one Battalion and 313 Brigade was located at Maulvi Bazaar with two battalions. In Nov, when additional troops were made available, these brigades were reinforced. Nevertheless, this ad hoc organisation was enough to cause some confusion amongst the staff of 4 Corps and 8 Mountain Division.

Khan, who was the Deputy Chief Martial Law Administrator, was given command of 39 Division and moved with his Headquarters to Chandpur. 117 Brigade at Comilla was put under his command along with 53 Brigade which, earlier earmarked to defend Dacca, was moved to Fenny, near the border. Thus by denuding his only strategic reserve and deploying it along the border, Niazi played into India's hands. Maj Gen Jamshed, the Director General of EPCAF, was nominated as GOC 36 Division and with his Headquarters was made responsible for Dacca and the Northern Approach.[40] He had 93 Brigade of two battalions and was allotted two battalions from 27 Brigade, which had moved from Mymensingh to Bhairab Bazaar.[41] By creating these two additional divisions, Niazi had succeeded in truncating 14 Division and diluting its cohesion. The planning process at Niazi's Headquarters came in for severe criticism by the Hamooder Rahman Commission, which scathingly commented that '.....the planning, if any, was hopelessly defective and there was no plan at all for the defence of Dacca.'[42]

The Indian planning process is worth a critical study as are the personalities of those involved in it. Luckily for India it had Prime Minister Indira Gandhi at the helm with General SHFJ 'Sam' Manekshaw as head of the Chiefs of Staff Committee.[43] Both were opinionated and headstrong and surprisingly got along well together. As Defence Minister, Babu Jagjivan Ram, whose sharp brain has been given little credit, ensured that at the highest levels, all the

---

40 Both these senior officers, with excellent pre-war reputation, were severely indicted by the Hamooder Rahman Commission, for corruption.

41 There is some doubt whether these battalions ever came under his command except for elements which escaped from Bhairab Bazaar.

42 P 402/34. **Report of the Hamooder Rahman Commission of Inquiry into the 1971 War, Vanguard Books, Lahore.**

43 The Chiefs of Staff Committee rarely functioned smoothly. Sam's personality white washed its shortcomings. Luckily for the Country, the other service Chiefs, Air Chief Marshal PC Lal and Admiral SM Nanda, were outstanding in their own right and made their plans within the bare bones of an overall strategy. However, as Jacob pointed out, '....there was no clear political aim nor was there an agreed strategy or coordinated control of operations.' Jacob. Op cit. P. 161.

ministries remained in step and the apex 'Secretaries Committee' decisions were urgently implemented.[44] Also, the authority of what Jacob disparagingly referred to as the 'Kashmiri Mafia'[45] could not be discounted. Knowing well the influence they exercised over Mrs Gandhi in the corridors of power, Sam cleverly cultivated them. His close association with DP Dhar, much resented by his Chiefs of Staff colleagues and subordinates, allowed him immediate access to the Prime Minister and enabled him to bypass the normal channels. Sam was a charismatic personality, thoroughly professional, confident of himself and with unimpeachable integrity.[46] He could also be domineering and never suffered fools gladly. Because Mrs Gandhi had a soft corner for him, he could get away with bullying or ignoring people with powerful influence, who later took their own revenge on him in petty ways. Sam had an excellent eye for selecting the right people but at times, his excessive sense of loyalty to subordinates was also a weakness, exploited by some of them.

The theatre responsible for operations against East Pakistan was Eastern Command with Lt Gen Jagjit Singh Aurora as the Army Commander. Gen Aurora was a close acolyte of Sam. He had served long years under him and was fully trusted by him. It was also rarely that he disagreed with him. As a staff officer Aurora had proved his credentials though there have been doubts raised about his ability as a commander.[47] However, his planning process was most thorough and his frequent visits to various formations made him familiar with the ground. Though he did not get along too well with his subordinates, he used his staff officer's eye to vet the plans in detail and made sure they were in step with what the Army Headquarters wanted. As Army Commander, the buck stopped with him. If there

---

44 '.....was perhaps the best Defence Minister we have had.' Jacob. Op cit. P 154.

45 Jacob. Op cit. P 33. They included the two Dhars DP and PN, PN Haksar and TN Kaul. They were instrumental in formulating and directing policy during this crucial year in India's history.

46 'He was a very straight man …….had a very strict consideration of character.' **Gen KV Krishna Rao in conversation with the Author at Secunderabad on 21 Mar 10.**

47 Jacob, Sukhwant Singh and Lachhman Singh, in their respective books, have all cast doubts on Aurora's capabilities.

had been any strategic failures or the overall plan had proved faulty, he would have had to accept responsibility. He was lucky in his Chief of Staff, Lt Gen JFR Jacob, who had been specifically selected by Sam and posted to Calcutta to complement Aurora. A man with professional integrity, he had a sharp brain and was well aware of the strategic nuances of the planning process. Luckily he got along well with the Corps Commanders, who were at times constrained by their relationship with Aurora. His close coordination with the staff at Army Headquarters resulted in resources being released in time for operations. A great deal of credit for the successful formulation of the offensive plan is attributable to him and the staff at Command Headquarters.[48]

The two Directors of Military Operations (DMO) at Army Headquarters, who were closely associated with the conceptualisation and execution of the offensive plan, were active players on the stage of War. Maj Gen KK Singh was the DMO till Aug 1971 and thereafter went on to command 1 Corps in the Western Theatre[49] during the War. Sam had been impressed with him when he went as General Officer Commanding 4 Corps immediately after Lt Gen BM Kaul had been relieved. KK was the Brigadier General Staff (BGS). A man of few words, he was most thorough in examining a problem from all angles. Regardless of what his superiors felt, he would unhesitatingly give his opinion on any issue he was required to address. He ran a good team and the plan for the Campaign, prepared by him, had the strong backing of the Chief.[50] Unfortunately, KK's innate caution resulted in a flaw in the plan which subsequently affected the conduct of operations. Maj

---

48 One needs to somewhat discount the impression created in his books that **he** was solely responsible for the successful conduct of operations. By constantly indulging in verisimilitudes and harping on his contribution to India's victory, Jacob does himself less than credit. He forgets that he was a staff officer while Aurora, despite his faults, was the Army Commander.

49 The caution he exercised in conduct of 1 Corps operations came in for some criticism.

50 'KK's examination in depth meant dissecting issues threadbare from all angles............ The Chief had implicit faith in KK.......' P. 66. ***The Liberation of Bangladesh* by Maj Gen Sukhwant Singh, Lancer Publishers, New Delhi, 1998.**

Setting The Stage

Gen IS 'Inder' Gill, a paratrooper with a tough reputation, took over from KK and remained the DMO for the duration of the War. A very sound professional, he remained unaffected by people's reputation when voicing his opinion. Sam respected him and he got along well with Jacob as well as Sagat, which was of great help to them during the War.[51]

As Jacob has mentioned, Eastern Command became aware by end Apr that it was required to prepare for war against East Pakistan. Once it became clear that the Army was unlikely to be dragged into this war before winter, enough time was available for preparation of the plan, allotment of troops and earmarking of resources. Despite the driving force of Sam it was still a close run thing as all the resources could not be assembled till well until the last month. The legendary thoroughness of KK combined with Sam's close scrutiny led to delays and a broad framework of a plan was only ready by Jul 71.[52] Briefly, it involved:-

- Blockade and isolation of East Pakistan.
- Segmenting the enemy's defences to prevent reinforcement or withdrawal.
- Bypassing of fixed defences and securing communication centres.

As an objective, Dacca was not suitably defined.

Sam was well aware of the risk he was taking in making formations available for the offensive. The Western Theatre could not be denuded accept to juggle with some strategic reserves. In addition, he was most loath in pulling out troops opposite the Chinese. This led to some tension with the planners at Eastern

---

51 '.......a down to earth man without whose support and understanding it would have been impossible for me to have functioned effectively.' P. 54. Jacob. Op cit. Gill also had a high opinion of Jacob. As quoted by Shubhi Sood from the extract of Maj Ashok Krishna's book *India's Armed Forces: Fifty Years of War and Peace*. P. 205. Sood. Op cit.

52 P. 68; Sukhwant Singh. Op cit.

Command[53] who, under Jacob, had already prepared an outline framework by end May 71, which emphasised on Dacca being the ultimate objective.[54]

The Offensive was to be along three major thrust lines, each allotted to a Corps. Headquarters 2 Corps, under Lt Gen TN Raina, was raised for the Western thrust line, to be focussed on Jessore. It took under its command 4 and 9 Infantry Divisions. The North Eastern thrust line was the responsibility of HQ 33 Corps, under Lt Gen ML Thapan,[55] deployed to face a Chinese threat from Sikkim/Bhutan. It would now look southwards. It was primarily to utilise one of its own formations, 20 Mountain Division. A couple of brigades from Army Headquarters reserves were also allotted.

The Eastern thrust would be the responsibility of 4 Corps. There was no alternative but to split the Corps Headquarters in two on account of the distances involved. The main headquarters, under Sagat, was required to move to Tripura, while the rear headquarters would remain at Tezpur to face the Chinese threat under the COS, Maj Gen (later Gen and COAS) OP Malhotra. For the offensive, Sagat was allotted the counter insurgency formations, 8 and 57 Mountain Divisions, deployed in Nagaland and Mizoram[56] respectively and one of his reserve formations, 23 Mountain Division. Since Sam

---

53 P. 88, Jacob. Op cit. The Chinese threat may have changed the strategic objectives and prevented allotment of adequate troops, thus delaying the outcome. It is also possible that the statement made on 10 Jul 1971 by Chou en Lai to Kissinger in Beijing that China will act in case India invades East Pakistan, made India's strategic planners very cautious. It did not help matters that the Chinese found Manekshaw 'insufferably arrogant.' Pp 225 – 227. **Myth and Facts: Bangladesh Liberation War by BZ Khasru; Rupa Publications, New Delhi 2010.**

54 P. 60. Jacob. Op cit.

55 Thapan had a difficult relationship with Aurora, primarily on account of Sam's antipathy. By all accounts he was a sound professional.

56 Gen Krishna Rao, then commanding 8 Mountain Division, was asked by Aurora about the formations that could be made available. He was confident that the complete Division of six brigades could be pulled out. In the end except for one brigade, the Division Headquarters and five brigades were pulled out. However, only two brigades served under his command. **In conversation with the Author.**

was wary of further denuding any forces facing the Chinese, the Northern thrust towards Dacca, via Mymensingh, was made the responsibility of 101 Communication Zone and given minimal resources.[57] Maj Gen Gurbax Singh Gill, a fine commander, carried on with whatever he had until he got injured and was replaced by Maj Gen Gandharv Nagra.

Aurora was briefed on the plan in Jul[58] in some detail and he thereafter visited all the formations to outline their tasks. He visited Tezpur that same month and had a discussion with Sagat in the presence of the division commanders. Krishna Rao recollects[59] flying to Tezpur from Nagaland on 12 Jul to hear for the first time what his role was likely to be. He and Sagat were old friends. At that time though the intelligence was limited and the Corps role had not been finalised, Sagat warned Krishna Rao that when it came to the crunch he would use his Division for the ultimate objective.

Sam, with KK, visited Calcutta in the beginning of August. The Plan was laid out in detail to the staff at Headquarters Eastern Command. It was then that another major controversy of the War raised its head. KK was 'sceptical about the feasibility of capturing Dacca within the time frame of a short war'[60] and felt that the orthodox techniques of the Indian Army and shortage of bridging equipment would make Dacca unattainable. When the plan was presented, Khulna and Chittagong were made the terminal objectives, without a mention of Dacca. Obviously, the aim was

---

57 This was the only thrust line which had no major water channel facing it and was initially given only 95 Infantry Brigade. Subsequently, another brigade was allotted. Both were from Nagaland. Inder Gill and Jacob deserve some credit as they realized the significance of this thrust and kept on reinforcing it. Whether there was enough dynamism in it is another question.

58 P.72, Sukhwant Singh. Op cit.

59 **In conversation with the Author at Secunderabad on 21st Mar 2010.**

60 P. 72, Sukhwant Singh. Op cit. Inder Gill was explicit in stating that '…..the objectives given to Eastern Command in the Army HQ Operation Instructions were the areas up to the main river lines. Dacca was not included as an objective.' The emphasis for Dacca was only changed in late Nov. P. 98. **India's Armed Forces: Fifty Years of War and Peace by Maj Gen Ashok Krishna, AVSM. Lancer Publishers, New Delhi, 1998.**

to liberate maximum territory and choke East Pakistan. Jacob immediately voiced his objections but the weight of KK, supported by Sam and Aurora, carried the day.[61] At a later stage, the Navy agreed to blockade Chittagong[62] and its priority was reduced. Nevertheless, the lack of emphasis on Dacca affected the planning and conduct of operations down the chain.

The most affected was 2 Corps as its objectives were completely divergent and it would lose its momentum by the time the Padma River was reached.[63] 33 Corps was given objectives to slice the Hilli – Gaibanda neck, despite objections by the Corps Commander, who feared that he would lose momentum for a thrust southward. The Northern thrust, which had the best chance to reach Dacca, remained at a lower priority.[64] 4 Corps was tasked to reach the Meghna River and contain Sylhet. Time and resources permitting it was to capture Chittagong.

It has been mentioned that Aurora's strategy was deliberately to carry out a multi pronged offensive and it was neither sound nor tactically correct to plan for Dacca at this stage. Gen Krishna Rao, while in conversation with the Author, gave the analogy of the 'broad front' strategy practiced by Eisenhower during his advance through France in World War 2. In this case the analogy may not be particularly apposite as our strategists seemed to have lost sight of the ball. In his decision to micro-manage his operations, Aurora did not permit enough freedom of action to his subordinates. In also not giving a clear directive about Dacca, Aurora gave no opportunity to his subordinate commanders to lay down intermediate objectives,

---

61 P. 66. Jacob. Op cit.

62 Sagat was particularly unhappy on the priority being given to Chittagong in his sector.

63 The Territorial Army Brahmaputra Flotilla of the Inland Waterways was ordered to move to Faridpur, on the Padma, to enable ferrying across formations of 2 Corps for advance to Dacca. This never came about. P.65. Jacob. Op cit.

64 There is an opinion that if Sam had been less reluctant in allowing move of troops from the formations deployed opposite the Chinese, the Northern thrust may have got additional resources at the beginning, which may have made an appreciable impact on the thrust to Dacca.

Setting The Stage

which would enable them to 'direct their full energies towards Dacca'.[65]

Different commanders reacted differently. Raina acquiesced to the plan but faced violent opposition from one of his division commanders and did not succeed in running a happy team throughout the War.[66] Thapan had serious professional disagreements with Aurora which soured the pitch between them and affected the ensuing operations.[67] Gurbax Gill, already lacking favour, was too junior to raise serious objections. However, the planners seemed to have realised the importance of his thrust line and subsequently allotted extra resources, including a paradrop at Tangail.[68] Sagat had served under Aurora and Sam earlier and was dissatisfied with his tasking. Those who served with him then realised that as the days went by he became reticent in the presence of Aurora. As the war progressed their relationship became strained as Sagat started keeping his cards close to his chest.

As a representative of the Military Operations Directorate, Sukhwant Singh was deputed in September to make a tour of all the formations preparing for the offensive. He had a meeting with Sagat and discussed his objectives. Sagat did not sound too happy but was cautious in voicing any complaint. However, the very mention of a race to Dacca '...brought a glint into his eyes....once battle was joined Sagat Singh was not the one to be bound by petty

---

65 P. 47, Lachhman Singh. Op cit. The Official History (unpublished) is also critical about this tendency towards over centralization.

66 Raina took over command of his Corps in late Oct. By then Eastern Command had war gamed the Plan. It required effort on his part to bring about changes.

67 Sukhwant Singh has been highly critical of Thapan and blamed him for the operationalisation of a Corps plan, which in no way contributed towards the capture of Dacca. Others are more generous towards him.

68 Maj Gen HS Kler, MVC, who commanded 95 Infantry Brigade during the War, feels the induction of the second brigade, 167 Infantry Brigade, at such a late stage, made no appreciable difference to the conduct of the Campaign in his sector. **In personal communication to the Author.**

constraints.....He would head the race to Dacca.'⁶⁹

Sagat was well aware of the magnitude of the problems he was facing. The first of these was a nearly non-existent logistic base. Tripura, the launch pad for the offensive, was an Indian state, projecting into East Pakistan. This made it vulnerable to any offensive intent of the Pakistan Army. It had an airport at Agartala, adjacent to the International Border. The railhead at Dharmanagar was at the end of a rickety 240 km single, metre gauge railway line from Gauhati. It was nearly 1400 kms from the broad gauge railhead at Barauni.[70] Part of this distance (21 kms) was traversed along the border with East Pakistan and prone to sabotage.[71] There was a single lane road from Gauhati, passing through Shillong and the picturesque dales of Jovai and Khleriat. It was not meant for military traffic and prone to disruption. The bridges were weak and required to be strengthened, thus increasing the turnaround time.[72] Being at the end of such a tenuous logistic link, the State's infrastructure was poorly developed. In addition, several million refugees had flooded in from East Pakistan and had to be housed and fed. Tripura itself was hilly and thickly forested, its towns connected by poorly maintained brick lined roads. Except for Agartala, no other town in the State could boast modern facilities to lodge or support a large body of troops.

That be said, Tripura was the ideal springboard for launching an offensive into East Pakistan. The bulge it formed gave options to the military planner to look in three directions. Dacca was barely 80 kms away from its border. Since Sagat's main task was to secure the

---

69 P. 89. Sukhwant Singh. Op cit.

70 '....the hill section of the railway, between Lumding and Dharmanagar was an additional bottleneck. This section could not take more than 10 trains a day, each hauling only 30 wagons.' P. 258. Lachhman Singh. Op cit. In addition, the Dharmanagar siding could take only two trains at one time when the minimum requirement was for three to four.

71 Saboteurs succeeded in disrupting the railway line on at least four occasions. Once 8 Mountain Division troops started moving in they took over the responsibility of guarding the railway line.

72 Without this, getting the medium guns to Tripura would have been impossible.

East bank of the Meghna River, it was on the River that his gaze first fell. The Meghna is one of the mightiest rivers of Bangladesh. It is not a Himalayan river. Its catchment area includes the hills of Mizoram in the South to the blue mountains of Meghalaya in the North. These receive the largest monsoon precipitation in the world. All the water flowing off these mountains descend towards the plains of Bangladesh via several wide and fast flowing rivers, which join and form the Meghna. The two most prominent among them are the Barak and the Gumti. The Barak originates in Manipur, receives a vast amount of rain from the hills of Eastern India and is more than 300 metres wide near the international border. Just before it enters East Pakistan it bifurcates into the Surma and Kusiyara Rivers flowing on either side of the Atgram-Zakigunj salient. While the Surma flows westward through Sylhet, the Kusiyara flows nearly parallel and south of it. They eventually join again turn south and become the Meghna. During the monsoons they invariably burst their banks creating a vast sea of water. The area around Sylhet has low lying hillocks. The ground in between remains water logged and forms perennial lakes called *hoars*. Some of these dry up or turn marshy. Obviously, cross country movement gets seriously affected. South of Agartala, the Gumti collects the outflow from the hills of Tripura, flows westwards, north of the Lalmai Heights and then joins the Meghna at Daudkhandi. The River, though only 100 metres wide, created a unique set of problems for the engineers as two divisional offensives were to be carried out north and south of it.[73] Further South was the Dakatia Nala, followed by the Fenny River and other rivulets and nalas, which were all major obstacles to cross country movement.

North westwards, between the Gumti and the Meghna, was a unique river system called the Titas. At some stage in the distant past, as the drainage into the Meghna came roaring through the hills bringing vast amount of silt, it blocked the extended loop

---

73 'Since the weight of the Corps offensive was astride this river, it had to be bridged at a number of places. But we did not have the bridging equipment. At least one of the bridges had to be strong enough for medium guns and light armour.' P4. Jagdev Singh. Op cit. The Axis would also be nominated as the Corps Centre Line.

created by the River near Ashuganj. The River than ploughed a direct channel southward. This created a large lagoon between Ashuganj and Akhaura with numerous water channels forming a trellis across the terrain. 'The monsoon downpour……. floods this area like an endless lake, the main river overflowing into a maze of lakes, rivulets and swamps…..when the dry months set in the water slowly percolates back into the Meghna through connecting lagoons and rivulets.' The water hyacinth grows extensively in these waters and 'floats with the rise in the monsoon floods, but somewhat regulates and slows the flow-back in the dry months by chocking the outlets.'[74] Fed by tributaries from Tripura, the Titas had a constant water flow and was also navigable at many places. The Meghna was navigable throughout its length as also along its tributaries. The main river ports at Daudkhandi and Chandpur were connected to the interior by tarred roads, which flanked the Lalmai Heights. Chandpur had the facility for docking of sea going ships, while Daudkhandi was located just opposite the approach road from Dacca.

The railway line from Dacca crossed the Meghna on the only bridge over it, at Ashuganj. The bridge was slightly less than 3000 feet long with each span being over 400 feet. Just before crossing the bridge a branch line bifurcated northwards to Mymensingh from the town of Bhairab Bazaar. After crossing the Meghna, the railway line ran southeast cutting through the Titas Loop to Brahmanbaria and then to Akhaura, a town opposite Agartala. Thereafter it branched north and south to Sylhet and Chittagong respectively. The line, a legacy of pre-independence India, ran close and parallel to the international border and was an ideal target for the Mukti Bahini. It was constructed on high embankments that were used by the Pakistan Army to build concrete emplacements to dominate the surrounding countryside.

The road network was as sparse. The main road in the area

---

74 P 37. **The Bridge on the River Meghna: The Dash to Dacca by Major General Ashok Kalyan Verma, AVSM. KW Publishers, New Delhi, 2009.**

was the so called C & B Road,[75] which linked Dacca to Chittagong via a ferry at Bhairab Bazaar. It was however possible to move jeeps over the railway bridge after suitably decking it. From the town of Brahmanbaria, a road ran north to Sylhet via Maulvi Bazaar. Though one could approach Sylhet from further west, the main communication network was east of the Meghna running through Brahmanbaria. This would prove significant as the Campaign developed. Southward, the road ran more or less parallel to the rail embankment and passed through Comilla and Laksham to Chittagong. Comilla was the largest town east of the Meghna and was dominated by the Maynamati Cantonment which was on the Lalmai Heights. Laksham was an important communication centre from where the railway line bifurcated in three directions to Chandpur, Noakhali and Chittagong. The road network was slightly better developed south of Comilla. However, as all these roads were on embankments and crossed the rivers on permanent bridges, they could be used effectively by the Pakistan Army if it carried out a tactical battle taking advantage of interior lines. The towns which have been mentioned were nodal points and incorporated by Niazi into his fortress defence.

---

75 '……C standing for China and B for Bengal. The road had apparently been designed and supervised by the Chinese. It was a fairly good road, of 12 feet carriageway and 9 feet grassy berms on either side. The quality of bituminous work was high…..' P 154. Jagdev Singh. Op cit.

CHAPTER SIX

IV CORPS: INTO THE RING

*Tempt me no more; for I
Have known the lightning's hour,
The poet's inward pride
The certainty of power*

- C Day Lewis

Sagat became aware of the role he was to play in East Pakistan when Jacob tentatively sounded him out in May. He had a firm idea of what he was required to do once Aurora visited Tezpur in July and discussed his role in the presence of his divisional commanders. Thereafter Sagat flew to Tripura and carried out a preliminary reconnaissance of his likely launch pads and logistic bases. The complete lack of any infrastructure and the near illusory supply line alarmed him. He also met the BSF senior officers and leaders of Mukti Bahini and the East Bengal Regiments. The latter had all been thrown out of their bases in East Pakistan and were either consolidating themselves or undergoing training. Tentative raids and minor sabotage activities were going on. He and the Brigadier-in-charge Administration, Brig KG Pitre, decided on the locations of the maintenance areas, the staging areas for the formations and the location of the Corps Headquarters. The Command Headquarters had nominated Brig PK Lahiri, the Sub Area Commander, Jorhat, to improve the lines of communications and set up the Maintenance Area at Dharmanagar, which was subsequently used by 8 Mountain Division. Lahiri was fat and looked jolly enough but he set to with a ruthlessness, which got things moving. A brigade of 57 Mountain Division had already moved to Tripura to safeguard the State against any Pak adventurism.

As July turned into August and the incessant monsoon rains turned the plain into a vast sheet of water, Sagat started getting worried. Without firm executive orders from Army Headquarters, resources and formations could not be moved with the urgency required. Though corps and army engineer units had started to establish the infrastructure, troops and equipment were not forthcoming at the speed desired, even though the Brig in charge Administration at Eastern Command, Brig Chajju Ram, had got things moving. Sagat managed another reconnaissance in Aug, once Aurora had further briefed him and defined his role in greater detail. During this visit the urgency of what was required to be done became more apparent as the monsoons and the lack of infrastructure started telling on the build up schedule. Work on the Corps Maintenance Area at Teliamura was still chaotic[1] and the Corps Headquarters complex was yet to be established. He was particularly dissatisfied with the progress on the Udaipur Maintenance Area, being established for 23 Mountain Division.[2] No bridging equipment[3] had arrived though Command had re-allocated BRO resources and earth moving plants for improving the road.[4] The State had to be prepared to receive approximately 100,000 troops, 30,000 tons of stores and nearly 5000 vehicles of all types. A 700 bedded hospital, with air conditioned operation theatres, was yet to come up. The morass being created by the monsoons was frustrating the effort of the engineers who had hired a vast number of refugees[5] to work on various sites. On Sagat's insistence

---

1 The Maintenance Area was stocked by 15 Sep, once Sagat wielded the stick.

2 This was only ready by 01 Oct. Supplies and stores had to be moved nearly 180 kms by road from Dharmanagar.

3 The equipment was not forth coming till the very end. Jacob mentions that he had to hound KK to release it as a final act before he proceeded on promotion to take over command of 1 Corps. P.173 Appx 1, Jacob. Op cit.

4 There seems to have been a mismatch in engineer planning. While bridging equipment was scarce, some engineer stores were overstocked.

5 There is not enough credit given to the refugees. Without their help the infrastructure for the Corps offensive would not have come up. They lived miserable lives but worked

nearly 400 mules were also inducted, rations for whom had to be catered for.[6]

Army Headquarters Operation Instructions were issued on 16 August, immediately followed by the Command Instructions.[7] Sagat discussed his tasks in some detail with Aurora over two meetings in Tezpur. The offensive part of his tasking specifically spelt out that:-

- Comilla was to be captured by D plus 7 (D being the day that the offensive was to be launched).

- The Meghna River line was to be secured at Chandpur and Daudkhandi by D plus 18.

- Approaches to Sylhet were to be secured and, if possible, Sylhet captured. No timeline was given.

- Agartala was to be secured by the capture of Akhaura.

- Chittagong was to be isolated and thereafter captured after the other tasks had been completed.

Knowing the importance of Dacca, Sagat particularly asked Aurora as to the tasking for capture of Dacca. He was informed that this would only be decided once the progress of the overall offensive was known. 33 Corps was expected to reach the confluence of the Brahmaputra and the Ganga, while 2 Corps was to reach Goalunda Ghat. At that stage 'regrouping would be done and fresh appreciation and plans would be made.' He was told that he should be ready 'to lose 23 Mountain Division.'[8] There were a

---

with dedication right through the monsoons. Of course once the Pooja month set in, they downed tools.

6 'It would seem strange.....that we were going to use mules in the plains......the mules were of tremendous help to us in carrying ammunition.....and supplies...(by) going cross country in unexpected directions.' **Sagat in conversation with Col Pyare Lal.**

7 Maj Gen KK Singh was most thorough and despite Sam's and Eastern Command's impatience, the Operation Instructions were only issued by mid August. Thereafter Command issued its own Instructions more or less immediately.

8 **Sagat in conversation with Col Pyare Lal.** Ibid. The Division was likely to be allotted to

couple of other implications of the Operation Instructions. Since Sagat was not expected to go beyond the Meghna, there was no allocation made for inland water transport. Secondly, the Mizo Hills were made a part of his area of responsibility, possibly because they had a border with East Pakistan. He was also expected to complete his tasks by D plus 18 ie secure the Meghna River line and isolate Sylhet. The Operation Instructions were pretty detailed in their tasking and highly cautious, which Sagat found to be irksome. He was nothing else if not a good soldier and an impression seems to have been created in those early months that he would strictly adhere to orders in an unimaginative manner. He had however started keeping his cards close to his chest and was bent on exploiting any fleeting opportunity that may occur.

Sep was a critical month. The rains showed no sign of abating and the constant battle to build and maintain the infrastructure to sustain the offensive was physically and morally sapping. The uncomplaining and stoic attitude of the refugees, without any home or permanent means of livelihood, never ceased to amaze and inspire their supervisors. The Corps Headquarters moved to Teliamura by the second week of Sep with four transport platoons[9]. They found the undulating hill sides dotted with quaint looking bashas linked with brick lined tracks. Sagat himself was in Tripura by Sep first week and was staying at the Raj Bhavan where Jagdev found him to be 'fairly nonchalant'[10] when he met him to discuss his difficulties.

On 09 Aug, India had signed a 'Treaty of Friendship' with the USSR, which gave it some confidence in its dealings with neighbouring states and the USA. On the other hand, Yahya had offered a general amnesty to the rebels on 04 Sep, which did not

---

2 Corps for operations for the capture of Dacca.

9 Ultimately 18 transport platoons were inducted with 300 additional civilian vehicles. A large number of this 'third' line transport was utilised for 'first' line duties ie in direct support of infantry units as the formations, being organised for mountain warfare, were not equipped to operate in the plains.

10 P 12. Jagdev. Op cit.

have the desired impact. The Pak Army had established its sway over the Region with an iron hand 'and had taken to leisure and merry making'.[11] Unfortunately, this was not so for the rank and file. In their effort to secure the Border against the Mukti Bahini, the Army had made the troops move constantly, tiring them out and denying them much cohesion.[12] Fed up of their constant pin pricks, it also decided to become more aggressive. Shelling of refugee and Mukti Bahini camps became a regular feature and attempts to sabotage the railway line increased. In one such incident near Karimganj, a patrol led by Capt (later Brig) Ransher Singh Ranawat, 9 Guards, managed to defuse an explosive device just before an overloaded passenger train went over it.[13]

One of the major problems faced by Sagat and his staff was the inadequacy of artillery. Since all the divisions joining his Corps were mountain formations, with two of them involved in counter insurgency operations, the artillery complement was negligible. In addition, the field guns had limited capability which was telling on their fire support proficiency.[14] At that time the Corps had only one medium regiment and had to be allotted additional resources by the Army. The divisions deployed opposite the Chinese were denuded of artillery to make up the requirement for the offensive so that

---

11 P 77. Jagdev. Op cit.

12 Sagat narrates an incident in which a Pakistan Army havildar, made a POW, was asked who his Commanding Officer (CO) was '……this senior NCO did not know his name………. he narrated how in the previous two months……he had moved from one location to another. Never spending more than two nights in one location.' **Sagat in conversation with Col Pyare Lal.** Op cit.

13 **In conversation with Brig (retd) RS Ranawat, KC, SM, at Udaipur on 16 Feb 2011.** The device consisted of 10 Kgs of Amatol Explosive with a rhythm activated device also attached to a radio transmitter and clock. Ranawat took a blade from his anti-snake bite kit and cut the wires. He had no training in bomb disposal and did not have the time to wait for an engineer expert. Subsequently he defused another device.

14 The field complement consisted of 3.7 inch howitzers (subsequently upgraded), 76 mm Yugoslav guns with a limited range of only 6000 yards and the freshly inducted 75/24 field guns.

by Nov there was only one medium gun facing the Chinese.[15] The Commander of the Corps Artillery, Brig 'Ted' Dartnell, had served under Sagat in 17 Mountain Division, and was particularly keen on counter bombardment resources, which only medium regiments could provide. Luckily the bare minimum resources were made available just prior to operations being launched.

The requirement of air support presented its own unique set of problems. The airfields available were at Gauhati and Kumbhigram (near Silchar). A Mig 21 Squadron was based at Gauhati, but because of the distances involved, the air cover was not available south of the line Comilla – Dacca. It was then decided to extend the length of the Kumbhigram Airfield runway, using army engineers and the BRO, on an emergency basis. The dozers lengthened the landing strip and the engineers laid pre-fabricated bituminised rolls as no other option was available. Even then the runway remained short and only Hunter aircraft could be deployed.[16] Sagat was unhappy at this state and on his insistence a Mig 21 squadron was made available to the Corps from Dum Dum Airfield near Calcutta. However, the distance precluded the use of anything but the front guns. INS Vikrant was moved into the Bay of Bengal to provide air support to the offensive near Chittagong, but the results were indifferent. To improve his air cover, Sagat had requested for Agartala airfield to be activated, which was done, once the threat from Akhaura was eliminated and a Gnat squadron was ultimately located there. During the Corps offensive the Air Force managed complete air superiority by 6 Dec and was able to provide 50 to 60 sorties of offensive air support daily.

To any other commander preparing for a major offensive, the

---

15 Col Satish Dewan (then Capt) has recounted the problem in graphic detail of moving his medium regiment from the high altitude area facing the Chinese in NEFA, on bad roads, in the teeth of the monsoons, to its deployment area in Tripura. **In personal communication to the Author.** See also pps. 23-24 **Operation Bangladesh by Col PK Gautam. Manas Publications, New Delhi, 2007.** The Officer served with 24 Medium Regiment throughout the Campaign.

16 "….because of the shortness of the runway, after three to four landings, the aircraft tires had to be changed." **Sagat in conversation with Col Pyare Lal.** Op cit.

responsibility for conducting a counter insurgency campaign in an area on the periphery of his launch pads would have been, to put it mildly, an irritant. Sagat took this as an opportunity when the Mizo Hills were put under his orbit. He had already fought a successful campaign there and knew the area and the dynamics of the insurgency very well. He did a minute review of the forces deployed and decided he could milk a few commanders and troops to give his offensive that extra edge. Brig Anand Swarup, the Commandant of the Counter Insurgency and Jungle Warfare School, was pulled out with his staff to form 'Y' Force (subsequently christened 'K' or Kilo Force).[17] To find troops for them Sagat took a gamble and pulled out the only two infantry battalions there. 31 Jat and 32 Mahar had been specially created as 'I'/ 'Insurgency' battalions for the Mizo Hills. As a precursor to the Rashtriya Rifles but with fewer teeth, their organisation was not created to fight a conventional war. They were put under command Anand Swarup, who was also allotted two East Bengal Regiment (EBR) battalions, A BSF battalion and a CRPF battalion. A minimal artillery element was allotted to him and he was expected to tie down the enemy north of Chittagong.[18] The Mizo Hills were put under a DIG (Brig) of Assam Rifles (AR) with four AR battalions and two battalions of armed police. He was asked to shift to Aizawl from Silchar and redeploy his troops to isolate the area from the Chittagong Hill Tracts.[19]

The Mizo Hills gave another priceless dividend to Sagat. In his words, 'Since I had very few troops left in the Mizo Hills; for casualty evacuation and to have the capability to switch troops from one

---

17 As per Jacob, the offer to command this ad hoc formation was initially made to Brig Shabeg Singh by Aurora, but he refused the opportunity fearing for his military reputation and preferred to remain in command of the irregulars in Tripura. Anand Swarup got an MVC and subsequently became a Lt Gen. Shabeg died ignominiously during OP BLUESTAR.

18 Imbued with Sagat's drive and vision his subordinates would prove what even such ad hoc forces could achieve.

19 'However, since I knew the problems in the topography I was able to redeploy these forces at important locations and thereby kept the insurgency in check.' **Sagat in conversation with Col Pyare Lal.**

location to another, should a threat develop, I requested that a helicopter squadron be made available to me.'[20] What he got was the 110 Helicopter Unit, consisting of the aging Mi-4 helicopters, which had been deployed for counter insurgency operations. It had barely 10 to 11 serviceable helicopters and could only take 10 men. They were to be phased out of service and were to be replaced by the larger Mi-8. Sagat was hopeful of getting these helicopters but they never arrived and he had to make do with the existing fleet. Being a paratrooper and fully aware of this third dimension, he intended to use them unconventionally when an opportunity arose. On account of their limitations, Sagat was mandated to utilise only one company for heliborne operations. He was required to make detailed plans and submit them well in advance. He gave a suitable non committal reply and submitted no plans.

The Mukti Bahini was a potent force and could have been made more effective. The pressure from Army HQ and Lt Gen Aurora had created a large reservoir of man power armed but only partially trained. In the months prior to the offensive they did succeed in jittering and tiring out the Pak Army. On the other hand, the units of the EBR were being prepared under dedicated leadership to become an effective part of the Corps offensive though they continued to suffer from a shortage of trained rank and file throughout the War.[21] The shortage of officers to command the sub units was critical from the outset and was never fully made up. Nonetheless the Indian Army did start an officer training establishment.[22] Col Osmani, their C–in–C, had always been fairly vocal in his faith in regular units and sceptical of the efficacy of ill trained irregulars and their impact on a post war Bangladesh. He had succeeded in convincing India of raising additional EBR battalions of which three were under

---

20 ibid.

21 Meanwhile, more than 90,000 irregulars were raised (though approximately only 50% were fielded).

22 One reason for this shortage was the institution of the Inter Wing Allowance, in which Bengalis serving in the Western Wing got a handsome allowance and vice versa. Once the crackdown started, a fair number of Bengali officers were in the West and remained there until repatriated.

raising.²³ All the effective battalions of EBR were located in the Corps Sector and served under Sagat. Most of them had dedicated officers commanding them, who rose to high positions in the post 71 Bangladesh Army. One of the most outstanding was, Maj (later Maj Gen) Khalid Musharaf, the Commanding Officer of 4 EBR.²⁴ As 2ic, he had managed to extricate his unit from Brahmanbaria where it was repeatedly attacked by the Pak Army. Thereafter it had occupied the Belonia Bulge and was evicted by the Pak Army after holding out for nearly four weeks.²⁵ It was now located at Sonamura, Central Tripura, where it was reorganised and undergoing training. 2 EBR, commanded by Maj KM Shafiullah (later major general and the first chief of the Bangladesh Army), also managed to extricate itself after a harrowing ordeal which took it from the outskirts of Dacca to Meymensingh and then to Ashuganj.²⁶ They were now in the forests of Teliapara opposite the Sylhet District.²⁷ Shafi was a straightforward soldier and could be relied upon to do his best in the coming ordeal. 8 EBR was commanded by Zia-ur-Rahman (the future President of Bangladesh), the most charismatic and idealistic of the military leaders. Unfortunately, his hatred of the Pak Army²⁸ and some incidents of extreme behaviour of his troops made him somewhat of an enigma. He was prickly about his independence

---

23 Though they participated in the War, according to Sagat, '....their effectiveness was only 40 percent.' Jacob feels that the trained cadres would have been better employed in making the Mukti Bahini more effective. P 93. Jacob. Op cit.

24 He was assassinated in the coup engineered in 1975, which ushered in Army rule in Bangladesh. He had a sharp professional mind and an easy going personality. P 7. Jagdev Singh. Op cit and p 10. Verma. Op cit.

25 'Ultimately a fully fledged brigade operation was launched against the Battalion... .....a company of SSG was dropped by helicopters behind the Battalion....' **Sagat in conversation with Colonel Pyare Lal.** The episode has been confirmed by **Col Nadir Ali**, who led the SSG sub unit. Op cit

26 It is ironic but 2 EBR was evicted from Ashuganj by a daring heliborne operation by the Pakistani Commandos.

27 It was from here that the joint Bangladesh command under Col Osmani was announced on 04 Apr 1971. P 5. Verma. Op cit.

28 This is somewhat surprising because his wife and children lived in a Pak Cantonment throughout the conflict.

and status though few doubted his dedication and professional competence. Zia was made the commander of 1 EB Brigade/ 'Z' Force (consisting of 1 and 3 EBR and a battery of 3.7 inch howitzers) when it was raised, thus acknowledging his place in the Bangladesh military hierarchy. Since the Force had been organised in the Garo Hills, Sagat offered it to Krishna Rao who unhesitatingly accepted it under Zia's leadership.[29] How the traumatic changes brought about by the crackdown and ruthlessness of the Pakistan Army changed people's character and lives are perceptibly, though unwittingly brought out by Qureshi. 'I had known him (Zia-ur-Rahman) since 1967........I had liked him: he was intelligent, mild-mannered and very easy to get along with.....one got the impression that he was not narrow minded or parochial, but a gentleman with a broad outlook on life....One could not think of him as an intriguer, a traitor, a rabble-rouser, or a murderer (under his orders it seemed all the Pakistani elements in his Battalion, including the Commanding Officer, were killed). On the other hand, Maj (later Maj Gen) Khalid Musharaf, an ex SSG colleague of ours, who was always vocal in propagation of Bengali culture and Bengali nationalism and had been trained in the 'dirty tricks' of guerrilla warfare, had behaved differently' (he had disarmed the Pakistanis and handed them over to the BSF).[30]

Meanwhile, the Pak Army methodically and ruthlessly set about shoring up its defences as well as dealing with the insurgency in the country side. The first thing they did was to ensure that all the airfields were securely held to enable them to move forces rapidly and flexibly. For preparations of defences they used the civilian population extensively, as Martial Law had given them strong executive powers. To give one example; in an act of cruel unscrupulousness they used food and material provided by the UN for cyclone assistance for their own ends. Some of the material

---

29 'He gave me little cause for complaint and was always willing to carry out orders, at times leading from the front.' **Krishna Rao in conversation with the Author.** Sagat also had doubts whether Zia would be able to get along smoothly in the other formations.

30 P 92. Qureshi. Op cit. One wonders if the history of post independence Bangladesh would have been different if Khalid had not been killed in the coup of 1975.

was siphoned off for defence works and the refugees from the cyclone were made to work on the defences. From the money paid to them they were made to buy food, which was otherwise to be given free as aid for cyclone relief![31] Most of the defences 'were made in......railway buildings and other double storied structures'. The defences of the Lalmai Hills were made in two tiers and cost Rupees 29 Lakhs. All strong points and communication hubs were extensively dug in and the defences of some border outposts had communication trenches, ditches and weapon emplacements. As the IA realised to its consternation, they were a tough nut to crack.

The civil communications in the Eastern Wing had been well developed with the help of a Japanese firm and were based on microwave. All boats had been commandeered. The newer and faster ones were equipped with machine guns and searchlights. Some of them were also equipped with the Bofors L60 anti-aircraft guns and were used for firing in the ground role. Identity cards were issued in the villages to keep control of the population.[32] In addition, Village and Sector Defence Committees had been organised out of politicians co-opted from the Jamiat and the Muslim Leagues. They kept a close eye on the population and patrolled the surrounding area to keep a watch out for intruders and would often be able to detect them. Keeping overall control were detachments of the Pak Army assisted by the EPCAF and Razakars, who were frequently shifted from one critical area to another as they were not adequate to maintain a strong security grid. As the border started getting restive the pressure on these sub units continued to mount. By Oct-Nov Indian build up and activity clearly indicated that India would likely go whole hog in finding an end solution in East Pakistan. Niazi's vaunted strategy should have been in place centring on a defence of strong points and girdling Dacca with a strong defensive ring. This is what the Indians expected and had planned for. Instead,

---

31 More than one writer has claimed that the indifference and near callousness shown by the Authorities in the aftermath of the devastating cyclone of 1970 was one of the factors which led to universal resentment and sparked the Revolution.

32 These were successfully copied by a civil printing press in Calcutta and used by the Mukti Bahini when they infiltrated inside.

some kind of a strategic hubris seems to have gripped Niazi and he frittered away his forces in bitter battles along the borders.[33]

Another aspect Sagat was concerned about was training. He was not too bothered about the physical fitness of his men and their ability to operate in small teams. They had already been operating against some of the toughest insurgents in one of the worst terrains in the world. He had to gear them up to conform to conventional battle drills and procedures and to operate as a homogenous combined arm.[34] Two of his divisions had no artillery which, when it came, had to be dovetailed into the organisation. Tanks and engineers were other arms which were required to coordinate their tactics and functioning down to sub unit level. On the other hand, the formation and unit commanders had different priorities as they tried to prepare themselves for war. Jagdev remembers how he had to approach Sagat to force the Division Commanders to release his units from logistic tasks in order to carry out training for war.[35] Intent on creating a 'strong sense of belonging' in his command, Sagat toured extensively, talked to the men and emphasised on their superiority.[36] Sagat also held several war games, talked to the commanders and 'by searching their minds as to how they would do…….their tasks, I was able to forge the Corps into a team where we all had each other's trust and were in each other's mind as to what is required of us and what we expected to achieve.'[37] During this critical period Sagat remained constantly on the move, supervising

---

33 Pp 128-129. Qureshi. Op cit. He sums it up clearly and acridly.

34 'All these battalions had not fired their heavy weapons…..one of the main concerns was that they fired their weapons….they got together as battalions; the brigade commanders got to know their battalions and the division commanders saw their entire division together'. **Sagat in conversation with Col Pyare Lal.**

35 '…when the formation commanders told him about the Chief Engineer exerting pressure for more time for training, I think he told them firmly to get on with it.' P 14. Jagdev. Op cit.

36 '… my seeing them under training and my emphasizing all the time that they were fitter than the Pakistanis and their field craft was far superior.' **Sagat in conversation with Col Pyare Lal.**

37 Ibid.

critical aspects of training. Satish Dewan recollects how he visited his regiment and inquired minutely on its activities. He never made notes and never forgot. All on the spot decisions were invariably acted upon. In his case the shortage of ammunition for training was shortly made up when the Regiment received four bogies of medium gun ammunition for practice firing.[38] Sagat also succeeded in achieving something more valuable. In the short time available to him during the border skirmishes he tried to assess the mettle and fighting ability of his commanders, officers and units. Being a good judge of character he was rarely disappointed. His subordinates also came to realise his relentless zeal and near ruthlessness to get the job done. Some discerned his vision, gained his confidence and were able to produce results, which perhaps surprised even them. As the War was to show, Sagat had this priceless quality of realising the potential and capabilities of his men to produce results beyond their own expectations.

Minor skirmishes near the border were going on for some time but it got seriously active in Oct as both sides tried to jockey for moral superiority. While the Pakistanis retaliated against the pinpricks of the Mukti Bahini by either shelling or firing across the Border, the Indian Army tried to ensure that its launch pads remained secure and the population centres were not affected seriously.[39] The escalating two way cycle, at times spiralled out of control with severe casualties on both sides. While there were minor company and battalion level actions, there were three brigade level operations which resulted in the elimination of any residual Pak military threats to Indian Territory. For reasons of pride and the fear of losing control of any part of East Pakistan, Niazi's

---

38 **Personal communication to the Author.**

39 There were at least nine to ten border actions of a major nature which took place in the Corps Sector commencing from Jun onwards. Some of these actions resulted in heavy casualties to both sides. The Pak Army was bent on making it clear that it would be no pushover. On the Indian side this led to apprehensions about whether our troops would be able to sustain a bitter campaign. Perhaps this was partly responsible for the cautious approach to the War taken by Army HQ. On the other hand the EBR units gained confidence and performed reasonably well in these operations.

stand fast decree led to some battles which were the bitterest in the entire Campaign. The Pak Army lost soldiers it could ill afford,[40] while the Indians got a foretaste of things to come whenever they tried to batter their forces away in direct attacks.

On 27 Oct, the Army Commander visited Teliamura to attend a Corps war game. At that stage the 4 Corps HQ staff seems to have realised that Eastern Command, perhaps on orders from Sam, was likely to shift the goalpost and make Dacca an objective. Sagat reiterated to Krishna Rao that as planned he should be prepared to give a brigade to him once the crust of the enemy defences had broken and the advance had progressed well into the hinterland. Though not too happy, Krishna Rao did not argue.

The first brigade action started off innocuously enough in the area of Kamalpur opposite the Sylhet District of East Pakistan. As the monsoons started tapering off by end Sep, the Mukti Bahini activity, which included raids by the EBR, increased exponentially. By Oct, the entire border region in 4 Corps Sector had come alive with fire. Special attention was being paid to economic dislocation without causing hardship to the civil population. The area opposite Kamalpur had no strategic or tactical significance and was left in the hands of the EBR and Mukti Bahini to manage. They were raiding the tea gardens to either target the power plants, the machinery or the tea godowns.[41] Kamalpur was a medium size town with an airfield and was overlooked by the sand hills of the Dhalai Tea Estate in East Pakistan. On the Indian side the area was hilly except around the Town through which the Dhalai River flowed into the Sylhet District. The area around the River's vicinity was marshy and an impediment

---

40 Col Ahmed Mukhtar Khan, who commanded, 30 Frontier Force Regiment during the Battle of Dhalai, asserts that Pakistani Army units were losing eight to ten men every day in these border engagements. The casualties were kept hidden by the Command HQ to avoid adverse criticism at home. See web page of Pakistan Military Journal **Frontier Defence** at www.defence.pk/forums/military-history/9201-battle-dhalai-bangladesh-campaign-1971-a.html.

41 The intention of the Mukti Bahini was to destroy the tea which 'could not be sold for foreign exchange that would be used to suppress the liberation movement.' **Sagat in conversation with Col Pyare Lal.**

With Maj Gen Krishna Rao & Gp Capt Chandan Singh at Shamshernagar

With Maj Gen BF Gonsalves and Brig Tom Pande at Dhalai

to tactical movement. The Pakistanis had fortified the area of the BOP and buildings of the Tea Garden, which were all approximately a kilometre east of the River on slightly higher ground to avoid the marshes. The depredation being caused to the tea industry worried Dacca and they moved troops close to the Border without appreciably denting the Mukti Bahini capability. Finally, fed up of these continuous pin pricks, the Pak Army heavily shelled the town of Kamalpur on 14 and 20 Oct, causing casualties and leading to an exodus of the civil population into the interior. Since the area was under the responsibility of 1 EBR, they were tasked by 57 Mountain Division to capture the BOP, whose strength was estimated to be approximately two platoons of EPCAF/ razakars with some regular troops.[42]

Unfortunately, the EBR was not fully aware of the strength of the defences, which consisted of concrete emplacements, ditches laced with mines and *punjis*, communication trenches and machine guns, some mounted on *machans* for better observation (after the Battle nearly 54 bunkers were discovered). They succeeded in capturing the area of the Patrakhola Tea Estate, by an outflanking movement from the west, but came in for a surprise when they tried to occupy the built up area of the Dhalai Tea Estate. Despite an impressive assault on the Dhalai BOP on 26 Oct, they were severely rebuffed and were forced to withdraw as they lacked intimate artillery support. Sagat told Maj Gen BF 'Ben' Gonsalves, GOC of 57 Mountain Division, that he did not want an EBR defeat, especially when they were meeting success elsewhere.[43] In any case the

---

42 Despite active Mukti Bahini operations inside East Pakistan, the Indian Army possessed very little intelligence of enemy dispositions as the irregulars seemed unwilling to close onto Pakistani piquets. Throughout the Dhalai Operation the IA seemed to be on the back foot. Brig Jagdev even goes on to say that the Pakistanis seemed to be better informed than our commanders. 'They were always, or almost always, well posted about the Indian strengths and movements.' P 102. Jagdev. Op cit. '…..the members of the Mukti Bahini ……………… would not go anywhere near the Pakistani troops to obtain identifications.' **Sagat in conversation with Col Pyare Lal.**

43 The EBR had successfully carried out operations to capture the minor communication hubs of Kasba and Saldanadi between Akhaura and Comilla. They had withstood counter attacks by regular troops and had held on doggedly. 4 EBR had particularly

Army was not to surrender any moral superiority. And so the fateful decision was taken to use regular troops to capture the BOP and the built up area, leading to a near uncontrollable spiral of violence.

With Brig RN Mishra after Battle of Akhaura

61 Mountain Brigade, commanded by Brig (later Maj Gen) Shiv Dayal Singh Yadava, was deployed in the relative vicinity though the brigade HQ was located beyond Agartala. Yadava moved with his 'Rover Group' to Dhalai on 28 Oct, the same time that 2 Jat, deployed in small groups and spread over 30 kms[44], was hastily assembled and sent to Kamalpur, which they reached on the evening of the same day. The Commander of 2 Artillery Brigade (now affiliated with 57 Mountain Division), Brig 'Tom' Pande,[45] also moved to Kamalpur around the same time to coordinate the artillery support. 'Ben'

---

distinguished itself.

44 One company was in support of 1 EBR and located in reserve.

45 Brig KP (Tom) Pande commanded 2 Artillery Brigade, which had a counter insurgency role in the Tirap Frontier Division of NEFA and was in support of 2 Mountain Division. He with his HQ, and whatever artillery units could be made available, was moved in Aug 71 to support of 8 Mountain Division, which was without any artillery complement.

Gonsalves moved from Agartala by late evening on 28 Oct, after meeting with the Army Commander, who was supposed to address his troops on 29 Oct. There was some anxiety that the enemy would get enough reaction time and reinforce the defences if the attack was delayed much longer. Lt Col KS Dalal, CO 2 Jat, was thus ordered to put in an attack earliest. With minimal reconnaissance and hardly any time for orders, Dalal reluctantly decided to launch his attack during daylight hours on 29 Oct. His hastily cobbled plan hoped to utilise the limited cover provided by the tea bushes to assault the BOP from the west. Simultaneously, a feint from the marshy ground to the east was expected to deceive the enemy long enough to enable the attackers to close onto the defences. Unknown to the Indians, the enemy on the night of 28 Oct had reinforced the whole area with another two platoons of regular troops with the result that in addition to the BOP, the Factory, Twin Huts and Coolie Lines each had a platoon deployed with interlinking fields of fire.[46] The GOC of Pak 14 Division, Kazi Abdul Majid (under pressure from Niazi and not a favourite of his), had decided to himself monitor the battlefield.[47]

The initial manoeuvring by the Jats proved successful and by first light 29 Oct, the attacking two companies were poised north west of the BOP while the feint on Coolie Lines succeeded in distracting the enemy. The two companies moved forward but their heart was not in it as they got badly entangled in trying to hack their way through the overgrown tea bushes and came under very effective small arms fire. Dalal realised that the opposition he was facing was likely to be more than the couple of weak platoons envisaged. A half hearted attempt by the reserve company to manoeuvre from further west went nowhere and at approximately 10 AM and 300 metres short of the objective, the attack was called

---

46 Ahmed Mukhtar Khan has claimed that his Battalion was deployed in an area extending over 60 kms and he could only spare one company and subsequently two platoons for the defence of Dhalai, which was mainly held by the Razakars. Op cit.

47 Once he started to take an active part in the Battle (Mukhtar claims he personally lead one of the counter attacks) he cobbled together another two company worth of troops from other units of his Division.

off. The Battalion had suffered only one casualty. When Sagat heard of this he was furious. He was seeing off the Army Commander at Agartala and decided to proceed to Kamalpur immediately. By now he and Aurora were not in the best of terms and it's likely that the debacle at Dhalai coloured his subsequent implacable attitude. Taking the BM of 61 Brigade, Maj (later Lt Gen) OP Kaushik along with him, he landed at Kamalpur[48], where he was met by Ben and Shiv. The luckless Dalal, who had just returned from his aborted attack, was also present. His justifications for failure were angrily overborne and Sagat ordered him to redeem the honour of his unit. It seems Dalal, seeing the strength of the enemy defences and his lack of knowledge of the terrain, remained unwilling to venture his unit. Sagat remained implacable. The contretemps were embarrassing for the Division and the Brigade Commanders as they could not adequately defend the lack of heart displayed by Dalal. For Shiv, the Brigade Commander, the situation was doubly difficult. He had earlier had a run in with the Army Commander during the War Game on 27 Oct and now he found himself trying to justify the action of his unit to the Corps Commander, who was a regimental officer and with whom his association went back to his youngster days. A man of honour, with a father who had served with distinction in World War 2 and a son, who was shortly being commissioned from the Indian Military Academy[49] into his unit, Shiv found himself in a near impossible situation. He had nurtured his brigade[50] and prepared it for war in the best way he could. He

---

48 This was the first time he was flown by Maj (later Lt Gen and Army Commander) GS Sihota of the Air OP Flight affiliated to the Corps Artillery Brigade. 'Our first impression was that he's a tough commander; don't take chances with him……..We came back to the Flight and told them that the Corps Commander is very tough and strict and you better do exactly what he asks you to do.' **In conversation with Lt Gen GS Sihota,PVSM, AVSM, VrC, VM at Chandigarh on 19 Sep 2009.** It was the beginning of a close association which continued till the end of the War with Sihota getting repeatedly involved in decisive actions initiated by Sagat.

49 He retired in 2010 as Lt Gen KS Yadava, PVSM, AVSM, SM, VSM

50 A fact acknowledged in a sentimental letter, in possession of the Author, written by his Brigade Major (later Lt Gen OP Kaushik). In conversation with the Author, Kaushik reiterated that Shiv was a man who had 'great self respect.'

now found his efforts going waste as Sagat berated Dalal. Losing confidence in Dalal in even adequately attempting to carry out his mission, Shiv decided that evening to go along with the attacking troops rather than conduct the Battle from the rear.[51] Meanwhile, Sagat allowed Dalal a night of reconnaissance on 29 Oct. The GSO 3 Operations of 4 Corps, Capt (later Colonel) Subhash Kaushik was in the Corps Operation Room responsible for updating the maps, and he heard Sagat telling his staff that evening, 'It seems that before fighting a war I have already lost it. I cannot accept this because this Unit they think someone else will move because they have come back. That means all units will not go. I have ordered them to go into the attack again.'[52] The debacle at Dhalai had cast doubts amongst all concerned as to whether the Indian troops would be able to achieve, what then seemed, the ambitious objectives set out for them during the forthcoming campaign. Things would only get worse in the next couple of days, forcing Sagat to do some heart searching.

On night 29/30 Oct, the Dhalai position got further reinforced with troops cobbled together by Majid and included some SSG elements. There were now nearly three companies deployed. The sub units were bleeding away due to heavy Indian artillery fire but continued to remain defiant. There were five reconnaissance patrols sent by 2 Jat on 29 Oct night but they could not obtain any worthwhile information though they had a vague idea that additional reinforcements had moved in.[53] This time Dalal decided to avoid the Tea Garden and attack from the East. He intended to capture Coolie Lines and Twin Huts with a company each. One

---

51 OP Kaushik, who was close to both Shiv and Sagat mentions that Sagat, who had a good idea of what this debacle would do to the self confidence of 2 Jat forcefully told Shiv, 'Brig, your prestige is at stake! Make sure that this Battalion captures it (Dhalai); and I want only this Battalion to capture, no other unit!' OP Kaushik in conversation. Op cit.

52 **In conversation with Col Subhash Kaushik, VSM, at Secunderabad on 21 Mar 2010.**

53 The estimate made by the Brigade that there was now a battalion worth of troops seems more out of hindsight. At that stage there was no inkling as to enemy force levels as the reconnaissance had not obtained any worthwhile information on enemy dispositions. Throughout the Battle, Majid continued to send troops in.

company was detailed to establish a block and isolate Dhalai, while the fourth company, reserve for the first phase, would capture the Factory and from there attack the BOP. The battalion had no reserves left and Shiv allotted him a company from 7 Rajrif, which was moved at short notice from some distance. The Battle had now become complicated but Shiv continued to control it from an adhoc skeleton HQ, which was manned by the 2ic of 12 Kumaon, who was officiating as the BM.[54]

The attacking echelons moved after midnight to their forming up place. By then it 'was raining cats and dogs. Worse were the leeches. I never understood how they managed to get through our clothing, pants, and on to our legs biting the flesh and bloating themselves on our blood.'[55] The companies managed to reach their forming up places by 3 AM on 31 Oct despite heavy going through the marshy area and paddy fields. The CO realising that troops were likely to lose their way in the pitch dark asked the artillery to fire on the objective to give them a sense of direction. This was done and around 4 AM the attack commenced with resolve. By 5 AM one company had captured Coolie Lines and the area of Red Huts. Unfortunately, the other company, which was to capture Twin Huts, lost its way and strayed towards the Coolie Lines. There it got defiladed by effective enemy machine gun fire. Thus despite a brave attempt, which got it a foothold on Twin Huts, the Company was thrown back by a determined enemy counter attack and suffered heavy casualties.

Shiv Yadava was moving with the reserve company, which was now ordered to move to Coolie Lines and capture Twin Huts. The Company was commanded by Maj Pritam Singh. When it reached Coolie Lines, the position was under effective counter attack by the 2ic of 30 FF, who succeeded in recapturing a part of it.[56] Now

---

54 Kaushik returned to Agartala to prepare the Brigade HQ for move though up till now it was still not anticipated that the Battle would get prolonged.

55 **Personal communication to the Author by Col (then Capt) RN Balagopal.** He was the Anchor OP with the company of 7 RAJRIF.

56 Major Raja Javed Akhtar. One of the most outstanding officers of Pakistan Army. **See**

in the words of Shiv, "I, therefore, asked the reserve company commander, Maj Pritam Singh (a very brave soldier) to come on his right flank and clear the opposition. He came across a Pak bunker continuously firing. I asked him to destroy the bunker, which he did with the help of a rocket launcher and we saw the bunker blow up. Just then a Pak soldier emerged from the debris and began to run. Maj Pritam Singh raised his sten gun to fire at him but......... the sten gun made a 'click' noise indicating that the magazine had no ammunition. The Pak soldier had a good chance to escape but, realising that the Indian Officer had no ammunition and no time to change the magazine, turned back to fire at Maj Pritam Singh. But something very strange happened, which happens perhaps one in a million times in war....in his enthusiasm the Pak soldier had fired off his ammunition.....so his sten gun also made the 'click' noise. He again had the chance to run and escape but decided otherwise. With a bayonet fixed on his sten gun, he charged at Maj Pritam Singh. Pritam is a tall and strong man. Hitting the oncoming bayonet on the side, he caught the Pak soldier and a scuffle began. At that moment one of Pritam's men came and bayoneted the Pak soldier. When he fell he said to Pritam in Punjabi, 'this is no act of bravery; the fight was between us two but you have got me killed by this other man.' The Pak soldier who turned out to be an NCO (non commissioned officer, a Naik) died soon afterwards."[57]

Shortly thereafter Pritam got hit on his ankle by machine gun bullets. Seeing him fall some of his men started to cluster around him. Dawn was breaking and fearing that such a group would be a prime target to a watchful enemy, Shiv moved to disperse them. It was then that the same machine gun, 'seeing another officer,' fired a burst and hit Shiv on his right leg below the knee. The officers were bandaged as best as could be, given morphine shots and moved to a nearby thatched hut where other wounded men had been placed. Gonsalves was dismayed to hear that Shiv had been wounded. He immediately appointed 'Tom' Pande to take control

---

Ahmed Mukhtar Khan. Op cit. See also p. 164 Salik. Op cit.

57 Quoted from a hand written paper of Brig SDS Yadava. **In possession of the Author.**

of the battle and get Shiv evacuated. 'It was about 0700 hours on 31 Oct when 'Tom' Pande reached our location and conveyed....... that the Company (of 7 Rajrif) should advance to Red Hut and extricate the Commander......the company advanced towards Red Hut against heavy enemy fire. It was really heavy going, what with thick paddy fields and slushy mud with heavy downpour. During the attack a bullet stopped me in my tracks. It was about 0900 hours.'[58] Maj Avtar Singh, the second-in-command of 7 Rajrif (Rajputana Rifles), who had been specifically told to ensure Shiv was evacuated, realised that the Company had been bogged down and collected a platoon and moved forward, desperate to reach Coolie Lines. Throughout this period, all movement was being effectively interdicted by Pak artillery/mortar and small arms fire. The troops were in the middle of the paddy fields, without any cover, when Avtar too was injured. His troops dispersed and with the rest of the Company struggled back to the base at Ganganagar.[59] Meanwhile 'Tom', though under shelling, had collected whatever troops were available and had dispatched them under the Quartermaster of 2 Jat to reinforce those on the objective. They, however, encountered the withdrawing company of 7 Rajrif and also fell back.

The battle continued until midday and the position was counter attacked four times throughout the afternoon by the Pak Army, which succeeded in getting a foothold again. By 4 PM the situation had become critical and Shiv now called upon a *Subedar,* who with his platoon had been made available to him, to attack this lodgement and avert a situation which might turn very dangerous. He also asked two young artillery officers, who were directing fire to 'bring down medium gun fire on this Pak position, which was less than 100 yards from where we were......and to forget the safety

---

58 **Balagopal.** Ibid. He had to crawl back to their base, bleeding heavily, before he could be evacuated.

59 Avtar lay injured on the battlefield for four days before he was found and evacuated. By then maggots had started eating into his wounds and he had survived by sipping the little rainwater that fell on him. His unit was overjoyed to find him. Sagat, who was in Kamalpur, personally ensured that he was taken in his helicopter and evacuated to Teliamura. **Maj Avtar Singh in a personal communication to the Author.**

regulations....' The artillery fire proved most effective and caused severe casualties to Pak troops including killing Maj Javed who was in the midst of launching another counter attack.[60] The *Subedar*[61] successfully reduced the lodgement and Coolie Lines were secured. Shiv and Dalal realised that the strength of the opposition was much more than anticipated and informed the GOC. 2 Jat had suffered heavy casualties. There were nearly 70 killed and injured and they did not have the strength to progress the attack any further.

Sagat was in Teliamura when he heard of the series of debacles. He was disquieted to hear loose talk amongst his headquarter staff that perhaps the Indian Army did not have the gumption to fight such battles of attrition. He also received a call from Ben Gonsalves, who recommended that the battle be called off, as further attacks would serve no tactical purpose. Sagat spoke to the Army Commander to obtain his clearance to appoint Tom Pande as the Brigade Commander as he was impressed with his positive and bull dog attitude. While giving his go ahead the Army Commander, to Sagat's dismay, also seemed of the opinion that Dhalai no longer deserved any further attention. Accepting a debacle was just not in Sagat's nature. His ruthless and dogged streak, so evident when he was commanding troops in Sikkim and Mizoram, made him determined not to give up the Battle of Dhalai on a losing note, especially as he had still not been fed authentic information on the strength of the enemy there. He was particularly annoyed with the report that one company of Jats had lost direction as they had not taken the simple measure of moving on a compass bearing to their objective. A helicopter was immediately summoned and Sagat

---

60 Ahmed Mukhtar Khan and Salik. P 164. Ibid.

61 "Commander Sahib I will either throw the Pakistanis from their positions or if I am not able to do so, I will not come back to show my face to you." Shiv Yadava. Ibid. There was a *canard* afloat that some artillery officers abandoned their positions during the Battle of Dhalai. This is not true. Shiv was full of praise for the bravery of the forward observation officers whose effective artillery fire at very close ranges was a battle winning factor. The Artillery suffered several casualties. There is also a skewed account of the Battle with incorrect timelines written by Lt Col Quazi Sajjad Ali Zahir of the Bangladesh Army (The Return of a Hero) which discredits Shiv and glorifies Pande.

flew down to Kamalpur in bad weather. Flt Lt Jayaraman, one of the better pilots, kept his finger crossed and heaved a sigh of relief when he landed at the Airfield.

The airfield was a scene of chaotic activity with materials of war lying around and large number of injured troops awaiting evacuation while more were trickling in. The unfortunate and injured company commander of 2 Jat was accosted by Sagat, when he landed there, and was harshly berated by him. Meanwhile, Tom Pande had done his own analysis and was of the view that since Coolie Lines was firmly held, there was no reason why the Dhalai operation could not be continued. He convinced Ben of his views and these were conveyed to Sagat, when he met them. Both of them were caked in mud and seem to have done some heavy legwork. It was obvious that Coolie Lines could not be approached during daylight. Sagat agreed with Tom and Ben that the position had to be held and reinforced. 7 Rajrif, which was nearly 100 kms away, had been collected from its dispersed location and was ordered to move to Dhalai. Before Sagat left, he spoke to Shiv on the radio set. His voice was weak and he seemed in much pain but he confirmed that though Coolie Lines seemed to be surrounded it could be held if reinforced early. His own gut feeling confirmed Sagat gave orders for Dhalai to be captured. He was adamant that the Battle must not be a defeat for Indian arms. Before he left he obtained re-assurance from Tom that Shiv would be evacuated well before nightfall and ordered that a helicopter be kept on standby to fly him to the Teliamura Field Hospital. However, Shiv could only be evacuated once it became dark and some reinforcements had moved in. An enemy counter attack at 4 AM on 01 Nov was rebuffed but it made Tom anxious to expand this lodgement and improve their fragile hold on Dhalai.

Now it was the turn of 7 Rajrif. Lt Col S Devesan, CO of 7 Rajrif, was informed at midday on 31 Oct that his Battalion would be required to reach Kamalpur earliest as the situation there was critical. After passing orders for the Battalion to move he left immediately and reached Kamalpur the same evening. The GOC and the new Commander briefed him on the situation. With the little time available, he managed to do a limited reconnaissance before nightfall and discussed his plans with Tom. He gave his preference for an attack through the tea garden but was dissuaded by Tom who told him of the predicament faced by 2 Jat in their first attack. The choice was to go through open country, which Devesan was reluctant to do despite the support of all available artillery.[62] Tom's thrusting nature seems to have jarred with Devesan and somewhat marred their short relationship. Both Ben and Tom were also insistent that in view of 2 Jat's precarious situation, the attack must be carried out earliest and not at night, as Devesan proposed. The plan now required two companies to attack the BOP from the southwest while one company would demonstrate opposite Twin Huts to distract the enemy. All the available recoilless guns were to be deployed at the fire base held by the EBR to destroy the bunkers of the BOP just prior to the attack. The pouring rain only aggravated the situation. Transport was late in arriving and by the time 7 Rajrif reached Kamalpur it was past 2 PM on 01 Nov.

It did not help matters that Tom refused to relent in delaying the attack and kept breathing down Devesan's neck. Devesan knew that Sagat was in Kamalpur and, perhaps out of a sense of desperation asked to speak to the 'Big Big Tiger'. In the manner typical of him, Tom replied, 'I'm big and I'm strong, you speak to me'. Under the amused eye of the Corps Commander, he then left to meet Devesan and give a pep talk to the company commanders. In hindsight, all this desperate rushing around seems baffling, though at that time the situation continued to seem critical. Though the Jats had partially redeemed themselves by their conduct during the second attack and thereafter, the reports from Dhalai showed that the enemy was bent on retaking it and was launching counter

---

62 The artillery support available at Dhalai consisted of two batteries of 23 Mountain Regiment, a medium battery and a light battery. All the mortar platoons were put under central control. Tom had come to Kamalpur to coordinate this fire but it was now being done by the CO of 23 Mountain Regiment, Lt Col Jagjit Singh (he was earlier the Adjutant of the National Defence Academy). The artillery fire at Dhalai was the heaviest concentration of fire carried out throughout the entire Campaign by 4 Corps.

attacks one after another. The lodgement at Coolie Lines was nearly surrounded and hanging on by, what seemed to the defenders, the skin of its teeth. Sagat remained adamant that Dhalai would not be a defeat for Indian arms and Tom, having committed himself, had put his newfound status at stake. Ultimately, despite the best effort by 7 Rajrif, the attack was delayed by half an hour, much to Tom's annoyance, and went in at 5.30 PM.

Things turned out better than expected. The artillery fire was effective, the demonstration distracted the enemy, a fair number of bunkers were hit and the pouring rain and the dark provided enough cover for the two companies to approach close to the objective and charge. There was some bayonet work once the troops managed to enter the trenches and the enemy fled. In a remarkable achievement, the BOP had been captured by 6 PM without a casualty. Now nearly two companies were concentrated in an area which used to house a platoon and should have rapidly exploited outwards. The Pakistani reaction was faster and they launched their first counter attack within half an hour. Since the assaulting troops were short of ammunition, which did not fetch up for some time, the CO ordered that all officers should man the machine guns. He himself got behind one. The third company also fetched up onto the objective around 2 AM on 02 Nov and was tasked by Devesan to exploit northwards. Meanwhile, the enemy had not given up yet and while launching some faint hearted counter attacks shelled the BOP with heavy artillery fire, which included a large number of air bursts.[63] The Battalion endured enemy attempts to recapture the BOP successfully throughout the night but suffered a trickle of casualties. At 7 AM, Devesan was discussing the defensive fire plan with his battery commander, Maj VP Khattri, when a shell landed right amongst their midst. Khattri, a brave and resourceful man, was killed outright along with his party and Devesan was wounded. He was evacuated with difficulty

---

63 The Pakistan Artillery had proportionately a large number of air burst ammunition in its inventory and did not hesitate to use it liberally. At Dhalai it was estimated that at times nearly 40 percent of the ammunition fired was air burst.

and the Unit was headless for a short time. At that stage a little panic set in and part of the objective was vacated. Tom, who was on the Battalion net realised that the situation was taking a turn for the worse and managed to speak to Maj Poonia, a company commander, to take things in hand. Poonia and the officers rallied the men, who after some hand to hand fighting reoccupied the vacated portion of the BOP and aggressively exploited forward. By 4.30 PM Poonia and the Battalion entered the Factory and found it full of ammunition and corpses. Throughout the night the enemy kept on probing the defences and made half hearted attempts to re-capture lost ground but by now Gen Majid had very little fresh troops available and whatever he could gather were sub units from various battalions, who had already suffered grievously in repeated counter attacks and lacked cohesion. Nevertheless, the enemy still held Twin Huts and continued to fiercely dispute the capture of the Factory area and its adjacent high ground.

While 7 Rajrif was engaged in its own battle, Tom thought it was an ideal opportunity to mount an attack on Twin Huts and capture it as the enemy would have got distracted and would be hard put to find any reinforcements. At around 11 AM, 2 Jat were ordered to attack. Unfortunately the aggressiveness of the enemy, who had just mounted another counter attack on Coolie Lines, reinforced Dalal's defensive mindset. A captured prisoner revealed that another Pak sub unit had moved into the Twin Hut area. Thus when the troops had been formed up on the northwest for launching the attack, Dalal informed Tom that the position was strongly held and he apprehended severe casualties. It was midday and Sagat was present when this conversation was going on. He was amazed at the resilience of the defender and not wanting 2 Jat to face another debacle, allowed Tom to call off the attack.

The objective was now assigned to 14 Guards, part of 73 Mountain Brigade, which had been already concentrated at Dhalai for just such a contingency. The same weary story was repeating itself. The Battalion had been hastily collected and moved to Kamalpur. While the Unit was organising itself the CO, Lt Col Vijay

Channa, collected his officers, who after being briefed by Tom, managed to carry out some reconnaissance from the Coolie Lines. The foibles of war were not to allow the Battle a neat conclusion. While the reconnaissance party of 14 Guards was moving to Coolie Lines a patrol of 2 Jat discovered that Twin Huts had been vacated by the enemy and occupied it. For reasons not clear the position was abandoned before the Guards could occupy it and the enemy promptly re-occupied it. The Guards however, remained under the impression that the position had been vacated by the enemy. Vijay Channa was unwilling to stroll into an enemy defence and regardless of reports of its vacation he decided to put in a tactical attack at 9 PM, with artillery support. Sure enough, as the troops advanced they were welcomed by the sound of machine gun fire and had to carry the place at the point of the bayonet. Twin Huts was finally captured by 1 AM on 3 Nov. By now it was obvious that the enemy had shot his bolt.

On 3rd afternoon Sagat, against the advice of Ben and Tom, decided to visit the BOP. Subhash Kaushik, who accompanied him, recounts a scene of devastation and the detritus of war. Piles of dead bodies,[64] large number of weapons and all types of ammunition were lying around. The defences were impressive with a number of concrete emplacements. The BOP itself was surrounded by a ditch with *punjis* embedded inside it. Sagat was met by Poonia and taken around. His leadership at a crucial moment had earned him a Vir Chakra. On meeting the Subedar Major, an old acquaintance, Sagat complimented him for the victory and then scolded him for having deserted Avtar.[65] While the visit was going on a Pakistani MMG, no doubt guided by an observer, opened up with a long rattle of

---

64 BBC estimated in a broadcast that day that approximately 300 Pak soldiers had died. By the time Sagat reached the BOP more than 70 corpses had already been collected by the troops and had been piled up for subsequent burial. Col Ahmed Mukhtar Khan himself mentions a figure of more than 80 killed till 31 Oct.

65 Avtar recollects the SM telling him with tears in his eyes that Sagat told him in fluent Marwari, "I give you sweets with one hand for having won Dhalai but on the other I kick you on your behind for abandoning your second-in-command on the battlefield." Avtar. Ibid.

fire. The impact was electric. All persons who had clustered around Sagat, jumped with comic alacrity to find whatever cover they could. When he had the occasion to look around, Subhash found Sagat standing exactly where he was with an amused look on his face. 'He showed no other expression as if nothing had happened; as though he was deaf.'[66] After everyone sheepishly got together, the visit progressed to the Factory area, which showed the same scenes of havoc. It was getting to early evening when Sagat turned back. On reaching the Airfield Sagat found Avtar waiting to be evacuated and looking remarkably resilient despite his nearly four day ordeal. Sagat held his hand displaying a flicker of emotion and gladly took him along to Teliamura from where he was evacuated to Calcutta.

For all practical purposes it seemed the Battle was over. 61 Brigade HQ finally fetched up and Tom, who was functioning with the same ad hoc headquarters established by Shiv, gave orders to his BM to reorganise the defences and move out 2 Jat, which had already incurred more than 100 casualties. The relief was planned to be carried out after 10 PM. It seemed the enemy heard all this on the radio and exactly during the period when the Jats were moving out launched a fierce counter attack on Twin Huts and the Coolie Lines simultaneously, while establishing a block on the withdrawal route of the Jats. The counter attack was beaten back with some hand to hand fighting and heavy artillery fire. The Jat relief got delayed by another day and they suffered some more casualties. 04 Nov was spent in strengthening and readjusting the defences and evicting any enemy hidden nearby. Coolie Lines were burnt to the ground to clear fields of fire. That evening the Jats were finally relieved and their unhappy ordeal by fire was over. On 06 Nov orders were passed to hand over the area to the BSF and Mukti Bahini and Dhalai passed into history.

I have delved in some detail on the Battle of Dhalai as it set a benchmark in the minds of opposing commanders. It was brought

---

66 Subhash Kaushik. Ibid.

home to Sagat and his commanders in a brutal manner that the Pak soldier, harried and dispirited though he may be, was no pushover. If properly led he held his ground and his battle drills seemed superior to the Indians. In adherence to Niazi's directions, he was willing to contest every inch of ground in East Pakistan to the bitter end. A vision of being bogged down in endless tactical battles seemed to grip the planner's mind. A question mark seemed to hang heavily over the capability of the Indian soldier.[67] Years of peacetime activities seems to have rusted his war fighting ability. As far as Sagat was concerned, he realised that the troops required battle inoculation before they could adjust to the brutality of war. He also had to review his warfighting concepts in the face of a determinedly dug in enemy unwilling to surrender ground.[68] The Battle throws a unique light on some of Sagat's character qualities, especially as a war leader. His ruthlessness in getting the job done; his reluctance to compromise on his orders, even with his superiors, once he was convinced of their rationale; his unwillingness to lose face; his supreme confidence in his own knowledge and ability even in the face of a reverse; his abhorrence in allowing troops to disgrace their unit's name by withdrawing from the of battlefield with the taint of defeat.[69] Dhalai was like a clarion call from Sagat to all troops and commanders in his Corps. It highlighted his unyielding and rock solid personality leaving no one in any doubt that he was a commander to fight a war uncompromisingly and to a victorious end and they had better follow him.

Unfortunately for the Pak Army, the Battle of Dhalai and similar battles prior to the outbreak of war only seemed to reinforce Niazi in his rigid mindset of holding ground and fight a battle of attrition. He did not realise, until it was too late, that his troops were a finite

---

67 Sodhi mentions how the losses incurred in the Battle of Dhalai created a sense of disquiet amongst the troops. Pp 143-144. Sodhi. Op cit.

68 Aurora remained an adherent of the direct approach right till the commencement of war, when the reverses at Hilli seemed to have convinced Command that attacking and capturing fixed defences was likely to bog down the Campaign. P 76. Lehl. Op cit.

69 Lt Gen OP Kaushik, who knew Sagat well, brought out some of these aspects in a wide ranging discussion with the Author. **In conversation.** Op cit.

resource and reinforcements were not available. While the Indian Army could call upon reinforcements up the logistic chain, he did not have that luxury. The 300 or so troops he lost in Dhalai could have been better utilised to fight the advancing Indian columns to a standstill in a more dynamic battle plan. In the Dhalai battle he uselessly frittered away the cohesiveness of nearly three infantry battalions as they were to realise once Krishna Rao commenced his advance.[70]

There were two more brigade size operations carried out in Nov to clear areas from where Pakistan could either interfere with India's offensive plans or itself launch some kind of an aggressive foray. Both operations centred on bulges on either flank of the Corps Zone. The first operation was designed to secure the Atgram-Zakigunj Bulge in the North. The Bulge, formed by the two distributaries of the Barak River, extended towards the Cachar District of Assam and directly threatened Indian road and rail communications, already targeted by Pak irregulars. It was decided to remove this threat by capturing the Pakistan defences of Zakigunj and Atgram on night 20 Nov. The operation was undertaken by 59 Brigade of 8 Mountain Div, which tasked 4/5 GR to capture the Atgram Complex and 9 Guards to capture Zakigunj.

4/5 GR, in the first of a series of bloodletting operations, which took a terrible toll on the Battalion during the War, launched two companies across the Surma River in a silent approach. The BOP of Amalsid was nearly 2 kms inland and dominated the high ground of Atgram, overlooking the River. The post had a series of interlocking trenches guarded by a company of Pak 31 Punjab, mujahids and elements of Thal/ Tochi Scouts.[71] Though the Gorkhas succeeded in crossing the River and infiltrating behind the enemy, he soon got wind of them. While approaching the high ground they were

---

70 **Ahmed Mukhtar Khan** brings out how the staff at Dacca tried to obfuscate the casualty figures in their reports to GHQ. This is a common characteristic in armies at the losing end, as Vietnam showed all too clearly. Op cit.

71 **Flash of Kukhries at Atgram by Maj Gen (retd) Ian Cardozo.** The article appears in the 5th Gorkha Rifles Regimental Newsletter of Apr 2009.

challenged by the shout of, '"*Kaun hai! Haath khare karo* (halt raise your hands)!"...........A few close by shouted *"Charge! Aayo Gorkhali!"* The shout of *Aayo Gorkhali* (the Gorkhas are here) remained in the air for a little while but soon it was the rattle of Pakistani machine guns, which tried to counter it.'[72] The rest of the platoons veered towards the sound of firing and entered the network of trenches and bunkers with kukhries and grenades. The CO of the Battalion, Lt Col AB Harolikar, believed that all officers must lead from the front and that's what they did. In one particular incident, the CO with the Maj Rattan Kaul, one of the company commanders, was inspecting a row of dead Pak bodies. He was suddenly attacked by Maj Azhar Alvi, the company commander of B Company, 31 Punjab, who was feigning death. In a close fight, Alvi was finally shot down by Sub Ran Bahadur Thapa and deservedly got the *Hilal-e-Jurrat.*[73] The Battalion itself lost two young officers. The enemy company ceased to exist as an effective force while 4/5 GR, with its kukhries, set itself a unique standard and reputation during the Campaign, which filled the enemy with apprehension.

In a simultaneous operation, 9 Guards with a BSF company was tasked to capture the Zakigunj Complex, across the Kusiyara River, which was held by a company plus of the enemy.[74] Supported by well concealed fire bases, the river crossing took place six to seven kms downstream around 9 PM and was detected at mid stream. There were shouts of *Allahu Akbar* and machine gun fire. This filled the troops with some apprehension. As the boats docked on the far bank, Ranawat recalled that the junior leaders had to physically get the troops moving. 'It was difficult to muster and then again re-muster them.' [75] Thereafter it was very slow going in the face of enemy fire, the slush, bunds and paddy fields. However, as the

---

72 **Personal communication by Brig (then Maj) Rattan Kaul.** He was one of the assaulting company commanders.

73 Cardozo. Ibid.

74 Since the Battalion attack took place after 4/5 GR had already attacked, the company commander with some troops had moved out or decamped.

75 **Ranawat in conversation**; op cit.

enemy fire was wildly erratic the men got more confident. The assaulting companies, under the 2ic were held up fighting through the built up area of Zakigunj and the CO's party found itself at the Forming up Place with only two platoons of the reserve company, just as dawn was breaking. Already heavily delayed, they had no option but to launch the attack expecting the assault companies to pass through them as their momentum ran out. 'We had to clear 300 to 400 mtrs; and in that we managed to kill 14 to 15 of the enemy......I cleared two to three bunkers with grenades through the loopholes and rear entry. I entered one bunker and found that the dust had not settled. Somebody went for my throat and since I had bent down to enter the bunker I was unable to grapple back. It was fortunate that the carbine, which was hanging in front, had been used by me and I pressed the trigger. The moving parts hit on an empty chamber. Since the bayonet was stuck it was providential that I lifted the sling down from my shoulder and shoved the bayonet into the fellow once, twice and then I fell unconscious. He was a massive pathan from the Thal Scouts. The boys with me dragged me out, found blood all over me and thought I was dead. I however recovered when some water was given to me.'[76]

At that stage the gallant artillery battery commander of the Battalion, Maj Chaman Lal, barely a yard away from Ranawat, was struck down by a machine gun bullet and bled to death while being evacuated across the River.[77] By then the momentum of the assault had fizzled out and it was lucky that the assaulting companies reached, passed through and finished the attack.

The Battalion had killed three JCOs and 21 men and had captured another 25. Barely had the success been reported around 9.30 AM, when the Battalion received a message that Sagat was

---

[76] Ranawat. Ibid.

[77] 'Under a hail of fire we dragged him behind cover and applied a shell dressing with the help of a torn piece from his own trousers. We should have had the sense to apply a tourniquet too but did not do so. Even the RMO, who was with the assaulting companies and eventually evacuated him, did not apply a tourniquet. It has been an abiding regret with me and continues to haunt me still.' Ranawat. Ibid.

arriving. He landed at Karimgunj and took a boat across the River. An exhausted Raghubir, who had moved with the assault, met him only to be greeted abrasively by the sardonic words, 'So Raghu you smashed a peanut with a hammer!' Raghubir stoically welcomed Sagat but these words continued to rankle him for years afterwards.[78] Sagat inspected the defences and was informed that the Battalion had killed two officers and buried them. Sagat was far too shrewd a person to accept such words at their face value. His remarkable ability to exactly assess the enemy's strength came into play and much to the indignation of those present, he asked for the bodies to be exhumed. And exhumed they were. 'To everyone's horror it was found that while one body had the epaulettes, the other, though having the pinholes, unfortunately had a bunch of keys hanging from its neck. Sagat said, 'Look, which officer in which army would carry his keys around his neck. On top of that he does not even look like an officer.' The Battalion decided thereafter not to claim the other body as an officer although he was wearing a captain's rank. What we realised about Sagat then was that the moment an operation was over he would land right in the middle at the earliest possible moment. He also had this remarkable ability to assess the essence of a battle field.'[79]

The last major operation before the Campaign began was the capture of the Belonia Bulge. The Bulge, approximately 25 kms by 8 kms in length, was like a dagger pointed at the heart of the southern part of the Corps Zone directly towards the staging areas and administrative bases of 23 Mountain Division. It had been held and bitterly contested by 4 EBR and now was firmly occupied by elements of Pak 53 Infantry Brigade, which Niazi, in a typical knee jerk reaction to the heating up of the Border, had moved from the defences of Dacca and put under command of the ad hoc 39 Division based at Chandpur.[80] The Bulge was held by two companies

---

78 Ranawat. Ibid.

79 Ranawat. Ibid.

80 Niazi had also created the ad hoc 91 Infantry Brigade which had only half a regular battalion with mostly EPCAF personnel. They were responsible for preventing any

plus of 15 Baluch, with elements of EPCAF and Razakars. The Northern portion of the Bulge had been cleared by 83 Mountain Brigade between 5 and 8 Nov, much to the disgust of Niazi, as it allowed an ingress route for the Indians, along the road and rail communications, straight to Fenny and then to Chittagong.[81] Sagat was not too satisfied with this operation as 'Rocky' had kept details of it close to his chest till the last moment. Once it was over, Sagat heard that though 2 Rajput and 3 Dogra, the Battalions engaged had done well, some of the enemy seem to have escaped through a Mukti Bahini block. Before the next phase of operations to capture the rest of the Bulge started, there was a fair amount of air activity from the enemy side. Pak Sabre jets strafed the Indian positions and 3 Dogra was credited with shooting down one of them. The AD claimed credit for damaging three.

The rest of the Belonia Bulge was cleared in two separate divisional level operations. They formed part of an elaborate deception plan initiated by Sagat by which he hoped to deceive the enemy into thinking that 23 Mountain Division was being tasked to capture Chittagong through the Belonia Bulge. The deception required establishment of an elaborate road system, setting up of a phantom communication network and actual employment of troops to clear the Bulge.[82] Maj Gen RD 'Rocky' Hira was a war-hardened veteran, a hands on man, who planned his operations meticulously and retained the respect, even affection, of his subordinates. He had an inkling that the enemy had fallen for the deception measures and moved a large number of troops into the

---

advance of the Indians from Fenny to Chittagong.

81 Maj Gen AS Chopra, then CO of 3 Dogra, recalls how just prior to the assault the GOC, Maj Gen (later Lt Gen) RD 'Rocky' Hira, visited the Battalion along with the Commander Brig AS Sandhu. Chopra remonstrated that it was far too dangerous to which 'Rocky' nonchalantly replied, 'Ajit, if this place is safe for you and your boys, it is safe for me.' **Reminiscences of a Battalion Commander by Maj Gen (retd) AS Chopra** as printed in the Dogra Regimental Journal, **Anubhav, Vol II, of Feb 2010.**

82 As per Sukhwant Singh, Sagat intended to lure 53 Brigade from its defences in Laksham and trap it in the Bulge prior to the advance of 23 Division towards Chandpur. P 152. Sukhwant Singh. Op cit. See also p 55. Gautam. Op cit.

Belonia Bulge. If he could trap these troops, his task for advancing onto Chandpur would become that much easier.[83] Like Krishna Rao, he was not fond of superiors breathing down his neck and though he could not keep Sagat out of the loop in his planning, he nevertheless made it clear that he was firmly in the saddle. The plan was simple. 181 and 83 Mountain Brigades were to advance from West and East respectively, link up at the railway line, and cut off and trap the enemy north of Fenny. Kilo Force was thereafter to lead the advance while the Division redeployed quickly and poised itself to advance onto the Meghna River line.

The first phase of the operation started on 16 Nov with 14 Kumaon of 181 Brigade being tasked to capture areas west of Phulgazi. The operation failed despite a heavy concentration of artillery fire. 14 Kumaon was pinned down, was unable to advance and suffered casualties. 'Tappy' Raina, GOC 2 Corps, who was tasked for a thrust from the western border of East Pakistan, heard of this debacle. 14 Kumaon was his own battalion and he was disturbed enough to speak to Sagat who, unfortunately for 'Rocky', had to get into the act. He would fly down to Bogafa, the helipad closest to the scene of operations, and spend time seeing the preparation and meeting commanders.[84]

On 22 Nov Sagat even decided to stay at Kilo Force HQ at Santir Bazaar. That day heavy air activity took place over East Pakistan and our aircraft shot down some marauding Sabres. Sagat was

---

[83] Rahim Khan the GOC and Aslam Niazi, the brigade commander of 53 Brigade, following Niazi's (no relation) diktats had decided to defend the Bulge in strength. The defences of Laksham were denuded and two Battalions, with a fair number of irregulars, were deployed in the Bulge to contest any Indian advance. This came under severe criticism by Justice Hamooder Rahman. P446/106. **Report of the Hamooder Rahman Commission.** Op cit.

[84] Unfortunately, around the same period, 19 Punjab, the battalion of the Army Commander, which was a part of 73 Brigade under 57 Mountain Division, had a minor debacle at a place called Chandrapur, resulting in a flurry of telephone calls from Command. These preliminary operations seemed to raise all sort of doubts among chair borne experts in headquarters, who seriously doubted whether Indian Army units had it in them to face, what seemed, a more battle hardened enemy.

peremptorily told to return to Teliamura as it was expected that the 'balloon would go up'. The last few days had been unpleasant for Sagat. Not only was he finding it difficult to fine tune the offensive plans with his subordinates, there was talk going on about the battle worthiness of his units. On top of that, petty squabbles with Eastern Air Command deprived him of his communication flight and he had to fall back on the Air OP Allouette flights.

The next phase of the operation started on 22 Nov when units of 181 and 83 Brigades moved into the Bulge. They were guided by men of 4 EBR with Khalid Musharaf very much in the lead. The independent squadron of 7 Cavalry was placed under command 181 Brigade. The initial move went off smoothly without the enemy even coming to know of the extent of the operations. Unfortunately, the attempt to trap the enemy failed as the two brigades could not link up that night. On account of some misunderstanding of orders, the armoured squadron of 7 Cavalry did not close the gap and a large number of the enemy escaped with their weapons and equipment. This did not improve matters between Sagat and 'Rocky'.

By the end of Nov, 4 Corps had poised itself for the coming offensive. Despite misgivings in several circles, Sagat felt confident that the troops had been suitably bloodied and would acquit themselves well.[85] On the other hand, relations with Aurora and some of his subordinates had become decidedly prickly as Sagat continuously interacted with them to fine tune his plans.[86] Every day one of the formations was visited and he held detailed discussions with the commanders. On 29 Nov, Aurora landed at Agartala and

---

85 'These events as a run up to the War were precursors to getting our resolve in place and more importantly getting everybody in the chain of command a good idea of whatever was missing, what needed to be done....in dealing with the adversary...all this put together got everybody ready that this was not going to be a walk over, let's get prepared for it.' **Conversation of Lt Gen Shamsher Mehta with the Author at New Delhi on 30 Sep 2009.**

86 Till end of Sep Sagat and Aurora seem to have got along well. It is only after the border heated up that the differences in their nature and outlook started manifesting itself. While attending the Dushera function of 1/11 GR, Sodhi recalls, 'Sagat Singh was all praise for Aurora. Offensive plan now as Sagat wanted it.' P 141. Sodhi. Op cit.

after visiting 19 Punjab, he and Sagat flew to the Belonia Bulge and landed at Phulgazi. The state of Pakistani defences was daunting. Aurora gave a speech to a large crowd and cheers of "Joi Bangla, Joi Hind" rent the air. There was no doubt about the feeling of freedom and exhilaration felt by the people.

Emboldened by his success in keeping the Indians at bay at most places, Niazi seems to have got the impression that the Pakistan Army, by contesting the frontier, had prevented the Indians from carving out any large enclaves from where an independent government of Bangladesh could function. He was convinced that India had no intention of liberating the entire territory. Despite the success at Bayra, near Jessore, the Indians seemed to have pulled back. He was bent on contesting every inch of the way. The fortress strategy already stood compromised.

CHAPTER SEVEN

IV CORPS: THE HAMMER

You must be master and win, or serve and lose,
grieve or triumph, be the anvil or the hammer.

- Johan Wolfgang von Goethe

Sagat issued his Operation Instructions on 12 Nov in which he spelt out the tasks to his formations.

- 8 Mountain Division, in the North, was to advance with a brigade each on two convergent axes from the directions of Dharmanagar and Shamshernagar and isolate Sylhet from the South in six days. Thereafter a brigade was to be made available to the Corps as reserve. Sylhet was to be captured only in case this Brigade remained with the Division. In a subsequent phase the Division was to capture Brahmanbaria. There were subsidiary forces tasked to assist the Division for operations in the Atgram – Zakigunj Bulge.

- In the Centre, 57 Mountain Division was initially tasked to defend Agartala. It was to capture Akhaura and box in the enemy 27 Brigade at Brahmanbaria. Thereafter the Division was to take over the operations being conducted by 61 Mountain Brigade to isolate Maynamati and capture Daudkhandi by D plus 8. If all went well the Division was to capture Chittagong.

- 61 Mountain Brigade had been put directly under command of the Corps and was tasked to cut off Maynamati from the North. After that it was to become a part of 57 Mountain

Division operations.

- In the South, 23 Mountain Division was to capture Temple Hill, a part of Lalmai Heights, and isolate the Maynamati defences from the south and west. Comilla was to be cleared and Chandpur was to be captured by D plus 8.

- Kilo Force was to operate in the Belonia Bulge, isolate Chittagong from the North and capture Fenny, if possible.

- A brigade of 8 Mountain Division was to be made available as corps reserve by D plus 6. It was expected to be employed either for the capture of Maynamati or Brahmanbaria.

If Niazi had played his part and Sagat had slavishly stuck to his Operation Instructions, the fortress defence would have effectively stymied the Corps as it got bogged down in reducing the nodal points in its route of advance. None of the critical objectives, which were essential for the liberation of the nascent state of Bangladesh, would have been attained without a bloody campaign that may have dragged on for months. However, while arrogance seemed to have made Niazi over confident in his military abilities;[1] Sagat's military mind was already straining to escape the constraints set by Eastern Command. During his last visit, Aurora had indicated that the Army had set its sights on Dhaka, even though 4 Corps was not expected to go beyond the Meghna. Sagat was evolving his strategy based on his experience at Dhalai and it made him averse from carrying out any direct attacks. His elaborate deception plan at Belonia, which went somewhat awry, was an attempt to confuse the enemy while he struck westwards.[2]

---

1 The Indian Army was 'helpless at the borders even after 13 days of attacks on 21 Nov ....We had succeeded in stopping the Indian onslaught on the border...' P 124/128. Niazi. Op cit. 'Gen Niazi's claim, in late November, of fighting an all out war was contradicted by the deployment pattern of his troops. Strung along the border as they were in penny packets.......' P 121, Salik. Op cit.

2 Justice Hamooder Rahman has severely castigated Niazi and his subordinates for the way they fought on the borders, '..removal of 15 PUNJAB from Comilla and 30 BALUCH from Laksham proved disastrous...' P446/106 the Hamooder Rahman Commission Report. Op cit.

Contrary to conventional wisdom about the planning process in 4 Corps, it needs to be clarified that it was not always Sagat who was brilliantly throwing ideas about a lightning advance. He was at times a restraining hand on his divisional commanders, who are wrongly depicted as a conventional foil to his brilliance. Hira had some difficult moments with Sagat as he wanted his Division to be focussed towards Chandpur from the beginning of its advance rather than lay siege to the Maynamati defences. Sagat, on the other hand, was unwilling to have fortresses holding out in his rear while his formations were swanning off into the enemy hinterland. Gonsalves has been praised by both Lehl and Cloughley[3] for his competence.[4] Krishna Rao, as always, brought a formidable and painstaking intellect into his own plans, always aware that his hands were tied firstly, by having only two brigades and secondly, by the deadline of D plus 6, when he would lose a brigade as Corps Reserve.[5] He was also aware of Sagat's warning that he might be required to play another role as Sagat seized opportunities as the War progressed. Brilliantly opportunistic, Sagat was never fixated on written directives. He would seize chance by the scruff of its neck and propel his Corps in directions that were still crystallising in his mind. By the time his campaign was over, he had made a mockery of all written instructions.

It was obvious that war, which some hopeless optimists thought could be avoided, was inevitable. Mrs Gandhi had skilfully orchestrated a political and diplomatic initiative that unencumbered her from any internal dissension. Internationally, she had managed either a sympathetic ear or had stymied any aggressive posture by either the Chinese or USA. She nevertheless realised that the

---

3 P 216. **History of the Pakistan Army: Wars and Insurrection by Brian Cloughley (Oxford University Press, Karachi, 2nd Edition – Revised, 2002)**

4 'A thorough gentleman and I mean thorough. Given a job he had the ability to put it together and deliver it. To some extent he was driven by Sagat.' **Lt Gen Shamsher Mehta in conversation.**

5 'Contrary to what people thought, our plans did not emerge during the first discussion, which anyway took place in Tezpur. The plans evolved as the intelligence picture was built up and over several discussions.' **Gen Krishna Rao in conversation.** Op cit.

military campaign had to be short and decisive. While Sam had promised her a victory he was not willing to hazard a guess as to the results of the Campaign. What was hoped was that when hostilities ceased, India would be in an advantageous position to establish the nascent state of Bangladesh.

Sagat worked feverishly against time and fine-tuned his plans. He would visit his formations every day and return late in the evenings exhausted but well satisfied with his preparations. He was not prepared for any distractions but distracted he was when Maj Gen Sujan Singh Oban, who had the ear of Mrs Gandhi, and his Special Frontier Force (SFF) were foisted on him by Eastern Command. Sagat met Oban and his subordinates in the last days of November and worked out the insertion of the SFF into the Chittagong Hill Tracts. They were expected to tie down Pak troops who may interfere on the flanks of any advance towards Chittagong. It was also hoped to trap the Mizo Insurgents. The SFF was moved into the Chittagong Hill Tracts on 12 and 16 Nov and they forced the withdrawal of Pakistani Army detachments, deceptively named 48 Baluch. A heliborne landing was carried out North of Rangamati on 29 Nov but it was unsuccessful in trapping the hardened veterans of the Mizo National Army (MNA).[6]

8 Mountain Division initiated the first act of the Campaign. Its two brigades moved on two axes converging on Sylhet.[7] 59 Brigade was tasked to move on an indifferent tea track, parallel to the railway line Kalaura – Fenchuganj - Sylhet. 81 Brigade was tasked to capture Shamsher Nagar Airfield[8] and then advance along a

---

6 The dramatic escape of the hard corps of the MNA into Burma is still the stuff of legend in Mizoram and is romanticized and well narrated by **Nirmal Nibedon** in his Book. Pp 165 – 168. Op cit.

7 59 Brigade was quietly moved out of the Atgram Salient and the operations in the area were handed over to the BSF. The deception was effective as Pakistan continued to have forces deployed in the area. 'The intention was to try and convince the Pakistani that we were taking the direct road to Sylhet.' **Sagat Singh in conversation.** Op cit.

8 'Gauhati was the only effective airfield from which air support could be given, so it was imperative to capture Shamsher Nagar Airfield to provide air support south of the line Comilla – Dhaka.' **Sagat Singh in conversation.** Ibid. Unfortunately the Airfield was

metalled road to the important junction of Maulvi Bazaar, cross the Kushiyara River at the Sherpur - Shadipur ferries and invest Sylhet from the South.

81 Brigade commenced its attack on night 29 Nov after a difficult build up over the Manu River. As Sagat expected, this attack reinforced the siege mentality and paranoia of Pak 202 and 313 Brigades[9] and no help was forthcoming to 14 Division when the attack on Akhaura developed. This had far reaching implications, which were brilliantly exploited by Sagat as his campaign developed.

On 30 Nov, after seeing off the Army Commander, Sagat visited Krishna Rao at Kailashahar to see how his advance was going. The attack on Shamsher Nagar had developed satisfactorily, though 10 Mahar and 3 Punjab, the attacking battalions, had suffered heavy casualties. 4 Kumaon had established a block behind the Airfield, which surprised the enemy and '...the Brigade Commander only discovered this when he came under fire....'[10] When he returned to his headquarters every evening, Sagat always had feedback from the front for his staff. This time they got a piece of his mind as the forward troops had complained of shortages in ammunition re-supply.

As it turned out, 01 Dec was a hectic day for Sagat. He intended to stay the night at Agartala so as to be close to the attack on Akhaura. This was a large scale effort and Sagat was worried about the repercussions on the city once the enemy retaliated with artillery fire. In the morning he did his rounds of all the divisions and had lunch with Krishna Rao. 'Bunty' Quinn and his Brigade had by then commenced their advance towards Kalaura.[11] By late

---

never used by the Air Force for various reasons despite Sagat's engineers making it operational in short time.

9   Only 'the 30 FF Company on the extreme right was allowed to join the neighbouring 27 Brigade.' P 165. Salik. Op cit.

10 P 165. Salik. Ibid.

11 By now the Corps intelligence staff realized that Krishna Rao's contention that he was likely facing two brigades and not one was possibly true. This was again a Niazi sleight

afternoon Sagat was back in Agartala, where desultory shelling indicated that the enemy had got the wind up. Meetings with 'Ben' and Ted Dartnell were followed by further discussions with 'Rocky', who had been summoned to Agartala and was patiently waiting for him. It was an exhausted Sagat who repaired to his room at the Raj Bhavan to freshen up before the long night ahead. It had got dark by the time Sagat reached the Tactical Headquarters of 57 Division where he was received by Col Hector Grant, the Col General Staff. 'Ben' was trying to grab a shut eye and Sagat did not disturb him but settled down with a glass of whisky to hear the progress of the Battle.

The Battle of Akhaura was the only battle fought as a division set piece battle by the Corps. 57 Division, with two brigades attacking in tandem, was to capture Akhaura in three phases. Phase One was by 73 Brigade, which was to capture area Karnel Bazaar – Gangasagar (5 to 6 kms South of Akhaura) and isolate Akhaura from the south.[12] In Phase Two, 311 Brigade was to capture Akhaura. In Phase Three, the Division was to exploit northwards to block any counter attacks from Brahmanbaria.[13]

In Sagat's own words, 'Akhaura being an important railway junction has a number of railway buildings. Adjacent to the railway station and to its west is the River Titas. The area around the junction is particularly flat and low; on the Pakistani maps this area is marked as a marsh. To the east and north of Akhaura town the Pakistanis had dug an anti-tank ditch. This could be seen from the rooftops from our side of the border. In the railway buildings......on the first floor they had made RCC fortifications using the windows as firing ports.

---

of hand where he had divided a brigade strength into two brigades. It now looked that while 57 Division had only a brigade against it, 8 Division faced an equal strength. It became all the more important to ensure that these forces were not allowed to slip towards Dacca. Krishna Rao emphasized this to 'Raja' Apte. **Krishna Rao in conversation.**

12 'The idea was to present a broad front to the Pakistanis and thereby deceive them of our real intentions.' **Sagat in conversation.** Op cit.

13 Brahmanbaria was the HQ of 14 Pak Division and the pivot from where troops coming from either Dacca or Sylhet could be moved north or south.

Bunkers at Dhalai

With Maj Gen Rocky Hira and Maj GS Sihota

At Burichang with Brig Tom Pande & Maj OP Kaushik

With Brig Anand Swaroop and Brig BS Sandhu. Planning the Op

They had also fitted searchlights to scan the area at night..... the Pakistanis had converted one side of the double railway track from Akhaura to Brahmanbaria into a road by removing the sleepers' to enable tanks and guns to move into the area. For the troop of tanks deployed there they had 'made RCC garage type structures with an opening on one side for the gun'.[14] The high water table prevented any kind of digging down. Pak 27 Brigade, under the courageous Brig Sa'adullah Khan,[15] was responsible for defending this sector. It had been allotted an additional battalion of Mujahids with several companies EPCAF. While most of 33 Baluch faced 73 Brigade, 12 FF was deployed to defend Akhaura and Gangasagar. Two companies of 21 POK (Azad Kashmir) Battalion were distributed for defence of Brahamanbaria (along with a company of 33 Baluch) and Akhaura town. The defences of Akhaura were formidable with a fallback onto the nodal point of Brahmanbaria. This being the HQ of 14 Division and a vital link between Sylhet and Comilla, Sagat did not expect any dividends to accrue by a slogging match along the embankments towards Ashuganj. Once Akhaura had been secured he planned to focus his corps operations on either flank of the Lalmai Heights and on towards the Meghna.

In the 57 Division operations room, Sagat found that he was literally twiddling his thumbs and drinking whisky as this was just the opening gambit of a battle which would last for five bitterly contested days. The Pak artillery shelling was becoming more than an irritant and Sagat found it annoying that Indian counter bombardment was slow in coming and rather ineffective. This led to a quick dinner and a drive to visit Ted Dartnell. They were old drinking companions since Gangtok days and over another glass of whisky Sagat berated Ted who, unfazed, defended himself. It

---

14 **Sagat in conversation.** ibid. Because of the low lying nature of the terrain and the numerous channels and ponds which dotted the country side, Pakistan could effectively make use of the bottlenecks they presented. It ultimately came down to the attacking troops using the road and railway embankments for their advance, while infiltrating through marshy ground and establishing blocks in the rear.

15 His book **East Pakistan to Bangladesh** is extensively quoted by Verma in his account of the Battle.

made not an iota of difference that the enemy started ranging onto the gun area where their argument was going on. While everyone else was cowering in trenches, Sagat and Ted continued their spat despite shells coming dangerously close.

Sagat's temper had not been assuaged when he finally left and he decided to visit 2 EBR, which was supposed to carry out a demonstration against the Pakistanis on the expected northern approach.[16] It was very dark and while driving on an indifferent dusty track, Sagat saw several vehicles which had got bogged down. While slowly bypassing these vehicles, Sagat saw a lieutenant from the ASC standing on the side with his jeep. On being summoned, he threw a sharp salute at the Corps Commander, who asked him if he could guide him to 2 EBR. The officer answered in a reassuringly confident manner. He then took the lead and shortly thereafter showed a clean pair of heels and was never seen again. He obviously had realised that the chaos in the convoy would be difficult to explain. Sagat had no other option but to return to the 57 Division Operations Room, where he took out his frustration on the hapless Grant. He returned late to the Raj Bhavan, told his personal staff to monitor the Battle and went to bed. The next morning at around 6 AM, the Pak Artillery lobbed a few shells into Agartala, some of which landed on the grounds of the Raj Bhavan fairly close to where Sagat was staying. While there was a general scurrying to find shelter, Sagat was seen standing on the balcony in a dressing gown with a cigarette in hand, enjoying himself, his temper obviously restored.[17]

---

16 2 EBR was part of Sierra Force commanded by Lt Col Shafiullah (later C-in-C Bangladesh Armed Forces), which had 11 EBR also under command (temporarily with 73 Brigade). Sierra Force along with 19 RAJRIF was expected to make the defenders think that the main attack, supported by armour, was to come from the expected northern approach and thus cut them off from Brahmanbaria. Shafi carried out his task despite some hiccups, which required Sagat to visit 2 EBR on 02 Dec. 19 RAJRIF carried out a determined attack on 03 Dec but suffered casualties as the rest of 311 Brigade attacks were postponed on 04 Dec.

17 **Brig JS Goraya, Artillery,** in an unpublished article (in the possession of the Author) describes how the counter bombardment resources were mustered and the single 105 mm Pak gun permanently silenced on that day.

The Battle of Akhaura was hard fought as the terrain favoured the defender. Sagat visited 73 Brigade on 02 Dec and found Brig (later Lt Gen) ML Tuli methodically carrying out his tasks. He was not to be hurried despite Sagat stressing the need for boldness.[18] It was during the Battle of Gangasagar that Naik Albert Ekka of 14 Guards, won a posthumous Param Vir Chakra (PVC), the highest Indian gallantry award. He was the only one to receive this award during the liberation of Bangladesh. By 03 Dec, 73 Brigade succeeded in linking up with 311 Brigade and cleared the road from Agartala to Gangasagar in some hard fought actions. It also established a block on the direct road going to Brahmanbaria. 14 Division had effectively been isolated from the south. At that stage part of the Brigade was pulled back as it was to be used for exploiting the break through.

The plan for the attack of 311 Brigade was formulated by Brig RN Mishra, VrC, after getting input from all his commanding officers.[19] Mishra had a good reputation as a soldier and was highly regarded by Sagat.[20] As it turned out he was the ideal commander to conduct such a difficult battle. Sagat's continuing faith in him ensured that he remained at the cutting edge of 4 Corps operations in future also. The Akhaura operation required 10 Bihar to infiltrate

---

18 Jagdev has hinted at the lack of intelligence and the inability of the Indian Army formations from fully getting to know the enemy dispositions. This made people like Tuli, who had an orthodox bent of mind, somewhat cautious. Pp 118-119. Jagdev. Op cit. 'While in London he acquired an anglicized pipe smoking style.' Goraya. Op cit.

19 311 Brigade had 4 Guards, 18 Rajput and 10 Bihar in its ORBAT. 12 Kumaon, part of 61 Brigade and 19 Rajrif, part of 73 Brigade were also put under command for the initial part of the operation. Verma claims that the attack incorporated the concepts his Battalion had learnt during the capture of Mukandpur BOP on 20 Nov and other engagements. P. 34 Verma. Op cit. 'It is odd that the three of us brought up in the same military tradition chose to do it three different ways.' The plan was discussed threadbare with even the Army Commander giving an input. **Himmeth Singh in conversation.** Op cit.

20 'I can say without hesitation that in Brig Mishra we had the finest of commanders that I could have gone to war with.' **Himmeth in conversation.** Ibid. 'He was very competent. Knew things at the grass roots and was a good mentor to his battalion commanders.' **Shamsher Mehta in conversation.** There were some contrary views which have been expressed by Verma (in personal communication to the Author) and by Jagdev in his Book.

and secure the area north of Gangasagar before midnight on 01 Dec. Thereafter 4 Guards was to infiltrate through and cut off Akhaura from the West and NW. This required the difficult crossing of the Titas River. 18 Rajput was to follow up on 10 Bihar successes and reduce the main defences around the town. To distract the enemy, 'S' Force along with 19 Rajrif was to demonstrate and divert the enemy's attention towards the North.[21] It speaks volumes of the panache and the leadership of the Brigade that the senior officers managed a nine hole game of golf on the Agartala Golf Course just prior to commencement of operations.[22]

The terrain and the close knit enemy defences delayed 10 Bihar efforts to find a gap for 4 Guards[23] by nearly two hours but by 2 AM on 02 Dec, 4 Guards had commenced its infiltration despite misgivings that the move would get day lighted. Luckily, heavy mist prevented the enemy from observing the movement and the Battalion succeeded in crossing the Titas[24] and positioning itself, though without its anti-tank recoilless guns. 10 Bihar kept on expanding the area it had captured on 02 Dec and in the process got hold of the 105 mm artillery gun which had harassed Agartala

---

21 Lt Col (retired) S Mukherjee, then a platoon commander in 19 RAJRIF, describes the shock of encountering a 20 feet wide by 10 feet deep ditch where their attack got bogged down. **Lessons Learnt in Close Quarter Battle from Live Battle Experiences by Lt Col S Mukherjee** as published in **The Infantry.** Mhow, Jun 2005.

22 They had made a vow to tee off at the Dacca Golf Course, the first morning after the Liberation. They did exactly that. Shamsher Mehta just beating Himmeth as the first to tee off. **As witnessed by the Author & confirmed by Brig Mishra.**

23 The Battalion was being commanded by Lt Col (later Lt Gen) Himmeth Singh. 'I have not seen or met another officer of that calibre since I joined the service and till I retired....A soldier, gentleman, leader in every aspect that he did, both in war and peace.' **Mehta.** Ibid.

24 Himmeth graphically describes the harrowing process of infiltrating an entire battalion through a marsh and then through a river 20 ft wide and 7 to 8 ft deep. He gives credit to his leading company commander, Maj Kharbanda, who found a local guide. The Battalion then in single file, painstakingly and literally on its toes succeeded in wading through a 'ford' six feet deep and under desultory enemy fire. **Himmeth in conversation.** Ibid.

so much.[25] 18 Rajput, which was to pass through 10 Bihar for attack on Akhaura on 02 Dec was held up as 10 BIHAR was still heavily engaged. 73 Brigade had also not succeeded in linking up. The Rajputs were therefore diverted to do the linking up and were also asked to link up with 4 Guards now facing difficulties across the River. Thus on 02 Dec night, two companies of 18 Rajput crossed the Titas Marsh. The Battalion, after a lot of effort, also managed to manhandle two 106 mm recoilless guns across the river, handing one over to 4 Guards in the nick of time before withdrawing.[26]

311 Brigade was to launch its attack on the main defences on 04 Dec morning and had troops poised at the forming up place waiting for close air support, which never materialised throughout the day. There was no other option but to postpone the attack to 04 Dec night. Sagat was furious and protested strongly to Aurora.[27] There is nothing more demoralising than to have troops hyped and waiting to attack for hours on end and then being told to postpone the attack. However, the postponement allowed the Brigade to reconstitute itself. 14 Guards relieved 18 Rajput to allow it enough time to participate in the assault. A delay of more than 24 hours had already occurred.

Meanwhile 4 Guards, now isolated across the Titas, was having severe problems in holding on to its lodgement and had already suffered several casualties. A determined enemy counter attack on 03 Dec was beaten back with difficulty with Maj 'Paunchy'

---

[25] Sagat made it a point to gift the 105 mm Pak artillery gun to the people of Agartala, after the War, as a tribute to their stoicism under adversity.

[26] Pp 58-60. Verma. Op cit.

[27] Sagat had positioned himself eagerly at the ATC Tower at Agartala Airfield to personally see the strikes. He wasted half a day waiting as the timings kept on getting postponed and finally left in a foul mood. He was getting fed up of his constant sparring with Eastern Air Command, which was located at Shillong and seemingly oblivious to ground requirements. On the other hand, the Air Force claimed that it was in the process of ensuring air supremacy and put close air support at a lower priority. Why this issue was not sorted out before the troops gathered for attack has not been adequately explained. This dichotomous debate on use of air still goes on.

Chandrakant having the most difficult time of it.[28] Kharbanda had actually re-crossed the Titas with his company and was deployed on an island created by a channel of the Titas, barely 200 mtrs away from Akhaura Railway Station[29]. By 04 Dec, the Battalion was in desperate straits with Kharbanda about to be overrun. Himmeth then appealed to the dashing and unorthodox 5 Independent Armoured Squadron Commander of 63 Cavalry, Maj (later Lt Gen and Army Commander) Shamsher Mehta for help. Mehta's tanks had got bogged down while infiltrating with 10 Bihar and had even been subjected to an air attack. A subsequent effort to send a troop to assist 4 Guards had met with no success. Only Shamsher with a few tanks had managed to reach east of the railway bund. On hearing Himmeth's appeal, he had no option but to do something himself. 'Shamsher drove his tank more like a prize steeple chaser. It came flying over the embankment in a manner that I have never seen – leave alone a vehicle, even a horse....... Kharbanda personally owes his life to this very gallant and prompt action by Shamsher and his tank.'[30]

The attack on the Akhaura defences finally got under way on the night of 04 Dec and became a slogging match without the expected breakthrough. 10 Bihar had already suffered more than a 100 casualties and suffered even more in the intense fighting.[31] By 2 AM on 05 Dec, the Pakistani brigade commander was getting desperate and asked for urgent reinforcements as he expected his defences to crack. Mishra, who was closely monitoring the attack,

---

28 '...I genuinely believe (Chandrakant) was a company commander very nearly unmatched in the Indian Army.' **Himmeth in conversation.** Op cit. He was recommended for the Param Vir Chakra (India's highest gallantry award) but received a Vir Chakra. **'Humour and Courage' by Himmeth Singh in Scholar Warrior, Spring 2013.**

29 The company had dug down without the enemy coming to know of it and 'nearly got the Pakistani brigade commander in their first volley.' P 51. Verma. Op cit.

30 **Himmeth.** Ibid. In an earlier incident Shamsher personally lead his tank to destroy some Pakistani bunkers which were impeding 10 BIHAR advance. P 272. **'Bihar Warriors: The Official History of the Bihar Regiment.**

31 One company had its entire first and second tier leadership either dead or wounded and only 20 men left to progress the attack. P 274. Ibid.

summoned Verma at around 3.30 AM and asked him to commence his battalion attack along the embankment and head for the railway bridge over the Titas. He was to ensure that the momentum did not flag. Despite an enemy tank attempting to hold up the advance, 18 Rajput troops reached the railway sidings and began a running fight with the enemy[32]. The bridge was reached. It was evident that the enemy was attempting to demolish it but Maj Sisodia 'charged across with Hav Chotte Singh's platoon.'[33] Unable to blow up the bridge, the enemy ran. It is to Mishra's credit that just as 10 Bihar attack was flagging, he unleashed 18 Rajput and prevented Sa'adullah from reorganising himself to carry out an effective counter attack. The companies of 12 FF, which had so doggedly held up the brigade advance, now started withdrawing in some disarray. The Battle of Akhaura was over and the way to Brahamanbaria lay open.

On 05 Dec, Sagat persuaded Sihota, the pilot of the Air OP helicopter who was flying him, to take a daring flight over Akhaura. Sihota cautiously approached from the South and on Sagat's prodding flew across the railway bund. They immediately noticed the Pakistanis troops pulling out from the defences with their packs and equipment. Realising the implication, Sagat flew south along the railway until he saw the Indian troops deployed along the embankment. He landed in their rear 'caught hold of Maj DP Singh, the company commander who had captured the 105 mm gun, and asked him to push through. The position was taken in no time.'[34] These daring helicopter forays by Sagat became common as the Campaign progressed and decisively affected its course in the days ahead.

As the opening moves of the Campaign commenced it became evident to Sagat that he had very little role to play before the contours of the various battles became clear. On 02 and 03 Dec he

---

32 They relieved Maj Ravi, 10 BIHAR, wounded and sheltering under the lee of a tank his men had captured, and continued the attack.

33 Verma. Op cit.

34 **Sihota in conversation.** ibid.

made a round of his formations and even some units, encouraging and persuading where required. It was clear that formal hostilities were imminent. Thus, when Sagat reached back to Teliamura on 03 Dec evening, he was informed of the Pakistan strikes in the Western Theatre and the formal outbreak of war. This had very little impact on 4 Corps operations except to signal 'Rocky' to commence his advance. Krishna Rao and Gonsalves were already deeply involved in the border battles and were now to implement their offensive plans with greater freedom.

Sagat had started setting a pattern to his activities, which he would follow for the rest of the Campaign. At the crack of dawn, fresh and cheerful, he would take off by helicopter[35] and visit units and formations as per a punishing itinerary which had been told to his subordinates a night in advance. Lunch, unless informed beforehand, was mostly impromptu from a picnic basket made of cane by the Tripura Handicrafts Corporation. Adequate provisions were made for the pilots too.[36] It was not unusual for Sagat to set the helicopter down in a clearing, which was immediately surrounded by hordes of locals (the pilots normally looking anxiously around). While he ate his sandwiches or *parathas*, he would cheerfully chat with the children and distribute sweets. He made it a point to range the entire frontage of his Corps Zone, the pilots refilling at various pre-stocked refuelling points. He returned by sunset, at times on an illuminated helipad. A quick bath was followed by an update by his staff in the operations room[37] and a chat with his division commanders. He was invariably at the 'A' Mess (where normally only his principal staff officers and commanders dined) before 9

---

35 Before leaving his *basha* he would ring up his division commanders, sometimes at 5.30 AM, to get a quick update. Krishna Rao, for one, resented this and persuaded him not to do so. **Krishna Rao in conversation.**

36 "....I must say he looked after the pilots very well. He would always enquire if we had our meals or were comfortable. He gave his reading material....." **Air Cmdre (retd) Mirza Ali, VM.** In personal communication to the Author.

37 Sagat had an inordinate trust in Maj Krishan Naidu, Bihar Regiment. A frail, superseded, alcoholic; his grasp of what Sagat had in mind and then ensuring its implementation made him a great asset to him.

PM to listen to the news broadcast by All India Radio (remarkably truthful). It was here, in a relaxed atmosphere and with a glass of whisky in hand that he would bounce ideas with his officers and get his strokes of genius.[38] Thus late at night, while dinner was being served, his aide and grade one staff officers would be found frantically shouting on the phone to irate counterparts, either changing his itinerary or bringing a twist into the entire Campaign. It was midnight by the time Sagat went to bed none the worse for wear despite the hectic schedule. He had a phenomenal memory, which he used to good effect, either to browbeat subordinates who tended to waffle or to grasp the intricacies of a situation. It seemed nothing escaped Sagat's eye.[39]

Though 23 Division's initial attempt to trap enemy forces in the Belonia Bulge had limited success, their offensive across the IB went better than expected. The troops facing 'Rocky' were commanded by Maj Gen M Rahim Khan, GOC of 39 Division, with his HQ located at Chandpur. 39 Division was an ad hoc formation created by Niazi and placed under command Rahim Khan, a pre-war favourite of GHQ and Eastern Command. He was expected to resolutely disrupt any offensive at the border itself with his defences based on the fortresses at Laksham and Comilla-Maynamati. He had under him 117 Infantry Brigade of three infantry battalions, which held the Comilla-Laksham Sector; 53 Brigade (moved from Dacca) with its HQ at Laksham and two battalions at Fenny and the ad hoc 91 Brigade, which guarded the approaches to Chittagong. The Maynamati-Lalmai Heights dominated the northern flank of any offensive which 23 Divisions planned to launch to reach the banks of the Meghna. Their defences were concretised and in concentric tiers. Any effort to capture them would involve set piece attacks, which would bog down the Campaign.[40] Laksham, as per Niazi's plan, had been

---

38 Much is owed to Messrs Mohan Meakins, the makers of Black Night Whisky, for their contribution to the Campaign.

39 Sodhi recounts an incident when a wrong situation report, which normally is read only by staff officers, was noticed by Sagat and came to haunt him. P 145. Sodhi. Op cit

40 The Pakistan Brigade Commander at Maynamati, Brig Atif, an internationally renowned

converted into a fortress. It was a junction from where the railway line from Comilla trifurcated to Chandpur, Noakhali and Chittagong. The gap between Laksham and the southern tip of Lalmai Hills was just 10 kms and could be effectively dominated by well directed artillery fire. While it was the shortest approach to Chandpur, no road directly linked Laksham to the river port.

The main road to Chandpur passed through Lalmai going southwest to Mudaffarganj. Thereafter it ran nearly parallel to the railway which ran east west from Laksham, even intersecting it at a couple of places. Between Lalmai and Laksham were two indifferent tracks which went westwards from the Border and eventually joined the main road to Chandpur. While Aslam Niazi's 53 Brigade had escaped the dragnet thrown by Hira in Belonia, he still retained his forces at Fenny, anticipating an offensive towards Chittagong. 117 Brigade had extended itself southwards with 23 PUNJAB deployed in Laksham and 25 FF covering the gap between Laksham and Lalmai. For someone who intended to use his fortresses as an anchor in order to carry out a flexible aggressive defence, Rahim Khan seemed to be playing into the Indian hands by deploying troops all along the border and that too east of the parallel running Dakatia Nala and its tributaries.

23 Division offensive planning went through a convoluted process. The Corps Operating Instructions, issued early in Nov, gave priority to the capture of Lalmai Heights before any forces could be sent westwards. Hira, who was looking west from the very beginning, wanted his division to be given objectives in depth. Sagat hesitated at first as he had a hard time getting in sync with Aurora's aims. Those who noticed his behaviour in Aurora's company during those days found him to be mostly reticent. However, the plans underwent a spectacular change during the closing days of Nov.[41] Sagat's ideas had crystallized and he decided to bypass the

---

hockey player, somewhat paranoid to the idea of being surrounded, shortened his defences and made them more cohesive. Maynamati and the southern portion of the Lalmai Heights were abandoned.

41 This was the period when Sagat realized that the Army had started to think of Dacca

fortresses and focus on Chandpur.⁴² This involved infiltrating two brigades on indifferent tracks between Lalmai and Laksham, both of which would be contained and invested, while the Division would make a sustained drive for Chandpur.⁴³ Now these plans were finalised at the last minute without suitable engineer inputs, much to the indignation of Jagdev, who had to allot and improvise scarce engineer resources.⁴⁴ 301 Brigade, commanded by Brig HS Sodhi would lead the advance followed by 181 Brigade, commanded by Brig YPS Bakshi. 83 Brigade, commanded by Brig BS Sandhu, would invest Laksham. 61 Brigade was to protect the northern flank of the advance and contain the enemy on Lalmai Heights.

The operation went off better than expected. While infiltrating, 1/11 GR of 301 Brigade ambushed two companies of 25 FF, dispersed them, capturing their CO and more than 200 men. A gallant tank assault on Mian Bazaar by the independent squadron of 7 Cavalry, dispersed the enemy, though with the loss of several tanks. A large enough gap was created through which a major part of 23 Division started moving to the depth areas. To the north, Pak 117 Brigade hemmed in by 61 Brigade was unaware of the fate of 25 FF till some survivors managed to get into communication.⁴⁵ 23

---

as an objective.

42 According to Sodhi, Aurora was much (perhaps too much) involved in the intense discussions, belying the assertions made by Jacob that he was a mere spectator. Pp 168-173. Sodhi. Op cit.

43 The Official history of the War (draft available at http://www.bharat-rakshak.com/LAND-FORCE/army/history/1971war/PDF/1971chapter13.pdf) mentions, 'This small mistake was enough for the hawk-eyed Rajput General. Taking advantage of the Pak reaction, Sagat Singh decided that Lalmai and Laksham were left with no mobile forces to dominate the gap....' and inserted 301 Brigade.

44 '... the Division decided to move itself....along a track which meandered all over the country to get to Buschi and ignored the well developed roads. The selected track ran through villages, skirting fish ponds and paddy fields, going over and through wet and dry streams and nullahs, and was barely adequate for cycle rickshaws and hand carts. It had no capability to take on sustained vehicular traffic....what was worse, this switch was decided barely a couple of days before the start of operations.' P 137. Jagdev. Op cit.

45 ' The mystery was resolved by a havildar of 25 FF who reached Comilla by about 11 AM

PUNJAB nearly met the same fate as 25 FF, when it was refused permission to withdraw into the Laksham defences as reports of Indian forces pouring into the rear were disbelieved. When the Battalion did withdraw, in some confusion, it suffered needless casualties, which affected its cohesiveness.[46] A fortress defence requires a certain amount of aggressive flexibility in the defender, who while withdrawing, is required to delay and cause casualties on the advancing enemy. In both the cases of 25 FF and 23 PUNJAB, withdrawal was denied them until it was too late and the troops either got trapped or withdrew pell-mell. Niazi's contradictory orders seem to have been misinterpreted on account of a rigid mindset amongst his subordinates. The lack of any major resistance during infiltration was a godsend to 'Rocky', who pushed his formations inside.[47] By first light on 05 Dec, 1/11 GR had occupied the vacated enemy defences at Buschi and the enemies lateral communication links had been cut.

Sagat landed near Buschi with a Mi-4 helicopter on the morning of 05 Dec and was briefed by an elated 'Rocky'. He was keen to have the officers of 25 FF interrogated quickly by his intelligence staff and on his return took Lt Col Akbar Baig, the CO of 25 FF and an artillery officer back with him. They were shown all due courtesies, so much so that when the helicopter landed at Agartala, Sagat sent his aide to buy toiletries for them, much to his annoyance. Sagat possessed this quaint notion of chivalry towards a defeated enemy, perhaps a throwback on his Rajput heritage, which disconcertingly emerged from time to time.[48]

After delivering the prisoners at Teliamura and refuelling

---

on 04 Dec.' p173. Salik. Op cit.

46 The reconnaissance for the attack on Chauddagram, which formed the hinge for an advance to Laksham, was carried out by 2/Lt VK Singh (later on General and COAS).

47 It was not all hunky dory as Sodhi testifies. Some units, fighting their first offensive action, were tentative in their approach much to the annoyance of Hira. P 194. Sodhi. Op cit.

48 His courteous behavior, even after the enemy had surrendered, was particularly noticed in Dacca and sometimes adversely commented upon.

the helicopter, Sagat flew off to 8 Mountain Division to land near Sagarnal, the site of a hard fought battle by 9 Guards. There was some shouting by the soldiers when the helicopter landed. It seemed the clearing was mined. Since there was no other suitable patch nearby, Sagat asked the pilots to stay put using the indubitable logic that as the helicopter had not been blown up, it was safe. Meanwhile, there was frantic stirring amongst the troops, watched by a grim faced Krishna Rao, as efforts were being made to create a lane to the aircraft. Sagat watched this agitated commotion for some time with growing impatience and then brusquely stepped out of the helicopter and coolly walked across, followed by his aide, who painstakingly ensured that he walked on the imprints of the General's shoes! The pilots horrified, preferred to remain inside. By the time Sagat returned, a lane had been prepared of planks. Sagat was full of good cheer as the day had gone well for him despite the slow progress. The pilots were not amused and subsequently complained to their superiors. That afternoon Sagat again got Sihota to fly him.

Sagat had landed right amongst the forward troops of 59 Brigade and was briefed by Krishna Rao and Quinn on the grim battles fought by them. The axis of advance was on an indifferent gravel track designed to serve the tea industry along the border. Kalaura and Fenchuganj were nodal centres with important lateral routes linking other towns of Sylhet District. The railway line leading directly to Sylhet had been rendered ineffective and was of little help to the advancing troops. 313 Pakistan Brigade, located at Maulvi Bazaar, was responsible for denying both the axes on which 8 Division was advancing and had nominated a battalion each to deny them. While 81 Brigade, advancing on the Shamshernagar – Maulvi Bazaar Axis was opposed by 30 FF (already much mauled at Dhalai), 59 Brigade was being opposed by 22 Baluch. Krishna Rao was operating under a restriction laid down by Sagat that he would have to give him a brigade by the sixth day and so was in a hurry. He was convinced that he had two brigades facing him while 4 Corps Intelligence were working on the assumption that only a brigade was deployed against his Division.[49] He rightly considered the 81 Brigade offensive more important and had nominated 59 Brigade as the designated Corps reserves. Not wanting to be relegated into a sideshow, he was pushing his commanders to produce results quickly.

22 Baluch had prepared formidable defences before Kalaura at Ghazipur and Kapna Pahar. The former defences were amongst the buildings and tea bushes of the hillocks comprising the Ghazipur Tea Factory with interlocking fields of fire, concrete emplacements, barbed wire and mines. Once the advance commenced the enemy caused some delay and withdrew in depth into the well prepared defences at Ghazipur. Sagat was impatient with the slow rate of advance and Krishna Rao had to ask 'Bunty' Quinn[50] to get on with it. 6 Rajput put in two attacks on 03 Dec but only partially succeeded in dislodging the enemy. By now Krishna Rao, in his own words, 'was annoyed.'[51] The next day he went down to Ghazipur with some difficulty and gave a piece of his mind to the commanders present, especially as the CO had prepared a sand model. He insisted on climbing to a vantage point to get his briefing. He was not satisfied with the forthcoming plans and forcefully told Quinn, "Bunty tomorrow by 6 o' clock I want to hear this is in our hands."[52] Before 6 AM on 5 Dec he got the message that Ghazipur had been captured. He spoke to Quinn, congratulated him and asked him to pass his congratulations on to 6 Rajput. Only then he came to know that the objective had been captured by 4/5 GR. Krishna Rao was surprised

---

49 Both were right in their assumption. Niazi had created the ad hoc 202 brigade out of the strength deployed in the Sylhet Sector. One battalion of 313 Brigade formed the core of this brigade along with two companies of 12 AK (POK) and various para military units. It was expected by Niazi and Majid that 313 Brigade would act as the link between Brahmanbaria and Sylhet and, if required, be able to launch a limited thrust into Tripura. Unfortunately by truncating 313 Brigade, Niazi had left it with no reserves and an inability to influence events.

50 A' quiet man but he had steel in him. He showed good leadership particularly at critical moments.' **Krishna Rao in conversation.** Op cit.

51 'We just can't fail and that attitude I conveyed to all concerned.' Ibid.

52 Ibid.

as 4/5 GR had already had severe casualties at Atgram and asked Quinn why he had employed them. Quinn replied, "Sir, you scared me like hell!" He thus took no chances and put in the Battalion. The first attack was launched by two companies led by the 2ic, who got killed. Col Harolikar, the CO, then led the other two companies and 'after some bloody khukri work through the trenches, Ghazipur was captured though the Battalion suffered heavy casualties and had by now lost seven officers dead and wounded.'[53] Krishna Rao insisted that 6 Rajput should not be allowed to get demoralised and thereafter it remained in the vanguard of the Brigade advance.[54]

Meanwhile, anticipating considerable delay at Ghazipur, Krishna Rao had asked Quinn to move 9 Guards, the third battalion of the Brigade, on a parallel subsidiary axis which would outflank the enemy. 9 Guards commenced its advance on 2 Dec and after clearing some delaying elements, encountered heavy enemy opposition on some steep knolls at Kapna Pahar. A fighting patrol led by Ranawat had a very narrow escape but succeeded in identifying the extent of the well prepared enemy defences. On night 3 Dec an attack from the rear was mounted by two companies led by the 2ic. Just as the attack was going in the troops saw a large convoy of vehicles coming from their rear. With no other option left, the two companies turned round and took up a hasty defence sandwiched between the defences of Kapna Pahar and the reinforcements. The CO now faced a major dilemma. He had only one company with him as his fourth company was still in the Atgram Bulge. He thus ordered a reluctant Ranawat[55] to take two platoons and attack Kapna Pahar. 'With two other frightened volunteer officers, as reluctant as me, we went back on our patrol route, divided two sections each amongst us and launched the attack. Before the enemy finally withdrew my small

---

53 **In conversation with Maj Gen Ian Cardozo at Dehra Dun on 28 Sep 2009.**

54 'They performed gallantly throughout the advance, captured Brahman Bazaar and at Fenchuganj captured a bridge across the Kushiyara River intact by charging across it in the teeth of enemy fire.' **Krishna Rao in conversation.** Op cit.

55 'I was emphatic in telling the CO that I was not a volunteer but he nevertheless nominated me.' **Ranawat in conversation.** Op cit.

force lost seven men in the fighting.'[56] It took nearly three hours of fighting before the defences were captured and required additional troops to move in from a flank. With the capture of Ghazipur and Kapna Pahar, 22 Baluch had been destroyed as a fighting unit. The Battalion HQ withdrew without informing its companies and went out of communication. All cohesion was lost. Ultimately only 50 stragglers made it to Sylhet.[57]

The Campaign up till 5 Dec was more of a slogging match with little scope for manoeuvre as the formations of 4 Corps broke through the crust of enemy defences close to the border. Now the depth beckoned and Sagat fully intended to exploit the disorganisation amongst the Pak units as they vainly tried to recover from the confusion created by Niazi's failed strategy of fighting forward. The nominated fortresses had been denuded of troops and the scramble back to re-occupy them was demoralising the Pakistani units, which had suffered much in the continuous bloodletting going on since Nov.

By 6 Dec, Sagat had started depending completely on the Air OP flights for his travelling, with Gurbax Sihota providing him the flexibility; going where he wanted and landing where he desired. The Pak Air Force had also been knocked out of the skies. Sagat used this day to see the progress of his formations and reconsider his strategy. No one was aware as to what he was about to unleash. Only on 5 Dec night, over a glass of whisky, was Jagdev informed that the axis of advance of 57 Division instead of going southwards towards Maynamati and Daudkhandi was likely to be shifted north westwards and he better go and see what he could do.[58] As he drove through Akhaura, Jagdev gives a graphic account of the utter chaos prevailing and the listless response of soldiers who had undergone tremendous strain over several days of battle. Realising

---

56 Ibid. Ranawat was awarded a Sena Medal for this action.

57 P 165. Salik. Op cit. Subsequently men from two companies succeeded in straggling into Sylhet.

58 P. 148 Jagdev. Op cit.

the enormous engineer effort now required, he got an additional engineer regiment allotted on this route for bridging the several river gaps which were likely to be found up to the Meghna.

Meanwhile the engineers were having an equally tough time on the axis selected by 23 Division. While the indifferent track was urgently being improved and the Dakatia Nala being bridged, 1/11 GR was tasked to head for the nodal centre of Mudaffarganj on the Comilla - Chandpur Road and preferably secure the bridges before they were blown up. The Battalion commenced its infiltration on the night of 5 Dec and amidst light opposition had reached and secured the town by 1 PM on 6 Dec. It was obvious that Pak 39 Division was fighting out of its depth. 53 Brigade was frantically trying to withdraw into Laksham from Fenny and had not succeeded till the morning of 6 Dec. Not really knowing where his units were, Brig Aslam Niazi had told them to harbour for the night. On 6 Dec, Maj Gen Rahim Khan decided to see things for himself and drove out of Chandpur in a convoy of jeeps. He ran into a block established by 1/11 GR at Mudaffarganj. The lead jeep was captured by the Battalion but Rahim Khan managed to turn round and speed back to Chandpur.

It was now that the classic fortress strategy could have come into play. Brig Atif with a battalion plus of troops held an impregnable Maynamati. Aslam Niazi had just about succeeded in getting adequate troops into Laksham. The gap in between these fortresses could have been sealed off, as it was intended to be, with some aggressive action. The Indian infantry units were still separated from their supporting elements and logistic support. This deadly potential was evident when a cleverly placed Pak artillery observer noticed a concentration of vehicles and communication antennas in a small forest at Buschi. 'Around 10.30 AM the enemy guns opened up with remarkable accuracy and caught the Indians in a trap.'[59] Hira had a narrow escape when his jonga was destroyed.[60]

---

59 P. 138. Jagdev. Ibid. See also p 77. Gautam. Op cit.

60 The Jonga had been lovingly modified by the Division EME and had been irreverently christened, 'Rocky's Gondola' by the officers. It seems Sagat was so impressed with it

'A part of the forest caught fire...The track.....got effectively blocked.' There were heavy casualties including the commanding officer of an artillery regiment and large number of vehicles, equipment and ammunition were destroyed. It took three hours to get the track functional again. Unfortunately, Rahim Khan was so shaken up that he barely took any coherent action for the next 36 hours, by which time it was too late.[61]

Shortly after Rocky had his narrow escape, Sagat, landed near his HQ. They had a burly Time-Life correspondent with them who called himself Hermit. While waiting for Rocky they heard the sound of some firing at a distance. To their astonishment Hermit jumped for cover abusing in the choicest Punjabi. Only then did they come to know that his name was Harmeet Singh.[62] Rocky drew up in a ramshackle vehicle looking none the worse for wear despite his narrow escape. Well aware of the potential for damage by the Pakistanis, Sagat reiterated that 83 and 181 Brigades must prevent any Pak attempt to pinch off the infiltration. 61 Brigade, which had been placed under command 23 Division for the break in phase, had reverted directly under control of Sagat and been moved the previous night around Maynamati. They were now to infiltrate to the west and north of Maynamati. Sagat flew onto the Belonia Bulge where he found that the enemy had vacated Fenny and Kilo Force had already made a triumphant entry. Obviously the pressure was telling on Aslam Niazi as he desperately tried to pull in his troops into Laksham.

Sagat now ranged the battlefield with complete impunity, no longer bound by Air force rules, as Gurbax Sihota unhesitatingly ventured or landed the helicopter wherever or whenever Sagat desired. Many a times Sagat would fly kms ahead of the forward troops. Meanwhile, 61 Brigade, spread over nearly 80 kms, had

---

that he had his EME modify his own vehicle on similar lines. **Col Ravi Bedi in personal communication to the Author.**

61 P 175. Salik. Op cit.

62 **Sihota in conversation.** ibid.

started concentrating for its new task by the morning of 6 Dec. Sagat had decided by now that 57 Division could not be diverted southwards as originally planned and would continue with its advance north of Akhaura. To fill the void, 61 Brigade was tasked to infiltrate north of Comilla-Maynamati, move cross country approximately 25 kms, effect a crossing over the Gumti River and cut off the Comilla- Daudkhandi Road at Chandina. This would effectively isolate Maynamati from the West. He expected 181 Brigade to block all approaches into the complex from the east and south. 'Tom', in his typical aggressive manner, had his patrols out up to Burichang and decided to commence infiltration on night 6 Dec itself.

Sagat, while flying back from Fenny decided to visit the Brigade. It was easier said than done as no one knew where the headquarters were located. After landing at a couple of places Sagat unerringly guided the helicopter to the Brigade HQ location. The place was in complete chaos, what with mules being loaded and jeeps being prepared for the advance.[63] Since 'Tom' was not there, the BM, Maj OP Kaushik, apprehensively went to receive him fully convinced that he was about to get a tongue lashing. As Sagat got down he smiled and said, "Hello Panditji, what's happening?" Kaushik replied that they were having lunch. Sagat then asked for a plate and relishingly ate the simple fare. Not a word was said of the chaos around. He asked Kaushik where they expected to be the next morning. He told him firmly 'at Burichang'. Sagat got up saying, 'See you for breakfast then.'[64]

After refuelling, Sagat landed at Akhaura, where he was met by Lt Col Sawhney, CO 10 Bihar. The grim detritus of war was visible; evidence that it had been a hard fought battle. Maj Gen (then Capt) Dipak Mukherjee clearly recalls what happened then. 'We had not slept for two nights, looked awful, were grieving for our officers

---

63 The sight and noise of a helicopter hovering over them in that chaos, so unnerved some of the muleteers that they fired wildly at it, much to Sagat's annoyance.

64 **Lt Gen OP Kaushik in conversation.** Op cit. He joined Tom and Kaushik for breakfast at Burichang next morning.

and men, dead and wounded, looking forlorn. The towering GOC read the situation very precisely and electrified the atmosphere. He hugged anyone and everyone around and though it was daytime had a few bottles of scotch opened and poured a bit in all our glasses, including the men. He then sat on a stool and chatted with us all. He brought a kind of aura and energy and told us to drink to our dead and wounded and not to grieve for them but to glorify them………. He told us of the weak opposition on the other side and that we would never get a better opportunity to avenge our casualties……. "Go, go get those bastards such historic moments come rarely!" His robust clarion call surcharged the atmosphere. What generalship!'[65]

By then Brig ML Tuli, who had been summoned, arrived. His Brigade had been tasked to take up the advance beyond Akhaura, for which purpose they had been pulled out of battle a day earlier to reorganise. Sagat, unhappy at the slow progress, gave a piece of his mind to Tuli. When he returned to Teliamura he had already crystallised in his mind the future course of the Campaign, something which even he may not have anticipated when the War had started. The enemy had been slow to react to his moves and he was the last person to give them a chance to recover.

---

65 **Maj Gen (retd) Dipak Mukherjee, YSM, VSM.** Personal communication.

CHAPTER EIGHT

IV CORPS: THE CROWDED HOUR

> *He either fears his fate too much,*
> *Or his deserts are small,*
> *That dare not put it to the touch,*
> *To win or lose it all.*
>
> - James Graham,
> The Marquis of Montrose

If one looks at 4 Corps operations in perspective it becomes clear that 6 Dec was the turning point when Sagat's decisive actions changed the tone and tenor of the Campaign. If he had followed his Operation Instructions, which were unimaginative and parroted the instructions given by Eastern Command, his campaign would have lumbered along conventional lines, no doubt achieving the objectives and deadlines set out for it. But now his war making instincts were alight with challenging prospects opening up before him. As OP Kaushik succinctly put it, 'While we looked for the next task or phase he was already thinking three steps ahead.' As he reviewed the battlefield, Sagat saw the great advantage that absolute air superiority gave him. He realised that the Pakistani generals, confused by the dichotomous nature of Niazi's strategy, had become tentative in their reaction capability. He saw the advantage that the local population with their support were capable of giving him and lastly he knew that at this stage audacity would pay far greater dividends than a plodding approach against a diffident enemy. By constantly moving around, personally checking up on the actions of units, he had his fingers right on the pulse of the battlefield and was now ready to grasp at opportunities. He had his sights on Dacca and saw no reason why the Meghna should prove an insuperable obstacle.

As the enemy's defences started disintegrating during the Battle of Akhaura, Sagat immediately visualised the potential of an approach on the undecked railway line to Ashuganj and the giant Meghna Bridge. He also knew that once 23 Division punched a hole through the gap between Laksham and Maynamati, it was only a matter of time before the Division reached Chandpur. He was more interested in Daudkhandi, which provided the direct approach to Dacca and was well pleased when 'Tom' Pande decided to commence his infiltration a day earlier. He had already allotted him adequate engineer resources, mules and jeeps so as not to inhibit his advance. As Jagdev says, 'the tracks which were to be used could barely take a loaded rickshaw.... there were two water obstacles.... of 60 feet. And finally there was the Gumti River, with a wet gap of 160 feet. The total length....up to the Comilla- Daudkhandi Road was 30 kms.'[1] However, as he goes on to point out, the engineers were involved with the plan from the very beginning and succeeded in executing it 'with aplomb'. Sagat was to give 61 Brigade little rest as he made them race to the River, while keeping Maynamati at bay.

8 Mountain Division had a slow start as it got held up at the border by the determined resistance of units of Pak 313 Brigade. However, with no reserves, the enemy was rendered nearly ineffective by 6 Dec. Krishna Rao well knew that Sagat's ambitions for Dacca would not be realised without additional troops. He had therefore already warned 59 Brigade. 4/5 GR, which had just captured Kalaura, was ordered to hand over the axis to the EBR and concentrate at Kailashahar.

What of the enemy? On 6 Dec all was not lost to him. In the South, the fortresses of Laksham[2] and Maynamati still stood with enough troops to make life difficult for an overstretched advance towards Chandpur. The Maynamati defences had specifically been

---

1   P 144. Jagdev. Op cit.

2   53 Brigade had withdrawn into Laksham from Fenny on 6 Dec.

designed to prevent any adventurism towards Daudkhandi. To the North, though he had lost the border battles, Maj Gen Majid still had troops to close any doors towards the Meghna. Niazi had created the adhoc 202 Brigade to defend Sylhet while 313 Pak Brigade was the reaction force, which was to move south and hit any offensive going towards Ashuganj. This is what Majid asked the Brigade Commander to do on 6 Dec. There was a flurry of messages between him and Brig Iftikhar Rana, who finally informed him that he would not be able to provide any troops as his units had been decimated in border battles. Majid had thus allowed the initiative to slip from his hands by not catering for any reserves and allowing two good battalions to be destroyed in rigid futile resistance to what was essentially a sideshow.

On 6 Dec, another personality, who had a decisive impact on the Campaign, entered the field. Group Captain Chandan Singh was the Indian Air Force Station Commander at Jorhat with a penchant for the unorthodox. He had no part to play in the War until Eastern Air Command detailed him to train and build up the nascent Bangladesh Air Force. They had two Otter Aircraft and an Allouette helicopter, which were fitted with various weapons and bomb bays. They were positioned at Kumbhigram and carried out clandestine offensive missions deep into East Pakistan, including strikes at Narayangunj and Chittagong. Chandan first met Sagat on 3 Dec evening and for him 'it was quite an experience. He was full of energy, dynamism and go.'[3] Sagat moved him and his Air Force to Kailashahar Airfield from where he targeted the enemy facing 8 Mountain Division.

On 5 Dec, when Chandan was with Krishna Rao, Sagat joined them and informed him that some MI-4 helicopters were likely to be placed under his command. On 6 Dec, Sagat rang him up to say that the garrison at Sylhet wanted to surrender. He was to fly over and accept the surrender.[4] That night, over his customary whisky

---

3 **Group Captain (later Air Marshal) Chandan Singh in conversation with Col Pyare Lal.**

4 There was no indication at all at this stage that Pakistani troops were keen to surrender from any of the fixed defences they were occupying. Sagat sometimes played cards very

in the officers mess, Sagat caught hold of a bewildered Colonel General Staff and ordered him to inform 8 Mountain Division to plan for an SHBO on Sylhet. Now poor Mohinder had never heard of this terminology either at Staff College or elsewhere. Loath to look and sound clueless when talking to the staff of 8 Division, he desperately looked around for enlightenment and was met with a studious aversion of eyes. Sagat watched all this with an amused look for some time and then kindly explained that he wanted 8 Division to launch a special heliborne operation on Sylhet.

Early on 7 Dec morning, Chandan took an Allouette and flew over the Sylhet airstrip. He was just about to land when he was fired upon. He got away through the skin of his teeth and landed at Shamshernagar where he found the 'omnipresent' Sagat. In some indignation he told him of his narrow escape. Sagat 'did not bat an eyelid. It made no difference to him whether I was hit or not. He said, "Well then if that is the case, we must now launch a heliborne operation against Sylhet."[5] He told Chandan that some Mi-4 helicopters (each was capable of carrying 1600 kgs but actually carried much more) were landing at Kailashahar. He was to take charge of them. He was now required to go to Kalaura, pick up 'Bunty' Quinn, the commander of 59 Brigade, and carry out a reconnaissance of Sylhet for a helilanding, which was to commence by 12 PM that day. Sagat had a dog eared copy of the US Infantry magazine, which showed a diagrammatic depiction of a heliborne operation. This he discussed with Chandan and that was it.[6]

Before Chandan arrived, Sagat had already had a detailed discussion with Krishna Rao[7] and it was decided between them that the battalion nominated to carry out the heliborne landing would

---

close to his chest.

5 **Chandan Singh in conversation.** ibid.

6 **Sagat Singh in conversation.**

7 In his memoirs Krishna Rao confirms that he only came to know of Sagat's intention on 7 Dec, when he rang him up early in the morning. P100. **In the Service of the Nation by Gen KV Krishna Rao. Penguin India, New Delhi; 2001.**

be 4/5 GR.[8] This was a surprising decision. 4/5 GR had already fought two bloody battles and was worn out with serious casualties. Nevertheless, it was a consensus amongst them that it would be this battalion. As Krishna Rao aptly put it, 'It was the best battalion in my Division. It had great pride and *esprit de corps*; a feeling that nothing will deter us (sic) and they were prepared to make any sacrifice.'[9] Sagat continued to insist, against all evidence, that the enemy had vacated Sylhet and the operation would be a walk in for the Division. Here he was guilty of some obfuscation. While well knowing that Pak 202 Brigade had unnecessarily dispersed its troops against the subsidiary advances of 5/5 GR from Jaintiapur (in Meghalaya) and the BSF from Charkhai (in the Atgram Bulge), he was more keen to pull troops into Sylhet rather than allow them to be moved southwards as clamoured for by Majid. The heliborne operation was the perfect ploy.

Chandan flew down to Kalaura, where he found 4/5 GR resting in some barracks and preparing to move back. The CO, when informed of the forthcoming task, showed understandable reluctance. Harolikar was a hard man but he was unwilling to have his men made into cannon fodder. 'Bunty' Quinn, the brigade commander, was informed of the urgency of the task. The heliborne operations had to be mounted and completed by sunset. 'Bunty' himself was reluctant to nominate so heavily mauled a battalion but in view of the explicit instructions received that '4/5 GR were to go in irrespective of the state of the Battalion', he had no choice. The reconnaissance was carried out and a landing site close to the Surma bridges was selected. While 'Bunty' was dropped back to get the troops ready, most of whom had never seen a helicopter, Chandan flew to Kailashahar to get acquainted with the helicopter crew. He was most impressed with them. They quickly got ready

---

8 Once this decision was taken it was not possible for 59 Brigade, which was in the process of concentrating at Kailashahar for move to Agartala, to be detailed as Corps Reserve. Krishna Rao persuaded Sagat to delay any decision and subsequently to accept 81 Brigade less 3 PUNJAB as the Corps Reserve instead. The orders finally came into effect on 8 Dec when 81 Brigade was poised to attack Maulvi Bazaar.

9 **Krishna Rao in conversation.** Op cit.

and by 11.30 AM five helicopters had landed at Kalaura.

The Battalion had hardly any officers and it was difficult to get them enthused and ready. However, Quinn got into the act and only by 4 PM could the first wave be launched. Chandan was worried, as before nightfall only two waves were possible. The first landing went off smoothly. When the second wave had landed, Chandan heard the ominous rattle of machine gun fire and found one helicopter could not take off as it had been hit. It was getting dark when the third wave, now in only three helicopters, all of whom had bullet holes in them, took off and dropped the troops without incident at Sylhet. This time the armed Allouettes provided some air cover. By the time they landed back it was pitch dark. As he mentions, Chandan was now in a quandary. He 'had no business commanding this detachment.... no proper night landing equipment. Thirdly, I was not sure of the serviceability of the aircraft.'[10] To his dismay he also found that only three pilots were trained for night flying. There was no other option but to train them and by 10 PM he had succeeded in getting seven pilots operational for the Mi-4 and three for the armed Allouettes. The Bangladesh Otters were also roped in and with the Allouettes provided continuous air cover. The rest of the night the sorties went in with six aircraft. By next morning one helicopter had been shot up and another had to make an emergency landing. It was in one of these sorties that Cardozo, freshly back from Staff College, was lifted into Sylhet. He found the men stoical as ever and Harolikar happy to meet him as now he had someone who could take over the Battalion if something happened to him.[11]

The operation carried on throughout 8 Dec and by the time it

---

10 **Chandan Singh in conversation.** Op cit.

11 "When I landed there it was chaos with artillery, mortar and small arms firing all around. My Johnnies, who had heard I was coming, came looking into the helicopters and on finding me jubilantly said, 'Kartoos Saheb aayo' and carried me on their shoulders. The Battalion was crazy. They did not bother about death or casualties once their enthusiasm was up." **Cardozo in conversation.** Op cit. He was subsequently injured and lost a leg on a mine, which he hacked off with a kukhri to prevent gangrene setting in.

was over, 66 sorties had been carried out with individual helicopters flying nearly 12 sorties – 'almost non-stop flying.'[12] The heliborne operation had succeeded in achieving its objective. Fearful of what the Indian Army intended, the Pak troops made no effort to escape southward. Their frantic attempt to withdraw into Sylhet was heavily interdicted by air. When the BBC announced that a brigade of Gorkhas had landed, 4/5 GR played on their fears and adjusted its deployment to depict a brigade frontage.[13] Despite troops being made available for a counter attack to dislodge the heliborne force, no attempt was made, thus allowing a link up to take place on 12 Dec. It was ironic that there were three brigadiers in Sylhet but none had the determination to remove this fragile lodgement.[14]

On 7 Dec the advance into the depth areas by 301 Brigade of 23 Division seems to have unnerved Brig Atif at Maynamati. While Laksham was now surrounded, the enemy started vacating Comilla. It became imperative that a force be detailed to occupy the Airfield. Lt Col (later Brig) LM Sabharwal had faced difficulties with Sodhi, so Hira put him directly under his command and ordered him to march north cross country for nearly 40 kms and occupy Comilla Airfield with all speed. The Battalion moved without much opposition and reached the Airfield as night was setting in. As Sabharwal mentions, 'we entered the Airfield and I foolishly marched on the tarmac with my men line ahead.'[15] The enemy did not react and the airfield was occupied. Later on the area in the vicinity was cleared after heavy fighting over a period of nearly three hours.[16] Meanwhile, 301 Brigade continued its advance towards Hajigunj well into the

---

12 **Chandan Singh in conversation.** Op cit. Statistics showed 1200 troops and nearly 10,000 kgs of load had been carried. It was obvious that the helicopters had carried more than their authorized weight.

13 **Cardozo in conversation.** Op cit.

14 Pp 167-170. Salik. Op cit. He points out that the troops observing the heli landing kept on looking over their shoulders for reinforcements and firm orders to launch a counter attack.

15 **In conversation with Brig LM Sabharwal at Dehra Dun on 29 Sep 2009.**

16 P 215. Sodhi. Op cit. The enemy lost nearly 70 soldiers killed and wounded.

night. There was hardly any opposition.

True to his word given to Kaushik, Sagat landed at Burichang for breakfast on 7 Dec and ordered 61 Brigade to detail 7 Rajrif to attack and make a lodgement on Maynamati. Sagat has come under criticism by Jacob for showing some kind of fixation for Maynamati, when he was advised to the contrary.[17] It is therefore worth rebutting this. Maynamati/ Lalmai Heights, if held in strength, effectively interdicted the Comilla-Daudkhandi Road as well as the gap between Laksham and Maynamati. By hemming in the enemy, it was imperative to create such a defensive mindset that he would lose any aggressive intent and look to himself. For this purpose, 2 Jat and 181 Brigade were tasked to carry out an effective demonstration against the defences from the north and east respectively, while 7 Rajrif was ordered to put in an attack on Lalmai Heights from the west. Sagat was so confident of the poor state of the enemy that 12 Kumaon, the only battalion left in 61 Brigade's kitty, was ordered to head hell for leather with tanks towards Daudkhandi. By the time the tanks linked up it was 4 PM. By 10 PM the Battalion had come into contact with opposition at Elliotgunj, midway to Daudkhandi.

While having breakfast at Burichang that morning, Sagat received a call from the Army Commander, which developed into an acrimonious exchange heard and witnessed by Kaushik. Aurora had an inkling of what Sagat was up to and told him in no uncertain terms that he was to desist from any attempt to cross the Meghna[18] and head for Dacca as that was not part of his task. Sagat unambiguously refused to oblige going so far as to speak familiarly, 'Jaggi, I am a Corps Commander. I am expected to exploit an opportunity. If an opportunity presents itself to cross the Meghna and give you an aim plus I will take it. I am not restricting you to the East Bank of the Meghna, I am giving you the West Bank and

---

17 P 121. Jacob. Op cit. He has reiterated his criticism in his Autobiography.

18 Aurora's apprehensions were well founded. Crossing the Meghna was a leap into uncertainty as there was no precedence of this kind. The Rhine, which the Allies crossed in World War II, was only 1/3rd the width of the Meghna.

beyond; you should be happy.'[19] The discussion closed with Aurora saying that he would meet him the next day.

Sagat was not in a happy frame of mind when he left Burichang and flew to Akhaura, where he learnt that 'Ben', to set an example, had driven his vehicle ahead of the forward troops of 73 Brigade.[20] Despite that, much to Sagat's irritation, 73 Brigade was not to be hurried. Sagat then caught hold of Brig Mishra of 311 Brigade and asked him to make an outflanking move from the North and head for Ashuganj, thus completely bypassing the waiting enemy at Brahmanbaria. He had something else laid on for 4 Guards and took Mishra and Himmeth on a helicopter reconnaissance along the Meghna.[21] Ben, who was with 73 Brigade, was then informed of what Sagat had in mind.[22] It later became obvious that the failure of Rana to move Pak 313 Brigade southwards was to prove telling for the fortunes of Pak 14 Division.

On the night of 7 Dec, Pak 27 Brigade, which after an orderly withdrawal was deployed to defend the strong point at Brahmanbaria, inexplicably withdrew to Ashuganj. 311 Brigade had by now been collected to make an outflanking move from the north to Ashuganj.[23] The northern flank of Brahmanbaria lay open to encirclement as the heliborne operation on Sylhet had killed any plans of intervention from that direction. As Salik mentions, 'We occupied the Brahmanbaria defences and waited for the enemy

---

19 OP Kaushik in conversation. Op cit.

20 'Ben' was in a towering temper and vented his ire within earshot of those present but Tuli would not be hurried. **Taped video conversation between Brig Mishra and Chandrakant in possession of Author.**

21 As Himmeth recalls, '…..Gen Sagat had a very definite grasp of what he was looking for and constantly directed the helicopter pilot to various areas he wanted me and Brig Mishra to view.' **Himmeth Singh in conversation.** Op cit. 'Himmeth had a completely positive attitude. He would weigh the odds and would never say no. He was most reliable.' **Mishra. Ibid.**

22 Mishra also claims that he volunteered his brigade to Sagat for operations across Meghna. **Ibid.**

23 Verma mentions that all this 'marching and counter marching' enabled the Pakistanis to make a clean break, which had consequences later on. P 90. Op cit.

hammer to fall on the anvil. As before they failed to do as we anticipated and infiltrated from the sides to threaten our rear. We also reacted as before and abandoned our positions......'[24] When he visited Brahmanbaria, Sagat noticed that Majid's 'Command Post... was so well fortified that it was fit for an atomic attack.'[25] The much vaunted strong point, where the lion hearted Majid (he had proved himself as such at Dhalai) was to make his stand, was abandoned without a whimper. Pak troops had demolished culverts and bridges across the Titas and in the organisational chaos, it was unlikely any guns would fetch up in time to support any action against Ashuganj. Nevertheless, Mishra was emphatic in ordering Verma to move his Battalion on an outflanking manoeuvre and reach the Meghna, approximately 8 kms to the NE. He was to interdict any movement from the north as well as attack Ashuganj from a flank during the main divisional attack along the railway line. 10 Bihar was also ordered to make their hook parallel to 18 Rajput, while 4 Guards continued to advance along the railway line.

On 8 Dec, 18 Rajput covered more than 30 kms and reached the Meghna by nightfall, while 73 Brigade made a slow deliberate advance ahead of Brahmanbaria. Unknown to them, while HQ 14 Pak Division had withdrawn across the Meghna to Bhairab Bazaar, Sa'adullah with most of Pak 27 Brigade was still east of the Bridge. That night Mishra ordered Verma to go for Ashuganj the next day, little knowing that shortly he would get caught up in events, which would change the shape of the campaign.

Aurora, perhaps realising that events in 4 Corps were getting beyond his control, paid a visit to the Sector on 8 Dec. His meeting with Sagat was not a happy one and an acrimonious argument

---

24 P 161. Salik. Op cit.

25 **Sagat in conversation.** Op cit. The command post was 'constructed of two and half feet thick RCC walls with an RCC roof and a single door. Outside this RCC structure, leaving a space of two and half feet was a bigger room with a RCC roof and walls. Thereafter leaving a gap of three feet there was a wall of sandbags all around. At the only entrance there was a steel door and to cover the door there was a RCC blast wall; and then another sandbag wall.'

developed between them witnessed by several people. Aurora, rather glumly got into the helicopter, which was piloted by Sihota. They first landed at Fenny and were greeted by a huge reception given by the locals. It was obvious that the people had suffered during the last few months and the breath of freedom felt heady. Thereafter they visited 'Rocky' at his HQ and flew onto Comilla. As the helicopter flew over the Airfield, Sihota suspected that the area was mined. He mentioned this to Sagat, who in his typical cavalier manner smilingly told him that 'I am sure you can land three wheels safely.... I was not too sure whether he meant it jokingly or otherwise but by now we had got so inured to his boldness that without a second thought I landed. By the time both the generals had got down, the civilians who were crowded along the fencing leapt over it and started running towards the helicopter. At that stage one of the mines blew up. Before things got any worse I quickly herded the generals into the helicopter and we took off.'[26] Sihota then located the patch which had been secured by 14 Jat and landed there. A huge enthusiastic crowd immediately collected around them and carried Aurora on their shoulder ignoring efforts by the troops of 14 Jat to keep them at bay. An iconic photograph of this event, taken by Harmeet, was subsequently published in international publications. Taking Sabharwal aside, Sagat prosaically asked him to ensure that all the mines were cleared from the area.[27] After shaking hands with the Jat troops, Aurora, much touched and pleased, got into the helicopter and landed at Agartala.

Over lunch and a visit to Akhaura, Sagat spelt out his plan for subsequent days and managed to convince Aurora. The contours of the battlefield were still shaping up but what Sagat would achieve on 9 Dec, perhaps even he had a nebulous idea. At that moment a message was received from Eastern Command to say that they wanted the Army Commander to return as there were indications (false as it was proved) that the enemy was preparing to throw in the towel. As Sagat saw off Aurora, he was content in at least

---

26 **Sihota in conversation.** Op cit.

27 **LM Sabharwal in conversation.** Op cit.

receiving Aurora's tepid support. He had the measure of the enemy and felt secure in the boldness of his plans.

Meanwhile, Krishna Rao had his hands full. 81 Brigade was poised to attack Maulvi Bazaar on 7 Dec night when Sagat suggested that he delay the operation by 24 hours. That night the enemy, fearful of what was happening at Sylhet, withdrew and Apte's Brigade walked in.[28] The enemy had affected a clean break and Krishna Rao, well aware of the approaching deadline for shedding 81 Brigade, goaded Apte to keep going.

At this stage he was however, more concerned with what was happening to his north where Brig MB Wadke's Echo Sector, spearheaded by 5/5 GR, was advancing very slowly. The CO of 5/5 GR and Wadke were at loggerheads and Wadke had issued him a written warning.[29] Echo Sector was to link up with 4/5 GR at Sylhet but at the rate they were advancing, this was highly unlikely. Sagat had not envisaged the Battalion getting isolated for long and expressed his concern to Krishna Rao.[30] Krishna Rao's Campaign was delicately poised. He was about to detach a brigade and lose momentum, without gaining Sylhet. He also had to nip any attempt by the enemy to withdraw southwards and affect the course of Sagat's grand design for Dacca.[31] It became imperative to squeeze the dithering brigadiers in Sylhet from all directions. So while Apte was tasked to secure the crossings over the Kusiyara, Echo Sector and the BSF were required to tie down Pak 202 Brigade.

---

28 Pp 102-103. Krishna Rao. Op cit.

29 Krishna Rao told Wadke, 'Madhu in war we do not fight on paper. You don't expect him to sit under a tree and write his explanation?' **Krishna Rao in conversation.** Op cit. See also p 105. Ibid.

30 Krishna Rao was unwilling to go back to Sagat and again ask for a delay in the move of the Corps Reserves, which were rightly required at the centre of gravity of the Corps Campaign. On the other hand he was unwilling to allow his operations to be relegated to a sideshow.

31 Sagat characterized the withdrawal of Pak 313 Brigade into Sylhet as a major tactical blunder. He was expecting them to use the steamers and go down the Kusiyara onto the Meghna. Their inability or rather unwillingness to do so effectively hamstrung Majid and reinforced his siege mentality. **Sagat in conversation.** Op cit.

On 8 Dec Krishna Rao visited 5/5 GR and found to his consternation that the Unit had been held up by a series of demolished bridges and was without any engineer assistance. He promptly allotted an engineer company and additional artillery support.[32] Thereafter the Battalion hastened its advance and had closed onto Sylhet by the time of the cease fire.

In the South, 53 Brigade under Brig Aslam Niazi had withdrawn into Laksham in some disorder but by 6 Dec the designated fortress had more than three battalion worth of troops.[33] After the narrow escape of Maj Gen Rahim Khan near Mudaffarganj, the brigade commander was displaying a distinct lack of aggression. However, on 7 Dec, two battalion columns moved out of Laksham for Mudaffarganj. There, in a brisk action against 301 Brigade, they were repelled. While one column was called back the other was ordered to Hajiganj. The ordeal of this column comprising troops of 23 Punjab and 21 POK is well described by Salik.[34] By the time they approached Hajiganj it had already been occupied by 3 Kumaon and 1/11 GR.[35] Without resupply and nowhere to go the column broke up into two and finally surrendered on 10 Dec.

301 Brigade units had fought some sharp actions and by night 8 Dec were well ahead of Hajiganj. With his troops stretched out, without adequate rest and replenishment, Sodhi decided to call a halt for the night and firm in. Meanwhile, there was no end to the ordeal for the injured of the Pak Army at Laksham. On 8 Dec they were loaded on a train, perhaps hoping to ride through to Chandpur. Simultaneously a train was despatched from Chandpur towards Hajiganj. It came under fire and went back. The wounded were

---

32 'The road from Dawki to Sylhet is on a high embankment........bridges over sixteen water courses........the Pakistanis had destroyed every single bridge....5/5 GR........had to fight its way past every water obstacle.' **Sagat in conversation.** Ibid.

33 23 Punjab, 15 Baluch, 39 Baluch and two companies of 21 AK.

34 P176. Salik. Op cit.

35 27 (Poonch) Medium Battery had to turn its guns round 180 degrees and engage an enemy column, which had come within 2000 mtrs of the gun position. P 81. Gautam. Op cit.

unloaded and taken back to the local hospital to suffer through two more agonising, interminable days. Rahim Khan, now realising that the game was up, begged Niazi to rescue him from Chandpur. Salik recollects that Niazi rushed out of his room in 'a dressing gown of red printed satin' and ordered Rahim Khan's evacuation by river.[36] A gunboat was ordered to escort him. It was obvious that the writing on the wall was clear to the military leadership of East Pakistan.

9 Dec, in Sagat's own words, 'was the most exciting day of my life.' If one particular day has to be studied to show as an example of dynamism and generalship, it has to be this day. The tremendous energy, ruthless focus, physical bravery and resolute leadership shown by Sagat on this day, is perhaps unmatched in our history. He well knew that his campaign was on the cusp of a decisive victory and he wanted to impose it through the sheer force of his personality. Though he intended to leave early, Sagat was held up by interminable telephone calls. This time he did not take Sihota as he had other tasks for him.[37] An Air Force Allouette, with two young pilots already infected by Sagat's enthusiasm, flew him on this historic day.

The first visit was to Burichang at 9 AM, where he ordered 61 Brigade to launch an attack on Lalmai Heights with 7 RAJRIF that night. He airily told the Brigade that there were only two companies there and it should be no problem for the Battalion, which had completed a 50 km infiltration move to its assembly area only the previous day. No time for night reconnaissance was given.[38] Sagat here was again guilty of dissimulation. As at Sylhet he deliberately played down the enemy strength to get troops moving.[39]

---

36 P. 177. Salik. Op cit

37 The evening previous he had told Sihota's Flight Commander that he wanted him to rest as he looked worn out. As it turned out 9 Dec was one of the most eventful days in Sihota's life. **Sihota in conversation. Op cit.**

38 'Later when we asked him why he chose 7 RAJRIF, he told that he knew the boys, their morale was high and moreover their Subedar Major (Rampat Ram) had once served under him as an NCO.' **Lt Gen OP Kaushik in an article in possession of the Author.**

39 Sagat had kept his cards close to his chest but he had decided very early that the

He then asked the pilots to take him first to Daudkhandi and then to Chandpur. Without blinking an eyelid they did just that. As the helicopter flew over Daudkhandi it was clear that it had been deserted by the enemy. The pilots then flew to Chandpur. 'I flew over at 3000 feet, 2500 and then 2000 feet to see if I would draw their fire, if not the Bangladesh flags would be drawn out. It so happened that when I was at 1500 feet over the town, I could see that the Pakistani trenches were unoccupied and soon the Bangladesh flags appeared'. Sagat then flew over the road towards Hajiganj. A few kms short of the town he saw Indian troops halted along the roadside. He landed on the road and was met by Lt Col TS Pall, CO of 3 Kumaon and Maj Inderjeet, the Armoured Squadron commander. He was not satisfied with their answers for tarrying on the road and took them up in the helicopter, showed them that Chandpur was deserted, dropped them back and told them to go 'hell for leather.' He also gave instructions to ensure that no ships/boats would be allowed to go upstream without interception.[40] He then again flew rearward looking for Sodhi, without knowing that Sodhi had been summoned to the rear by 'Rocky' who's staff had not permitted him to go forward in view of the movement of Pakistani troops parallel to the road.[41] Not finding Sodhi, Sagat landed amongst the advancing columns of 2 Rajput[42] and told the CO to hurry up and inform Sodhi that he wanted the whole Brigade

---

Comilla-Daudkhandi Road would be the Corps Centre Line. For this reason he had allotted large engineer resources, which surprised even his Chief Engineer. He wanted to doubly ensure that the enemy on Lalmai would have no offensive capability at all. It was only on 10 Dec that he told his staff that they should be planning for supplies across the Meghna for the forthcoming offensive on Dhaka, through Daudkhandi. By then of course, the rail bridge over the Meghna had been destroyed.

40 Ibid.

41 For Sodhi it was a three hour round trip in view of the bridges demolished en route. 'Rocky' had as diplomatically as possible told him that Sagat was dissatisfied with the slow movement of the Brigade. This was a bitter pill. Unfortunately Sagat's impression was reinforced when he flew over Chandpur. Sodhi justifies himself, perhaps rightly so. It's an interesting issue for military leaders to evaluate. There were enemy columns attempting to break through and Rahim Khan was still supposed to be in Chandpur. Pp 222-226. Sodhi. Op cit.

42 The Battalion was loaned from 83 Brigade to Sodhi when 14 Jat was moved to Comilla.

to reach Chandpur before lunch.

Thereafter Sagat flew towards Daudkhandi and landed in front of the leading elements of 12 Kumaon, where he bracingly told the young company commander that there was likely only a section facing him and he should immediately go and occupy Daudkhandi. He landed back at Burichang and met Kaushik, who was asked to ensure that 12 Kumaon commandeer all possible river crafts and await further instructions. He expected a reconnaissance in force to be carried out across the river and be informed of any enemy opposition on the opposite bank. Despite Kaushik's request, he refused to napalm the enemy defences at Lalmai as he was under the impression that Rahim Khan was inside. His quaint notions of chivalry were evident again. After refuelling at Agartala, the helicopter flew to 57 Division.

Stirring things were happening in 57 Division. Sihota recalls that he was preparing for a restful night on 8 Dec when he and his flight commander were summoned by Sagat to the Corps HQ and told to carry out a reconnaissance across the Meghna for a suitable landing zone for a heliborne operation on 9 Dec. That evening Chandan Singh had already concentrated the helicopter fleet at Agartala for, as he was cryptically told, an impending heliborne task. Before departing on his herculean labours on 9 Dec morning, Sagat had a long conversation with 'Ben' on the conduct of a heliborne operation to be mounted by 311 Brigade and 4 Guards. He had already done a preliminary reconnaissance with the Commander and CO on 07 Dec evening. In retrospect it seems amazing how Sagat had initiated three to four parallel preparations for what came to be known as the 'Meghna Air Bridge,' and all this without any of the furious staff activity which always accompanies such complicated operations of war. Chandan Singh recalls that he reached Agartala late on 8th evening and was asked to meet 'Ben', whom he met at Brahmanbaria at 10 PM. He was told that the heliborne operation was to be by a battalion group from Brahamanbaria across the river.⁴³ Without acquiescing immediately, Chandan went back and discussed the matter late into the night with the helicopter pilots. The problem was further compounded as new pilots had to be qualified for night operations. With his typical gung ho attitude Chandan resolved these problems and next morning informed 'Ben' that they were ready but he wanted to carry out an armed reconnaissance first.⁴⁴ Jagdev in some irritation describes how he was left in the lurch by Chandan, who had picked him up and then abandoned him at Brahmanbaria.⁴⁵

Meanwhile, Sihota flew down to Brahmanbaria where he picked up 'Ben', Mishra and Himmeth and took them on a reconnaissance to select a suitable Landing Zone close to the railway line. They were flying over the Meghna, with the bridge to the right, approx 2000 mtrs away, 'when suddenly there was noise of small arms fire. Our whole attention was diverted to looking for the source of this firing. Suddenly from just behind us the bridge blew up. Gonsalves became very concerned.... and by that time we circled round and came to the other side and re-crossed the River....... we then saw some troops withdrawing and tanks with troops mounted on them rushing back. With our complete attention now focussed on what was happening below, we now started going along the railway line. I had inadvertently come down to 400 feet when we heard the sound of firing. Bullets had gone through the rear of the cockpit and I saw Brig Mishra sitting frozen.'⁴⁶ 'Brig Mishra missed losing his head....... three bursts of bullets missing his head by no more than three inches.'⁴⁷ 'Ben' and the others had lost all taste for reconnaissance and asked to be dropped back. Sihota was told rather brusquely to complete the reconnaissance and be prepared to guide the Mi-4

---

43 As Jagdev notes, both Ben and Mishra did not seem much enthused on this day towards what any sane man would have considered a mad venture. P 160. Op cit.

44 **Chandan Singh in conversation.** Op cit.

45 'Then he smiled, a supercilious smile, and said that he was not in a position to fly me...' Jagdev. P 160. Op cit.

46 **Sihota in conversation.** Op cit.

47 **Himmeth Singh in conversation.** Op cit.

helicopters as they brought 4 Guards in.

The incident was viewed from the ground by Ashok Verma and his Battalion who were in the process of going through their own purgatory. 18 Rajput commenced its advance towards Ashuganj and had approached to within 150 mtrs of the Bridge, when they came under withering small arms fire from the embankments along the Bridge. Without noticeable artillery support, the companies wilted as their casualties mounted. It was obvious that the Indians did not anticipate such fierce resistance.[48] Meanwhile Majid, fearful of the Bridge falling into enemy hands, 'pulled a Sittang'[49] and blew it at 10.30 AM. This whole scene was witnessed by Ben and Mishra from Sihota's helicopter and it upset them. Unfortunately, the lack of coordination amongst the Indians became apparent as the plodding 73 Brigade was in no position to launch a riposte along the railway line. Tanks of 63 Cavalry, reached the fighting too late and themselves fell victim to enemy tank and recoilless gun fire. It was obvious that once Brahmanbaria had been abandoned, 'a mindset was created that the enemy was on the run.... it was no longer an advance to contact but more of a pursuit.'[50]

While Sihota returned to Agartala to have his aircraft inspected and refuelled, Sagat had refuelled at Agartala and picked up the flight commanders of the Mi-4 Helicopter Unit, Sqn Ldrs Vaid and Sandhu and proceeded on his own reconnaissance of the Landing Zone across the Meghna. After showing the pilots the areas proposed, Sagat asked the helicopter to return. Up till now he had no idea about the debacle that had befallen 18 Rajput and

---

48 The eastern bank was being defended by most of 27 Pak Brigade under the personal leadership of Brig Sa'adullah who mounted an energetic counter attack which nearly routed 18 Rajput. The complete Battle from the Indian and Pak view point is well explained by Verma in his book. Pp 93-107. Op cit

49 During World War 2, the retreating 17 Division, blew up the Sittang Bridge in Burma while most of the fighting troops were on the other side. This was an unmitigated disaster. In the case of Meghna, Sa'adullah had adequate river craft to get his Brigade across on night 9 Dec. Also there was no vigorous follow up by the Indians.

50 **SS Mehta in conversation.** Op cit. Mishra has similar comments. **Mishra. Op cit.**

also about the fate of the Bridge. However, as the helicopter was approaching the Bridge, a span of the Bridge was clearly visible, collapsed into the River. No doubt disappointed, Sagat was keenly watching the Bridge when he saw an enormous explosion at the silo at Ashuganj. The pilot was asked to proceed closer towards the Bridge and go lower. As it started descending the helicopter was now nearly over the Bridge. At that moment a medium machine gun opened up and straddled the helicopter; bullets went through the controls and hit Flt Lt Sidhu, the pilot. The passengers sitting behind were splattered by his blood and bone splinters. Sidhu collapsed, the helicopter made a dip but the controls were immediately taken over coolly by Flt Lt Sahi the co-pilot. Throughout this period Sagat remained unperturbed, even when a burst shattered the perspex near his head and a bullet grazed his temple like a vermilion mark. He was sitting next to Sahi and half smiling continued to encourage him. Sahi adroitly manoeuvred the helicopter out of range and flew it to Agartala.[51] As the helicopter landed and Sidhu was evacuated, Sagat saw that Sihota had just refuelled his helicopter after his close encounter and was again going to proceed on his reconnaissance. This was an excellent opportunity for a quick conference with Sandhu and Vaid. A tentative location for the landing was decided and Sihota flew off.

While Sahi ruefully inspected the badly shot up helicopter,[52] Sagat commandeered another AF Allouette, which had just been cleared to go to Shillong. He was annoyed and disappointed to find that the enemy had destroyed the Bridge and still held Ashuganj. He flew to Brahmanbaria to meet 'Ben' and assess the implications of what was obviously a debacle. As 'Ben' realised, he was not to be diverted from his primary aim. The heliborne operation was on and was to commence by late afternoon. On Chandan Singh's insistence, it was however, postponed for late evening. The Air

---

51 **Recollection of the Author, who was in the helicopter.**

52 Subsequently 64 bullet holes were counted. Some perforations were discovered in between the passenger seats. The dual controls of the Chetak had miraculously saved the passengers.

Force wanted the first wave to go in just prior to dusk and the balance of the heliborne operation to be carried out throughout the night, as they were apprehensive of enemy interference from Bhairab Bazaar.[53] Sagat met a red eyed and unshaven Himmeth, still looking impossibly debonair despite the scruffiness of his attire. 4 Guards had had no rest as they had been pulled out in the middle of their advance to Ashuganj. The officers and junior leaders were running around and frantically preparing the Unit for the heliborne assault. Sagat then met Ben and Mishra at the former HQ of Pak 14 Division and it was obvious to him that 18 Rajput had been caught unawares and unprepared to face the onslaught of Pak 27 Brigade. Instead of a weak company, as was suspected, there were nearly seven companies deployed in and around Ashuganj[54] while the assaulting troops barely had the support of two weak artillery batteries. Mishra blamed himself for losing focus as he had become more absorbed towards the impending operations of 4 Guards, while 2/3rd of his Brigade was biased towards Ashuganj.[55] To Sagat, Ashuganj had now become a sideshow. He wanted Ben to focus on the heliborne operation and that very night he wanted another unit to go across and contain Bhairab Bazaar. Majid was to be bottled up and allowed no further role in Sagat's relentless march to Dacca. While the most decisive move of the War was about to be played out, Sagat flew back to his HQ, where he finally got some shards stuck to his forehead removed.

Sihota again proceeded on his reconnaissance with further instructions to ensure that the Landing Zone was across any distributaries of the Meghna, near the railway line and outside the range of any artillery pieces at Bhairab Bazaar. He selected a suitable location at a place called Raipura and returned to Brahmanbaria where the flurry of activity had risen to a crescendo. He barely had time to brief the pilots who blithely gave him the heads up.

---

53 **Chandan Singh in conversation.**

54 Three companies worth of 12 FF were pulled out on night 8 Dec for the defence of Dacca. They were encountered by Himmeth when he crossed the Lakhya River.

55 **Himmeth in conversation.**

The Crowded Hour

The first wave of the Battalion mounted on the helicopters, the rotors started and they were off.[56] In Himmeth's words, "As 'Paunchy' and I got into the lead helicopter, we found 'Groupie' Chandan Singh sitting in one corner. I was a little surprised and asked him what task he had to play in the fly in. Back came a most pleasing answer. He said, 'One is never certain if you *pongos* will get out of the helicopter quick enough. I'm here to make sure you do.' I really do think that this personal gesture by the Group Captain, which was in no way called for, was the kind of thing that makes functioning of joint operations........ most conducive to success."[57] It had started to get dark by the time the fly in commenced. Sihota immediately lost visual contact with the Mi-4s and realised that they were flying at different altitudes. Then to his consternation, he found he could not identify the landing zone he had selected, which was nearly 2 kms from the River. In his typical decisive manner, he selected a sandy patch near the River, landed and asked the Mi-4s to follow him. As soon as they had done so he took off and headed back to Teliamura. He was in a cold sweat and did not 'sleep the whole night', any moment expecting some news of disaster.[58] 4 Guards landed at Raipura at 4.30 PM without any enemy opposition, the nearest being approximately 2 kms away. There was some desultory shelling but as most of the shells were landing a km away, the enemy soon gave that up. The fly in continued up to 3 AM by when the Battalion with some light mortar artillery had landed and consolidated itself.[59] The Air Force improvised the landing site with flour and hand held torches and completed its task in 47 sorties.[60]

---

56 'Everything was in such a rush that I had no time to even meet Gp Capt Chandan Singh.' **Sihota in conversation.** Op cit.

57 **Himmeth Singh in conversation.** Op cit.

58 **Sihota in conversation.** Op cit. "When I got up in the morning and we went to the Corps HQ, the first thing the old man told me was, 'Congratulations! Well Done!'"

59 **Himmeth Singh in conversation.** Op cit.

60 **Chandan Singh in conversation.** Op cit. '....the problem was landing on the treacherous terrain of Raipura.....it was only the highest professional skills of individual pilots that enabled us to carry on without a hitch.'

Surprisingly no enemy force ventured out of Bhairab Bazaar to contest the landing. Majid had his own problems. There were only two companies in Bhairab Bazaar when he blew up the Bridge. The rest of Pak 27 Brigade had to make a clean break and withdraw across the River in assorted river craft during the night.[61] By the time the Brigade could consolidate, 19 Punjab ex 73 Brigade had followed on their heels by boats and had started hemming them in from the south. A window for some aggressive action on 10 Dec existed but was never taken. 14 Division was allowed to wither on the vine.

The bewildering series of events from 7 to 9 Dec in East Pakistan seem to have unmanned Niazi, who repeatedly broke down, once pathetically in front of the Governor who was compelled to inform President Yahya Khan of the sorry state of affairs.[62] On 10 Dec, Yahya gave the Governor the authority to handle the situation but this seems to have been rescinded on the initiative of Bhutto, who was trying to galvanise the international community to help Pakistan. At that stage an impression seems to have been created that USA and China would come to the aid of Pakistan. While the situation on the ground continued to deteriorate, Niazi perked up somewhat. However, opposite 4 Corps his strategy had completely unravelled. Both his GOCs had become ineffective. Rahim Khan, escaping through the skin of his teeth from Chandpur by steamer, was attacked by the IAF despite a gun boat escort and injured. Majid with his troops was bottled up at Sylhet and Bhairab Bazaar, twiddling his thumbs.

On 10 Dec, Sagat first flew to Burichang to find out about the fate of 7 Rajrif. The Battalion had put in a night attack without much artillery support as the guns were firing at extreme range and their fire was inaccurate. The first phase at night was successful and the whole Battalion was trying to consolidate on the ridge line. Two company commanders had already been injured. At daylight

---

61 Pp 106-107. Verma. Op cit. He quotes extensively from Brig Sa'adullah's book **East Pakistan to Bangladesh. Lahore Law Times Publication, Lahore, 1975.**

62 Pp 193-198. Salik. Op cit.

they observed two enemy tanks had taken up firing positions to launch a counter attack. The attack was beaten back but the Battalion had started suffering serious casualties. Shyam Singh, the senior company commander on the objective, requested for air support. This was denied as the Air was busy softening up Dacca. The situation was reaching a critical state as the enemy tanks had slowly started trundling forward. The 57 mm recoilless guns with the Battalion were without sights and useless. A troop of tanks allotted to the Battalion for the attack had been left out because of mines. These tanks were now asked to move forward to support 7 Rajrif. However, the troop commander was most reluctant to move until he was compelled to do so.[63] Ultimately only one tank reached the objective and according to Mehta 'was instrumental in turning the tide of battle.'[64]

Sagat was at Burichang and heard the radio conversation going on between Shyam Singh, Brar and Pande.[65] 'Col Brar presented a very damaging picture. He told Tom that I have neither anti tank resources and nor are you giving me air support. If you can't help me I would like permission to withdraw.'[66] Tom now spoke to Shyam Singh and tried to get him to hold on. 'I very respectfully told him..... it is becoming difficult to withstand the fury of the enemy tanks. After a little pause the Brigade Commander asked me that if that was not enough then what exactly I wanted. My reply to him was the same ie to intervene and restore the situation.'[67] Now Sagat was hearing this conversation and he reiterated to Tom that air support was not possible. If 7 Rajrif was not in a position to hold on they had his permission to withdraw. This was conveyed to Shyam Singh but he refused to withdraw. 'It was a most critical moment for

---

63 Out of sheer frustration, the Brigade Commander asked the CO of 7 RAJRIF, Lt Col (later Brig) AS Brar to 'go and shoot the officer.' **OP Kaushik in conversation.** Op cit.

64 **In conversation with Shamsher Mehta.** Op cit.

65 'This was one of the lessons we learnt from Dhalai. We ensured communications remained open and were constantly monitored.' **Kaushik in conversation.** Op cit.

66 Ibid.

67 **Col (then Maj) Shyam Singh, in an article in possession of the Author.**

the Battalion....... Many men had sacrificed their lives..... An equal number were wounded and lying on the objective....... Almost every alternate minute, men were becoming casualties. We were facing this situation not because we had exhausted our will to fight but because the support promised to us had not materialised..... It was broad daylight. We were at a height on the ridge with open fields all around. The enemy was firing from either flanks and anyone caught in the open would be picked up like partridges in the desert. How could we leave behind our dead and wounded...... and above all how were we going to face our colleagues and our kith and kin on return, if lucky enough to survive.'[68] All this conversation was being heard on the radio set by the other company commander and the senior JCOs. It was a 'hard decision, which could have a lasting impact on the history of the Battalion.' At that stage the radio conversation, as narrated by Kaushik, went on something like this;

"Shyam Singh Bhati says 'I am not withdrawing.'

Col Brar: 'I am ordering you to withdraw.'

Bhati: 'Sir I am not withdrawing.'

Brar: 'I will hold you responsible for disobeying my orders.'

Bhati: 'You can hold me responsible but I am not withdrawing. I am sitting in my trenches. Pakistani tanks are in front of me. They are firing at us and I am firing back. They have stopped but the moment I leave my trenches we will be killed. I am not leaving this place'.

Col Brar again says, 'I will hold you responsible.'

Bhati: 'Sir you can continue to hold me responsible but I am not withdrawing from here.'

In my opinion the only man who acted correctly was Shyam Singh Bhati. Everybody had said you can withdraw but the company commander said I am not withdrawing and he was in an extremely

---

68 Ibid.

critical and dangerous environment."[69] At that moment a sortie was returning from Dacca. Kaushik contacted them and though they had no ammunition, he wheedled them into making a low pass over the battlefield, which was indicated by the Battalion. Subsequently, as Sagat had promised, the Battalion got continuous air support till the battle lasted.

Confident that 7 Rajrif would hold, Sagat flew on to Chandpur to a reception by the locals. 23 Division, with the help of tanks and air, had interdicted the withdrawal of the enemy on the Meghna and several boats and steamers had been destroyed while attempting to flee with troops. In one particular savage incident, a steamer was fired upon by tanks and grounded on a sand bank on the River. When a white flag came up a boatload of men from 1/11 GR[70] with an officer went to take their surrender. At that moment a machine gun opened up and killed a soldier in the boat. This incident was seen by the troops of the Battalion who were on the jetty. They got so enraged that ignoring the fact that hardly anyone knew how to swim, they commandeered whatever boats were available and paddled to the steamer, despite efforts by officers to restrain them. The Gorkhas of Eastern Nepal are most fearsome when truly enraged. These troops waded in with naked khukris and inflicted fearsome carnage until their blood lust was satisfied.[71] They had walked and fought for nearly a 100 kms over seven long days. They had also received reports on barbarity being inflicted on their comrades who were prisoners in Laksham. This incident was perhaps the snapping point.

While the surviving prisoners from the steamers were being collected, the column of Pak 23 Punjab, which had tried to reach Hajiganj and was by now in desperate straits, surrendered at Chandpur. Sagat was introduced to the CO of 23 Punjab, Lt Col Ashfaq

---

69 **OP Kaushik in conversation.** Op cit. In the attack the Battalion suffered 35 killed and 87 wounded.

70 One of those rare battalions nominated as the 'bravest of the brave' after the Kargil Operations, as it has an Ashok Chakra and Param Vir Chakra awarded to it.

71 A version is also given by Sodhi. P 233. Op cit.

Syed. He was reported to have drawn two balls on the surrender note sent to him by Brig Bakshi, Commander 181 Brigade. His troops were also reported to have been cruel to Indian prisoners. While 23 Division was not kindly disposed towards him, Sagat showed his typical courtesy (much resented by those present) and passed instructions that he and his men be treated properly. 23 Division had now completed its mission and had to be re-assigned. After a discussion with Hira and Sodhi on the future tasking of the Division, Sagat proceeded to Fenny, where he ordered Anand Swarup of Kilo Force to head for Chittagong.

Sagat then flew to Brahmanbaria where he told Ben to organise his HQ and Division to operate across the Meghna and head for Dacca. The helicopters were to be given no rest and the Titas Channel, leading to the Meghna, had to be cleared to permit steamers, stuck on the wrong side of the demolished Titas Bridge near Brahmanbaria, to start operating. Ultimately two additional engineer regiments were involved in constructing a bailey bridge over the Titas, clearing the Channel and making class 18 rafts to ferry guns and heavy stores across the Meghna.[72] Before he returned to Teliamura, Sagat insisted on visiting 18 Rajput, licking its wounds in Ashuganj, against the advice of Ben. They drove to the town, still under desultory enemy shelling, where Sagat collected the junior leaders of the Battalion and gave them a pep talk. This incident is well described and held out as an example of leadership in the ARTRAC publication on that subject.[73] Verma, feeling bitter about the way his unit had been mishandled, found this talk patronising.[74]

That day troops of 8 Division crossed the Kusiyara River at Sherpur and Fenchuganj.[75] The enemy in Sylhet Sector was now

---

72 Pp 156-158 and p 208. Jagdev. Op cit.

73 Pp 31-32. **Leadership. ARTRAC, Shimla, 1st Edition, 1999.**

74 "…..he seemed mocking us at the way we foolhardily flung ourselves at the Bridge." Major General AK Verma in a personal communication to the Author. That evening when he met the GOC and Brigade Commander in Brahmanbaria, Verma vented his bitterness. They had nothing much to say.

75 Sherpur and subsequently Shadipur were captured by 3 Punjab of 81 Brigade and

effectively bottled up.

On the night of 10 Dec, the defences of Laksham, in the Southern Sector, cracked. Heavy equipment and ammunition was discarded or destroyed and the injured with the attendant medical staff abandoned. The defenders broke up into three columns. While two columns (including one led by the Brigade Commander) succeeded in reaching the Lalmai defences, the column of 39 Baluch got entangled with the troops of 61 Brigade. They were fired upon through open sights by the guns of 23 Mountain Regiment, clashed with a patrol of 12 Kumaon and the B echelon of 7 Rajrif. They even fought a bloody action against the Mukti Bahini and blundered into 61 Brigade HQ where they were engaged by the Defence Platoon. Thoroughly demoralised, they wandered back and offered to surrender to the 12 Kumaon patrol led by Lt (later Brig) Sinha. Meanwhile Tom, driven by Kaushik, reached the location with his badges of rank removed. Kaushik introduced him as GOC Phantom Force (a designation given by Sagat to the Brigade). Lt Col Nayeem the unsuspecting CO of 39 Baluch was led forward and Tom in his typical style told him, "Colonel, I will speak to you later! First you deposit all your weapons in one place and make your men fall in on the other side. I will give you only 10 minutes to do it. After that you come and speak to me." Thus more than a 1000 soldiers of the enemy surrendered to a patrol of 12 men and the flamboyance of Tom.[76]

On 11 Dec, after a visit to 61 Brigade, Sagat went to Chandpur and re-tasked 23 Division, whose brigades were now given separate tasks. 61 Brigade was to be taken under command and with 181 Brigade, the Division was to capture the Lalmai Heights. 311 Brigade was to move to Daudkhandi, cross the Meghna and commence operations for the capture of Dacca. 83 Brigade was to operate in

---

Fenchuganj (that night) by 6 Rajput of 59 Brigade.

76 **OP Kaushik in conversation.** Op cit. He monitored their movement over nearly two days as the head clerk of 53 Brigade, captured by them, told them all he knew. Kaushik knew that the enemy column was nearly at the end of its tether and needed to be dealt with firmly.

conjunction with 'K' Force for the capture of Chittagong. These two brigades would operate directly under 4 Corps.[77] Thereafter, Sagat flew to Brahmanbaria. He was met by Ben and Chandan Singh. Though he was fulsome in his praise to Chandan, he refused to give a respite to the helicopter fleet. 'This time his plan was to lift an entire brigade and an artillery regiment, entailing a total of 150 sorties. Each helicopter had to do 14 to 15 sorties. The human may undertake the mission but the machine might fail. I did not mention this to him, as time was of great essence and these considerations were for subordinate commanders like me to bother about.'[78] While the helicopters were sent to Agartala for a scheduled maintenance, there was a joint briefing of the pilots and officers of 311 Brigade at Brahmanbaria. Sagat also carried out a reconnaissance of Narsingdi with Chandan Singh, going to the extent of foolhardily landing there when he saw Bangladesh flags flying. 'I landed and enquired if there were any Pakistanis and I was told there was one, the manager of the Khuda Baksh Mills and they had locked him up. And so I discovered that Narsingdi was safe.'[79]

10 Bihar was the unit to fly in. The Battalion had a rough time in the Ashuganj battle, where their CO, Lt Col PC Sawhney and Lt Col Verma of 18 Rajput had to personally intercede to prevent their troops from retreating further.[80] The Battalion had concentrated at Brahmanbaria Stadium by night 10 Dec and commenced its fly in by midday on 11 Dec. 'Sorties carried on continuously......... till early morning on 12th. At the end of this massive heliborne operation a total of 1628 troops were landed with their arms....... etc.'[81] Though three helicopters failed en route they were repaired and by the time the operation was over 135 sorties had been carried out. In addition to the infantry, elements of two artillery regiments were also helilifted, the field guns delicately slung under the Mi-4s. With

---

77 **Sagat Singh in conversation. Op cit.**

78 **Chandan Singh in conversation. Op cit.**

79 **Sagat Singh in conversation. Op cit.**

80 P 281. Chapter 24. **The Regimental History of the Bihar Regiment.**

81 **Chandan Singh in conversation. Op cit.**

Sagat personally monitoring, the build up continued relentlessly and elements of 73 Brigade were moved across by steamers on night 11 Dec.

On 12 Dec, 301 Brigade had been given 25 vehicles for concentrating at Daudkhandi. They were to cross the Meghna, firm in across at Baidya Bazaar and thereafter commence operations for the capture of Dacca via Narayangunj. 14 Jat, who were being relieved at Comilla and were moving to Chandpur, were the first to commence their move. Unfortunately the lateral road via Chandina was not functional so the Battalion (two companies were still at Comilla) had to go all the way back to Sonamura in Tripura and then drive to Daudkhandi. It was now 13 Dec and as they were being driven in the lorries, a helicopter landed on the road and Sagat emerged. He encouraged Sabharwal to hurry his troops and then took off. Sabharwal then took a jeep and rushed to Daudkhandi. On arriving there he found Chandan Singh waiting for him. Chandan informed him that Sagat had been waiting for him but had gone back. He was being provided helicopters to go across on 14th morning. Sabharwal asked him 'if I could carry some recoilless gun jeeps in the helicopters. He said 'No!' Then I informed him that I would not like to fly in my whole Battalion by helicopter and would like to take half the Battalion by 'choppers' and half by boat and land there simultaneously about thousand yards or so from each other. And do you know I was very surprised when on behalf of the Corps Commander he agreed. I was astonished that he readily agreed to such a big decision.'[82]

Meanwhile Sodhi went through the painful process of reeling in the rest of his brigade. This would involve skirting the enemy defences of Lalmai, going around Comilla and then on to the engineer track made for 61 Brigade; in between crossing the Gumti on a ferry. He was given only 25 vehicles. Hira had given him a more realistic target of concentrating at Daudkhandi by 16 Dec. Sagat was not willing to accept that and expressed his unhappiness to

---

82 **LM Sabharwal in conversation.** Op cit.

Hira on 13th of the slow progress of the Brigade.[83] Hira readily took the blame upon himself and made his engineers reconnoitre and prepare a track south of the Lalmai Heights. Troops of 301 Brigade moved on this track and by 9.30 PM on 13 Dec, the first lot had reached Daudkhandi.

83 Brigade, which had successfully captured Laksham, was moved south for the capture of Chittagong on 12 Dec. The Brigade was in position behind 'K' Force, waiting to be unleashed. Around the same time, 'Romeo Force' consisting of 1/3 GR and other troops came under 4 Corps for conduct of amphibious operations at Cox's Bazaar. The Force had sailed down the Hooghly into the Bay of Bengal under Naval command and transferred to two landing ships on 12 Dec. The landing, scheduled for 13 Dec, was postponed to 14 Dec. Unfortunately, the whole operation turned into a fiasco. An attempted landing on 14 Dec was badly botched and two men drowned. On the insistence of the CO, the naval commander landed a strong patrol by boat under Capt HS Klair and Lt KJ Singh, which secured the area and cut off any retreat towards Burma. The landing finally took place on 16 Dec.

Chandan Singh was getting very worried about the state of his helicopters and requested Sagat that he be given some time off for maintenance but Sagat was implacable. "He said, 'Chandan, the war is on so let's get on with it."[84] The helicopters started lifting the troops of 301 Brigade during the early hours of the morning on 14th into late at night and then again on 15 Dec. Unfortunately 301 Brigade could not position the troops in time. The sorties thus got delayed and whoever was available was flown in. Part of 12 Kumaon of 61 Brigade, not originally intended to go across, was thus flown in. Despite the best efforts of 23 Division and the growing impatience of Sagat, 1/11 GR, without one company, could only reach Daudkhandi by afternoon on 14 Dec and were flown across by late evening, while a truncated 3 Kumaon (only half the Battalion

---

83 'He looked upset at my not having reached Daudkhandi. Sagat Singh had been looking for me and wanted me to cross the Meghna River tonight!' p 237. Sodhi. Op cit.

84 **Chandan Singh in conversation.** Op cit.

was available) could only be flown in on 15 Dec. By the time the helilift was over, Chandan's boys had done 121 sorties, carried 1209 troops and lifted 38,000 kgs of weapons, stores and ammunition.[85]

By 14 Dec, when Sagat had moved his HQ into Comilla within enemy artillery range,[86] he had succeeded in pushing across the Meghna, 73, 301 and 311 Brigades and Shaffiullah's 'S' Force. It was the greatest improvised river crossing in Indian Military History. Artillery, including medium guns, was either ferried across or taken by helicopter. On that day, after repeated efforts, Shamsher Mehta got his tank squadron across the Meghna, well knowing that if the floatation failed, his tanks would disappear amid the turgid waters. Since the Corps had not been tasked for crossing the River, it had not been dedicated any resources. Against the orders and inclinations of his superiors and doubt and bewilderment of his subordinates, Sagat had literally lifted his Corps and propelled it across one of the mightiest rivers of the world.[87]

Across the river, the units had to improvise or carry everything on their backs as they advanced. The population, poor and without much themselves, gave everything they could. All forms of transport were used from tractors, to rickshaws and diesel locomotives.[88] Sagat recalls that he invariably carried a jerrican of petrol when

---

85 P 567, Chapter 13, History of 1971 War (Bharat Rakshak). Op cit

86 On return to Tezpur, Sagat made a sentimental speech on the Raising Day of the Corps of Signals where he praised the Chief Signal Officer, Brig GS Sidhu and his troops, 'He rose to every occasion, every demand and communications never ever failed. I don't think there is any parallel in history that a corps headquarters moved within enemy gun range as we moved into Comilla.' The Author is grateful to Maj Gen VK Singh for providing a transcript of this speech.

87 For reasons not understood, Jacob has continued to be parsimonious in his praise of Sagat, especially the Air Bridge over the Meghna. Against all evidence he called it a 'token crossing of the Meghna.' P 76. Jacob. Op cit.

88 4 Guards even used a fire engine. Himmeth had to put his foot down when one of his officers was seen sporting a fireman's helmet! **Himmeth in conversation.** Op cit. 'It was a heart lifting sight. Each jawan marching free hand with half a dozen civilians trailing, carrying his rifle, haversack, helmet and an artillery shell and cartridge tucked under each arm.' **Goraya.** Op cit.

flying across as there was always a stranded rickshaw available for him to use to go amongst the forward troops.[89] Through sheer dint of his personality and at times brutal goading, Sagat had succeeded in pushing across an entire division worth of troops across the Meghna, an obstacle considered impassable by the sanguine Niazi. They were now poised from two directions to assault Dacca. Niazi had done precious little to ensure a coordinated and cohesive defence. As Salik says, his ineffectual behaviour more or less forced Maj Gen Jamshed, the GOC of 36 (ad hoc) Pak Division, to take things into his own hands.[90] However by then it was too late.

If a date could be given where a historian could say that the fate of Dacca and East Pakistan was sealed in 4 Corps Sector, it would have to be 13 Dec. In the south, 83 Brigade had concentrated at Sitakund. The advance commenced on 15 Dec. While 'K' Force moved against half hearted opposition on the main road, 83 Brigade traversed a distance of 28 kms over the Sitakund Range and poised itself on the outskirts of Chittagong by 16 Dec.[91] The Brigade subsequently took the surrender of the Pak garrison on 17 Dec.

In the North, 81 Brigade less 3 Punjab had been relieved and had concentrated at Kailashahar on 13 Dec. They were airlifted and moved by road and had concentrated at Agartala on 15 Dec for heliborne operations against Dacca. Meanwhile, 59 Brigade captured Sylhet Railway Station on 13 Dec night in a hard fought action. All area south of River Surma was now in Indian hands. The noose around Sylhet was a strangle hold. To his elation Krishna Rao received instructions from Sagat that he should prepare his division for operations for the capture of Dacca. On 16 Dec the garrison at Sylhet surrendered along with the Pak troops all over East Pakistan.

Ben moved across the Meghna with a bare boned HQ on 13 Dec. Himmeth remembers a helicopter landing near his troops

---

89 **Sagat Singh in conversation.** Op cit.

90 P 202. Salik. Op cit.

91 The Brigade was guided by Lt (later General & COAS) VK Singh, who had reconnoitered the route.

and out stepped Sagat, Ben and Mishra. 'They wanted to know if there was anything they could do to help............ to follow up front line troops, to give them the kind of mental backing; kind of mental support that the commanders up above don't only want you to go off and try something dangerous but are willing with you to share your danger, was a feeling that I as an individual found most gratifying. A feeling which made me believe that with the kind of higher commanders that I had there was no way that the Pakistani's in Bangladesh could stop us.'[92] Sagat pushed the units to move forward regardless of their lack of logistics and physical state. Knowing that the population would neither let them starve or allow them to be surprised by the enemy, he wanted them to push on to Dacca before its defences could be organised. 57 Division advance was on two prongs. While 73 Brigade advanced westwards along the railway line, 311 Brigade was ordered to move on the direct road Bhairab Bazaar-Dacca. 19 Rajrif led the advance of 73 Brigade and found the enemy well dug in on both sides of the Balu River. To their delight they found the rail bridge over the river intact. Two companies were sent across the river from either flank at night, while the vanguard company was asked to engage the enemy from the home bank. These men had by now got intensely frustrated dug in under enemy fire for close to 48 hours and so led by their junior leaders spontaneously charged across the bridge and captured it before the unnerved enemy could blow it up.[93] By 14 Dec, 73 Brigade had contacted Tungi and cut off Pak 93 Brigade withdrawing from Meymensingh. They were then stopped in their tracks to avoid any inadvertent clash with 167 Brigade of 101 Communication Zone, which was moving south. By 14 Dec, 311 Brigade had also contacted the Lakhya River near its junction with the Balu and carried out a crossing over a broad front that night. There was now no obstacle for them before Dacca. That evening 65 Field Regiment fired into

---

92 **Himmeth Singh in conversation.** Op cit. A similar sentiment was expressed by Sihota when he went on his reconnaissance to 57 Division on 9 Dec. The alacrity with which Ben, Mishra and Himmeth volunteered to fly across enemy territory he attributed to the fearless leadership being shown by Sagat. **Sihota in conversation.** Op cit.

93 Mukherjee. Op cit.

the Cantonment, just before a ban was imposed on firing of any artillery into the City.[94]

Meanwhile at Baidya Bazaar, another pincer aiming for Dacca, Sabharwal recollects the ubiquitous Sagat driving out a recoilless gun jeep from a Mi-4 helicopter and asking him about the progress of his operation. 'For a Corps Commander to meet a battalion commander not once but thrice in the face of danger made us feel that we were someone special and he had our interest at heart.'[95] Sagat had already met Sodhi and Hira at Daudkhandi before Sodhi flew across with his Rover Group on 14 Dec. By 15 Dec, Sodhi had the situation in hand with 14 Jat and 1/11 GR leaning on the Lakhya River. 14 Jat had fought a sharp action and suffered a few casualties. Sodhi had taken off his shoes and was 'ruminating' on his plans when Sagat drove up in a jeep. He was not in the best of mood as he had got lost while guiding Sihota and had landed well ahead. Sagat took out his annoyance on the luckless Sodhi. He wanted Lakhya to be crossed that night. The Brigade was then to come under command 57 Division. By morning of 16 Dec, Sodhi got his bridge head. Soon thereafter the enemy surrendered.

Once it dawned on Niazi and his HQ that no help was forthcoming from either USA[96] or China and it was all a hoax to buy time, morale plunged. There were no troops to protect Dacca, which was now a determined target of enemy advance. None of his division commanders were either in a position to send troops or were willing to do so. Jamshed, who had only 93 Brigade (deployed on the Mymensingh Axis) under command, ordered its commander,

---

94 Goraya mentions that on night 13/14 Dec, he used medium guns to fire into Dacca. Op cit

95 **LM Sabharwal in conversation.** As another young officer, a colleague of the Author told him during the War, 'He speaks to you as if you are someone big and not a small fry who does not count. We want to achieve because we don't want to disappoint him.' **From notes kept by the Author.**

96 It is now evident that both Nixon and Kissinger seriously considered actively interfering in the War. A carrier battle group with a marine brigade was kept in readiness for such a contingency.

despite his imploring to the contrary, to withdraw to Dacca. This had disastrous results. The withdrawing troops could not affect a clean break and the block at Tungi further unhinged them. Niazi had already delegated his authority to the Governor and played no decisive part in the closing stages.[97] On 14th the Governor had convened a high level meeting at Government House, when it was attacked by Migs. Thereafter the civil administration ceased to exist and moved into the Dacca Intercontinental Hotel, disassociating itself from the West Pakistan Government.

The option available to Jamshed and his garrison at Dacca was to fight on the streets or surrender. Dacca was no Stalingrad. The fighting strength inside the city consisted of mostly odds and ends, including injured soldiers. They lacked cohesion and even heavy weaponry. Since Niazi had frittered away his reserves in fruitless border battles, there were no headquarters or troops available for an organised resistance. Those that succeeded in trickling in were the detritus of losing battles. The Dacca Cantonment lay to the north of the City and was easily approachable from there. 95 Brigade led by Brig (later Maj Gen) HS Kler was already making a push from that direction. The paradrop of 2 Para at Tangail, in the heart of the major organised resistance by the people, only accelerated the confusion and despondency amongst the Pakistanis. Niazi claims to have removed Majid from command of 14 Division and had put 27 Pak Brigade under command Jamshed[98] but this obviously had no effect, as Sa'adullah neither acknowledged this change of command nor moved his troops for the defence of Dacca. He and Majid[99] surrendered at Bhairab Bazaar on 17 Dec.

---

97 'He rode the chariot of time without controlling its speed or direction.' P 206. Salik. Op cit.

98 P 157. Niazi. Op cit. the remnants of 12 FF were withdrawn for the defence of Dacca.

99 'Gen Majid proved to be a difficult person. We were aware of his reputation (four soldiers of 10 Bihar were found at Brahmanbaria shot dead with their hands tied behind their back)........Gen Majid didn't want to be seen surrendering by his troops.....kept on dilly dallying.....was ashamed that he was contained by one under strength battalion." **Sagat in conversation.**

While Sagat was poised to enter Dacca form two directions,[100] Maj Gen GS Nagra, the GOC of 101 Communication Zone, with Kler's 95 Brigade was pressing down from the north and presented an immediate threat to the Dacca Cantonment. On 14 Dec they came across a road sign in Urdu indicating a road not marked on their maps. In Kler's words, '.... we checked with Qadir Siddiqui (the guerrilla leader), who confirmed it was the Chandra-Savak link road to Dacca. It was then decided to send 13 Guards and 2 Para under command of Brig Sant Singh on that route........ At 2 AM on 16 Dec they contacted the Mirpur defences,'[101] which had been hastily prepared just the previous evening. Nagra sent a note to Niazi (whom he knew since pre-independence days) and was escorted into the Cantonment by Maj Gen Jamshed. There they awaited the arrival of Jacob.[102] The War was over.

The dawn of the first day of Bangladesh Independence found Sagat saddled with a host of problems, which he was not prepared for. The Civil Affairs set up, which was to administer the new country, was yet to be established. The erstwhile East Pakistan administrative services, seen as a hand maiden of the previous regime, were defunct. Pakistani troops in large numbers were concentrated in various cantonments or towns, fully armed but without any wherewithal to guarantee their security against the vengeful population, once they were disarmed. The Mukti Bahini was a lethal mix of armed and unruly gangs out to seek revenge. In the beginning, before the Indian Army units spread out to assist the civil administration, there were unsavoury incidents of 'collaborators' (they included former Razakars, Bihari Muslims,[103] police and administration officials and locals who had worked for

---

100 In a major engineering feet, the medium guns had been ferried across the river.

101 **Brig (later Maj Gen) HS Kler, in a personal communication to the Author.** In his correspondence Kler emphasized that the operations of his Brigade were carried out as per a time table laid out by him during the planning stage and approved by Aurora. This included the paradrop of 2 Para. It is all the more surprising why this axis was neglected in the beginning by Army HQ.

102 Salik brings out the full drama of the closing stages of the War. P 201 Salik. Op cit.

103 Their repatriation to Pakistan has bedeviled relationships between the two countries.

the previous government) being singled out and killed. Tarred by a broad brush as traitors, fearful for their lives, they had either hidden themselves or barricaded themselves into ghettos, prepared to sell their lives dearly. The local political leaders, mostly affiliated to the Awami League, were starting to assert themselves. On the other hand the officers of the East Bengal Regiment also felt that they had inherited the true mantle of liberators.[104] They were just one among many competing factions jostling for control. In one incident, Zia-ur-Rahman, the Commander of 1 EB Brigade, insisted on sitting on the stage when Krishna Rao was to address a large audience of civilians in Sylhet. Though he took it with ill grace, he was firmly told to sit with the other brigade commanders in the audience.[105]

A skeleton Civil Affairs organisation had been set up under Maj Gen BN Sarkar at HQ Eastern Command. A Brig was appointed at Corps HQ and Lt Cols with one to two IAS/IPS officers at divisional level. Luckily, the military officers were all of above average calibre from the Schools of Instructions of the Army, which had been closed down for the duration of the War. Sagat had to immediately bring the situation in Dacca under control as the world media was focussed on it. He also had to pacify Eastern Bangladesh. Thus while retaining 57 Division inside Dacca and its environs,[106] the other troops were dispersed to other sectors, where the units and sub units became the hub for the administrative recovery of the new country. The Engineers and Signal Corps were immediately involved in the urgent task of nation building and tasked to get the communications through. Jagdev drove to Dacca on 17 Dec via Daudkhandi amid scenes of jubilation and chaos.[107] He met the Corps Commander in

---

104 Their own political ambitions and disenchantment was to drastically change the face of Bangladesh politics subsequently.

105 **Personal communication by Maj Gen (retd) KJS Jamwal, PVSM.**

106 61 Brigade was sent to the Chittagong Hill Tracts to round up Mizo Insurgents. However, their leadership had affected a dramatic escape into Burma before the arrival of troops.

107 Pp 222- 225. Jagdev. Op cit.

an office in the erstwhile Pak Eastern Command HQ. It was obvious that the reaction to the uninterrupted frenetic activity of the last few months had started to set in and he, 'looked tired and was reticent, speaking monosyllabically.'[108] Jagdev was ordered to get the mines removed and the airfields operational on priority and had no hesitation in utilising the support of the Pakistan Army and civil engineers.[109] Bridges on major roads also had to be constructed or replaced. It speaks much for the dedication of those involved that the work was completed well before the deadline set for Mar 72. There were constant pinpricks and Jagdev was particularly unhappy with the increasing arrogant behaviour exhibited by Zia, who was resentful of the consideration being shown to the Pak military prisoners.[110]

Sodhi's Brigade was moved out of Dacca to the Noakhali District. These were difficult times as there was a complete vacuum as the Pak Army had moved out on 06 Dec, giving an opportunity to the Mukti Bahini to hold sway. The administration of the area, with the help of former East Bengal civil servants, was set up painstakingly and rule of law established but as he says, 'We may have won Bangladesh its liberty but could never hope to win for it the synthesis of thought and form and the stability it desired.'[111] It was with a sigh of relief that he and his men received orders to move back to India. Lt Col Jagdish Jamwal was responsible for Civil Affairs under 8 Mountain Division. He had the complete trust of Krishna Rao and used his authority, sometimes autocratically, to get his job done.[112] It was a difficult time for people of his set up, which

---

108 P 218. Ibid.

109 'Here I must give credit to the senior Bengali civil servants, particularly the Chief Engineer..........His sense of duty was so high that he did not even go to see his Family but went straight to Dacca Airfield........worked non-stop for three days and nights....' **Sagat in conversation.**

110 Pp 237 – 238. Jagdev. Op cit.

111 P 269. Sodhi. Op cit.

112 'I had complete freedom of action. The first day I met him (Gen Krishna Rao) he said I will not have enough time to devote to you so wherever you go and whomever you meet.......... say Gen Krishna Rao has asked for it.' Jamwal. Op cit.

literally consisted of another officer, a civil servant from the IAS and a couple of jeeps. There was no template and they had to literally play it by the ear. Luckily, he had complete freedom of action and the Civil Affairs hierarchy at Corps and Command exercised minimum control except for receiving the daily situation report. Because officers of his ilk were especially selected, there was no hesitation from their superiors in allowing them their heads. For Jamwal, it worked very well and through persuasion, threats, coercion and liaison he established the writ of law, even though there was an occasional friction with own troops.[113]

In Dacca, Sagat carefully monitored the competing factions. He allowed Pakistani troops to retain their weapons till 20 Dec, while they were carefully concentrated in selected assembly areas. Pakistani troops from outlying areas were transported into Dacca cantonment escorted by Indian soldiers. As Sagat mentions, 'It was a funny sight – with an Indian soldier driving, with two other Indian soldiers in the front seat transporting a bus load of armed Pakistani soldiers.'[114] On 19 Dec, a formal handing over of weapons was carried out. The event was conducted in a two tier manner with officers surrendering their weapons first, followed by the troops at nominated locations. This was fraught with potential for trouble as thousands of Pak troops were lined up in military ranks under the over watch of a handful of Indian soldiers. Sagat was present to see the ceremony being organised under 101 Communication Zone at Dacca Cantonment. One by one, led by their superiors, the officers marched up and placed their weapons as per type and calibre, at specified spots. Subsequently, units marched up and followed suit. Soon large mounds accumulated, which were carefully accounted for. '.....a discrepancy of 5000 weapons was found. I, through Gen

---

113 'We were fighting to get the rights of a nation restored.' Jamwal. Ibid. The dedication of these people has not been properly recognized. One only has to look at utter chaos of post war Iraq and compare it with the smooth transition affected in Bangladesh.

114 **Sagat in conversation.** Op cit.

Niazi,[115] asked the unit commanders to hold an enquiry.'[116] Quite a few weapons were recovered from ditches and ponds by Indian Army patrols, when their location was pinpointed through these enquiries.

Sagat recounts a quaint but tense situation which was created on 17 Dec, when it was pointed out that Begum Mujib had been barricaded in her house in the posh Dhanamandi locality by a detachment of Pak troops, which refused to surrender. With explicit orders from Sagat to ensure that no firing was carried out, Ben proceeded to the site along with a detachment of troops of 14 Guards, commanded by Maj Ashok Tara. Tara found that the Pak army detachment was tactically deployed around the house. An assault would have lead to tragic consequences. Without orders from his superiors, the Pak NCO refused to surrender despite several entreaties. Tara then removed his helmet and weapon and walked out onto the street fully exposing himself. He persuaded the NCO to surrender, guaranteeing the life of his troops. He was taken in to see Begum Mujib and her family members. He found them hungry and dehydrated and provided immediate succour. On her insistence, his troops set up a perimeter and the Pak troops were escorted safely to the Cantonment.[117]

Sagat was worried about the lack of control being exhibited by the Mukti Bahini. 2 EBR had been brought into Dacca and Col Shafi and his troops had their work cut out in preventing them from wreaking vengeance on the Pak Army and collaborators. A British correspondent informed Sagat about the massacre of intellectuals which had been carried out near the brick kilns of Mirpur. He sent troops to the site. The gruesome evidence was all there to see. Jagdev himself recollects mass graves being located all over,

---

115 Sagat's old fashioned notions of chivalry were evident in the respect he showed towards Niazi. This was resented by some officers.

116 Ibid.

117 Ibid.

including Comilla and Sitakund.[118] There was a tendency in some troops to treat the property of the Pak Army as justifiable spoils of war. Sagat and his commanders made sure indiscriminate looting did not take place.[119] Some reports were received and troops involved were severely disciplined; wholesale looting, as alleged by Salik, was never carried out. As troops marched out of Dacca and then out of Bangladesh, their convoys were searched and items, which could not be accounted for, were confiscated. Some reputations were ruined and one Brigadier, who had particularly distinguished himself in the War, was even disciplined by a court martial. Jamwal recollects that Krishna Rao had told him to be particularly ruthless where any looting was concerned and he carried out his diktats implicitly.[120] A major matter of concern for Sagat on 17 and 18 Dec was the threat by the Mukti Bahini to storm the Dacca Intercontinental Hotel and pull out and lynch the members of the East Pakistan Government, who had sought shelter there. The Hotel had been declared a neutral venue by the UN and the International Red Cross and no weapons were allowed.[121] Armed guards comprising Indian Army and EBR personnel were provided for the duration until the Governor and his Cabinet were removed to a secure facility guarded by Indian troops inside the Cantonment. Now that the War was over, the international correspondents, trapped in Dacca, were desperate to move out with their scoops. Sagat was constantly importuned by them whenever they met him. He managed to organise a special aircraft and had them flown out.

On 19th Dec, the Army commander visited Dacca and expressed apprehension about large scale disturbances reportedly taking place, Sagat took him around to show him the masses moving

---

118 P 238-239. Jagdev. Op cit. Both Sodhi and Goraya make a mention of this unsavoury aftermath of the War.

119 Jamwal. Op cit. one of his primary tasks was to check on looting of any assets of the new Government and civilian property.

120 Jamwal. ibid.

121 The Author recollects surrendering his weapon at the checkout desk when he and some friends had gone for a cup of coffee at the Coffee Shop there.

around normally but was perturbed to find that Aurora reiterated this matter from Calcutta. It was obvious that some messages were filtering out unknown to the Indians. Investigations by the CSO revealed that the UN radio link with New York was functioning. The UN personnel had barricaded themselves and a Filipino Radio Officer, under tremendous tension, was sending these alarmist messages from the radio room. 'I discovered that the Chef de Mission, Mr Paul Mark Henry and 16 of his staff had locked themselves in and were transmitting arbitrary reports every four hours.'[122] Sagat had to personally convince him to open the door and promised to have all personnel evacuated. Sagat's relations with his superiors continued to remain frosty and this was made further evident during the visit of Sam to Dacca.[123]

The evacuation of prisoners was to be carried out from 19 Dec onwards. On the insistence of the Bangladesh administration and prominent people, all personnel were thoroughly checked for smuggling out any valuables. According to Sagat, hardly anything of value was found. However, the Bangladeshis insisted that large quantities of gold had been taken out after the crackdown started in March. An investigation through the postal authorities revealed that soldiers had been allowed to send small packages home in the normal course through the Post Office as well as carry a little gift for their families on repatriation. It was possible that these items were taken out then. On the 19th itself, Indian troops not required to pacify the countryside, were ordered to move back to India. It was apt that on that very day the Pak Army started surrendering its weapons and an advance party of the Bangladesh Government arrived from Calcutta. The next day Niazi and the other senior officers were flown out to Calcutta where they were to remain as prisoners of war. On 25th Dec, amidst jubilation throughout Dacca, the Bangladesh Government arrived. Shortly thereafter Advance HQ Eastern Command arrived to take over responsibility from Sagat, who went back to Comilla. Except for particular occasions, he did not visit the capital again.

---

122 **Sagat in conversation.**

123 Sam's charisma was evident the moment he stepped out of the aircraft. Not only was he a hero to the people of Bangladesh, he was held in awe and respect by his own men.

The Surrender Ceremony

After the Surrender with Lt Gen AAK Niazi and Maj Gen Gandharv Nagra

CHAPTER NINE

THE FINAL TRUMPET

Methought from the battle-field's dreadful array
Far far I had roamed on a desolate track:
'Twas autumn; and sunshine arose on the way
To the home of my fathers that welcomed me back

— Thomas Campbell

Sagat returned to Tezpur to a hero's welcome in Feb 1972. He was honoured by the citizens and prominent personalities of Assam. Hoards of congratulatory messages were received from all over the country. When he went on short leave to Jaipur, people from all walks of life feted and congratulated him. His achievements, though not fully known, were acknowledged fulsomely. His family was justly proud of him. Digvijay, just commissioned into 2/3 GR, had paid a short visit to him when he was at Comilla. At first hand he got an idea of his father's military genius when he met the officers who had participated in the Campaign.

Sagat got back to commanding his Corps in the same businesslike manner. Sam, the COAS, paid a visit to inaugurate the Tenga Valley Project, a military cantonment deep inside Kameng. In his brief social interaction with officers, he was fulsome in his praise of Sagat. Nevertheless, it was apparent that a certain tension existed between the two of them. Sagat set himself the same punishing schedule he had always maintained, by visiting his far flung posts and getting the operational plans up to date. His war experience seems to have mellowed him further. Lt Col LM Sabharwal, who had commanded 14 Jat during the War, was posted to the Operations Branch of the HQ. He recollects that he was invited to dinner that evening and next morning the General himself discussed his familiarisation itinerary with him. On one occasion he dropped him off by helicopter at one of the forward most post and asked him to return getting briefed on the way. 'By the time I returned to Headquarters, I knew the area and its operational ramifications like the back of my hand.'[1]

As always, Sagat got on best with the youngsters. In the evenings, whenever he would visit the bar at the mess, he would make it a point to join the junior staff officers and have a drink with them. He knew every Grade 3 staff officer in his HQ and would ask for one of them whenever any minor staff work was required. It seemed his awesome achievements had made him more humble and approachable. Col (then Capt) Subhash Kaushik recalls that Sagat had taken a penchant for playing croquet on the lawns of his house every evening. The foursome would include Sagat, with a senior staff officer, and two young officers from the Staff. The game would be played ruthlessly and seriously but after it was over, everyone would repair to the portico of the Flag Staff House where cold coffee or chilled lime water with light snacks would be served by the efficient Nair, his waiter.[2]

Sagat's coolness rarely deserted him. His ADC recalls that one day he was to go and receive the Corps Commander at the airport, on his return from Calcutta. Unfortunately, the plane landed and Sagat found only the Military Police pilots waiting for him. Without ado he got into the pilot jeep and left for his HQ, which was several kms away. The ADC with the vehicle fleet, which included a venerable Studebaker Saloon, driving frantically to the airport intercepted the pilot jeep on the road and tried to stop it. Sagat ordered the pilot jeep to drive on. Now the road from Tezpur Airfield to the Cantonment is on a high and narrow embankment. With great difficulty the fleet was turned round and the chase began. For several kms the Corps Commander was piloting his ADC

---

1 Personal communication by Brig LM Sabharwal.
2 **Subhash Kaushik.** In conversation.

as he refused to give way. The ADC, now in panic, threatened the driver, a doughty Rajasthani, with the direst consequences if he did not overtake and stop this farce. The driver, Havildar Bhan Singh, with two wheels nearly suspended in the air, overtook and finally succeeded in stopping the Pilots. Without even a harrumph, a grim faced Sagat, completely ignored his aide got into the car and was driven to his house. That evening the ADC was at the bar morosely quaffing glass after glass and being commiserated by his friends, as everyone was certain that his days were numbered. It was then that Sagat walked in, wearing his customary bush shirt and sandals (in complete violation of the mess rules), ordered a drink and started chatting with the youngsters as if nothing had happened. There was no mention of this incident then or later.

Sagat had become the Colonel of 3 GR, during the fag end of his tenure at Shillong. He would have preferred the Colonelcy of the Parachute Regiment but Inder Gill, who was to take over the Corps from him in Tezpur, got the honour instead. This was a disappointment to Sagat and though he remained a proud paratrooper, he discarded his maroon beret and wore a rifle green beret thereon. His Military Secretary, Maj (later Col) J Chanda[3] had obtained a beret for him from England of which he became quite proud.[4] He remained the Colonel of 3 GR for more than seven years and took his job seriously; visiting his battalions often. In 1973 he visited 2/3 GR, which was in Sikkim. Lt Col (later Lt Gen) Raj Anand recalls that Sagat must have wanted to meet Digvijay, but he was patrolling on the watershed and was not called to base. Neither by word or action did Sagat express his disappointment or make a mention of it. As far as he was concerned Digvijay was just another officer of the Battalion assigned on duty.[5] 4/3 GR was located at

---

3 For a strange reason Sagat insisted on calling him James instead of Jayanta.

4 The rifle green beret was obtained from Gieves and Hawkes, New Bond Street, London. It was a size too small but Sagat continued to wear it till he retired.

5 **Raj Anand in conversation.** When Digvijay got commissioned into the Battalion Sagat told Raj Anand, 'I expect you to treat Digvijay the way I treated you and if you remember, I was rough with you.'

a remote area in the Lohit Sub Division of NEFA. Sagat visited the Battalion every few months. The first time, when he went after the War, he gladly presented to the men all the perishables and cartons of cigarettes he had received as gift in Bangladesh. Whenever he visited Calcutta, it was 1/3 GR, located there, which looked after him and where he felt happily at home.

He and everyone in the Corps was expecting that he would get his promotion to an army command as a just reward for his achievements, especially as he had been recognised by the rare award of the *Padma Bhushan*. It thus came as a shock to all concerned when he was passed over for command of an Army and his junior got the appointment he so richly deserved. This unwarranted supersession has remained a mystery. Gossip and rumours had a field day. Sagat's so called womanising, drinking and other allegations had full play amongst ungenerous minds. There was even talk that he had smuggled valuables out of Bangladesh despite the fact that his was the only Corps where the Military Police check posts found little of substance. As a matter of record he had let no transgression go unpunished so much so that he sacked two of his most gallant brigadiers for moral perfidy and court martialled one of them, though with a heavy heart. Lt Gen Depinder Singh, in his biography of Sam, claims to be mystified by the friction between him and Sagat and the lack of recognition given to him.[6] Brig (then Capt) Behram Panthaki was an aide to Sam. During his correspondence with the Author he mentioned that Sam considered Sagat his finest field commander but was constrained in not promoting him because of a discussion he had with the Prime Minister, Indira Gandhi, who seemed to have a file on all the generals who took part in the War.[7]

---

6 P 288. **Field Marshal Sam Manekshaw: Soldiering with Dignity by Lt Gen Depinder Singh, PVSM, VSM.** Natraj Publishers, Dehra Dun, Second Edition, 2003. 'The Chief had excellent relations with the Army Commander, Jagjit Aurora, which continued with almost all formation commanders with one exception; there was always some degree of friction between him and GOC 4 Corps, which is surprising as Sagat's work was admirable and he succeeded in whichever operation he undertook'.

7 It seemed all senior officers participating in the War were closely observed by the

Sagat now knew that he had reached the end of a turbulent road. He had just about a year to retire and requested that he be posted to Mathura, in place of Lt Gen KK Singh, who was being promoted as Army Commander Central Command. KK and Sagat were old friends and though Sagat was senior to him, he was willing to serve under KK as GOC 1 Corps. A posting at Mathura would enable Sagat to settle down at Jaipur and take care of his family, which had remained sadly neglected throughout his service.

Sagat's tenure in Mathura lasted just about a year. It was perhaps the most contented of his service. Kamla, who had remained separated from him since 1965, joined him and his sons would frequently drop in. Veervijay, his third son, was a bit of a scamp and would prove a sore trial to him. Not afraid of his parents, the only person of whom he was wary was Chanda, who would put a brake on his exuberance. Ranvijay and Digvijay were both strapping young officers, the former having joined the Garhwal Rifles,[8] and were a source of joy to their parents. Ranvijay recollects that his Father never interfered in his choice of careers, even when he resigned from the Air Force and joined the Army.[9] The youngest son, Chandravijay, was on the threshold of a promising career in the corporate world.

Meanwhile Kamla, in her own unobtrusive way, was putting

IB, including Lt Gen Aurora, and thick dossiers were maintained on them. **Personal correspondence of Brig Behram Panthaki to the Author.** As an aside, the Author came to know of this as two gardeners employed in the house in which Sagat was staying at Dacca (the former residence of Maj Gen Kazi Abdul Majid), were caught stealing a carpet by the JCO ADC. They were thoroughly beaten up by him and were being handed over to the police, when mysteriously orders were received to let them go and recompense them. Some days later a senior police officer, on secondment to the Bangladesh Govt, sarcastically let the cat out of the bag in a party.

8 The Garhwal Rifles were initially raised out of 2/3 GR. Sagat felt that tradition was well served.

9 Ranvijay was bent on becoming a fighter pilot but that was not to be and he resigned during training. While undergoing the Young Officers' Course at Belgaum he got involved in some hijinks but never informed his father and was willing to face the music when he got into trouble. Sagat remained scrupulous in not interfering in his sons' careers.

her stamp on the life of the families in the Station. Soma Chanda, Jayanta Chanda's wife, best encapsulate the affection she inspired by her open and friendly nature. 'She had an eye for detail, was always cheerful and never threw her weight around though she was the General's wife. She was a mother figure and was never unpleasant to anybody. She was also a great sport.'[10] How great a sport is well illustrated by the sore trial the ADC was to her. Once he was going in the staff car on a personal errand when he found Kamla walking with a parasol on the road in the summer heat. He immediately got out of the car and asked her what on earth she was doing. In her most diffident manner, without a touch of sarcasm, Kamla informed him that she was expecting the staff car to come and pick her up to take her to the ladies club. Since it had not arrived she decided to walk. She asked the ADC to not worry about her as he must be busy with other work! On another occasion, as Soma recollects, the ADC took her to a social engagement a day earlier than scheduled. 'When she realised the mistake she did not throw a fit, nor was she cold and angry but laughed it away.' Her sunny temperament made those who came in contact with her bask in her glow. The personal staff of the General was always treated with great courtesy and his staff officers were accepted as members of the Family and had the run of the house.

Sagat got on with his job in his typical professional manner. The Corps was the premier offensive formation of the Army and he kept it honed up. The units and formations were spread across a vast area of Central India and Sagat travelled extensively for inspections, exercises, discussions and reconnaissance.

It seemed Sagat had hardly any time for personal work. This was all the more urgent as he had no place to settle down once he retired. With typical prescience, Sagat had acquired some scrub land on the outskirts of Jaipur from Major Govind Singh of Khatipura in the late 1960s.[11] He now set about methodically to

---

10 **Personal correspondence of Mrs Soma Chanda to the Author.**

11 Sagat anticipated the manner in which the urban development of Jaipur would take place. His property, which was in a barren area with no facilities in the vicinity, is now in

plan the construction of his house. He knew precisely the material he would require, the shape the house would take and how he would landscape it. The whole project would be implemented like a military operation. He was however, resigned to the fact that no construction would be carried out unless he supervised over it and that would only happen once he retired.

As per his wishes, Sagat's retirement functions were low key. He left quietly in Nov 1974. He insisted that the MES take over the Flag Staff House from him and only after the ADC gave him the clearance certificate did he leave by road for Jaipur. For a short while he stayed in the Cantonment till he had built three rooms on his land.[12] Those three rooms would be his home for nearly three years till the house came up. His family recollects that there were no facilities nearby and every day Sagat would take the car to the market to buy the daily necessities. Sun or rain, Sagat would be standing amidst the construction closely supervising it. Till the construction met his personal rigorous standards, he would not allow the work to continue. There were long delays mainly on account of shortage of money but he and Kamla remained philosophical about it and shaped their post retirement lives accordingly. There were possibilities of him going as a Governor to J&K or accepting the Lieutenant Governorship of Mizoram but nothing came of it as by now Sagat was unwilling to leave Jaipur.

It was not in Sagat's nature to cut himself off from society or responsibilities. He took on several commitments, including running a business, which he subsequently abandoned as his heart was not in it. He became a director in a few companies that included Krishna Strips and Modern Thread. He became President of the Lion's Club of Jaipur and for a time was a member of the Rotary Club. He was also President of a school where he introduced English as a medium of instruction. In 1980, he was persuaded to organise the Centenary Celebrations of the reign of Maharaja Ganga

---

the heart of a posh urban conglomerate.

12 These rooms now pleasingly form a part of the house and enclose a courtyard.

Singh, which he did in his inimitably thorough manner. He became a Founding Director of the Social Security Foundation, which succeeded in persuading the Central Govt to initiate the National Old Age Pension Scheme. Shri TD Khandelwal, his colleague and fellow Director still cherishes the friendship he developed with him and the qualities he displayed.[13] What stood out was that he was a man of his words. His extra-ordinary sincerity to help people surprised many a paper philanthropist. Where Sagat put his mark was as a Director of the State Bank of Bikaner and Jaipur. He helped a large number of people and had branches established in remote areas of Ratangarh, including one in his village.

There are many instances of Sagat going out of his way to help any armed forces veteran who came to him for help or justice. Once he took the bit between his teeth he would not let a matter rest until he had resolved it satisfactorily, even if it involved considerable expense on his part. The case of Subedar Lajja Ram Dhankar, Army Education Corps, is a remarkable illustration of Sagat's qualities. Dhankar had been posted as the Education JCO of one of the battalions of Sagat's Regiment in 1979. Shortly thereafter, the Unit got involved in some serious disciplinary problems. The Army is pitiless in these matters and in one fell swoop removed the entire junior leadership of the Battalion. By association, Dhankar fell into the dragnet and his services were terminated in Oct 1981, despite protestations of innocence. At that stage Dhankar had approached Sagat, who was in no mood to help as he was not convinced that Dhankar deserved help, especially as a visit to the Battalion did not elicit any sympathy for him. Dhankar had a strong sense of grievance and he was determined to clear his name. He filed an appeal to the Delhi High Court in Mar 82, which was turned down. A double bench of the High Court again turned down his plea. Dhankar then knocked on the doors of the Adjutant General (AG) of the Army and others in Govt to grant him justice, to no avail.

---

13 **In conversation with Shri TD Khandelwal at Jaipur on 1 Jan 2008.** 'He was a friend philosopher and guide to us. A soldier who never boasted about himself......... He was gentle and always straight forward..... Our Foundation was honoured by him rather than the other way round.'

What was particularly galling to his honour was the requirement for him to report to the local police station every month like a common criminal. At that stage Dhankar again contacted Sagat, who gave him a patient hearing. He got convinced that Dhankar was innocent and a victim of circumstances caught in the whirlwind of madness which had engulfed the Unit. Sagat wrote several letters to senior officers without any result. Thereafter he met the Adjutant General in 1984 and convinced him to take up a case for Dhankar's re-instatement in the Army. The matter was taken up and rejected by the Govt. The case was taken up again in 1986, to no avail. In 1988 Dhankar went with Sagat to meet the AG who impassionedly convinced him to help Dhankar in getting justice. However, two years elapsed and nothing happened. By now Dhankar had despaired and met Sagat requesting him to give up the case. Sagat refused to do so. He told him, 'to give up without firing the last bullet is cowardice' Thereafter he again met the AG in 1990, who now personally interceded with the Govt and convinced the bureaucrat in charge that justice would not be served if Dhankar was victimised any longer. Dhankar finally got a favourable decision in Aug 1990. Even now he recollects that Sagat would give up his leisure and own interests once he decided to help someone. 'I was neither from his community or social circle. We had no common friends. As a matter of fact I was a constant and bitter reminder of an unsavoury episode which he would have preferred to forget but because the General had this strong sense of justice and intense desire to help, he pursued my case relentlessly even though I was on the verge of giving up several times'.[14]

There were several cases where Sagat intervened, even in the teeth of community opposition, to help young brides and widows.[15] Brig Jagmal Singh recollects that whenever he wrote to the General about a problem he would go out of his way to resolve it. His brother Jeoraj recollects that he took particular interest in widow

---

14 In conversation with Sub Lajja Ram Dhankar at Jaipur on 01 Mar 2009.

15 One instance was of Maj Sajjan Singh, whose daughter's marriage he help annul because she was married under false pretences. He got her a job and then had her re-married.

re-marriage.

Ratangarh is the home of the Bidawat Rathores, a community to which Sagat belonged, as well as some renowned Marwari business families. The area is harsh, arid and unforgiving. It was but inevitable that such a severe milieu would produce a remarkable set of people, resilient and enterprising, able to overcome their limitations and put their stamp on their professions. One of Sagat's oldest friends was Ram Gopal Saraf, the quintessential Marwari business man who made his millions in trade in Calcutta and further East. Whenever Sagat went to Calcutta a visit to the Sarafs was de rigueur. Their friendship survived over the years and after Sagat retired, Ram Gopal asked him to establish a community centre at Ratangarh out of a trust he had established in the memory of his mother. As was his wont, Sagat went about it thoroughly, neglecting his own pressing family requirements. The Durga Dutt Saraf Jan Kalyan Trust Building now stands in majestic red sandstone in the heart of Ratangarh, where community marriages and other functions are performed regularly.

Sagat remained close to his village[16] and its people. Located in a neglected part of the Thar, Kusumdesar had barely any facilities. Cultivation, if any, was at subsistence level and most people kept cattle and goats. Sagat first set about renovating and repairing his ancestral home. For himself he constructed a spartan set of rooms at the rear of his *Haveli*, where he was perfectly contented to stay whenever he visited the village. He created a trust[17] and facilities for carrying out marriages of poor girls. He provided rations and utensils for community functions, a tradition now followed by his family members. He persuaded the PWD to tarmac the road between Ratangarh and Salasar and made it pass through the Village. He set up a branch of the State Bank of Bikaner and Jaipur, in the village as well as in the neighbouring areas. The one man branch at Salasar, which he had established, has now become a main branch and is

---

16 Damyanti, Sagat's daughter-in-law continues to be the Secretary cum Treasurer of the Trust.

17 In the memory of Digvijay.

With Ranvijay

Talking to Digvijay

'doing brisk business in mass remittances from the Gulf countries.' He ensured that a potable water pipeline was laid to the village as only brackish water was available there. A separate electricity line was laid to pump the water to other villages. He was also mainly instrumental in getting a senior secondary school allotted to the Village, which has now become a permanent examination centre.[18] Unfortunately, as Dr Ajit Singh recollects, a plot of urban land, which was allotted to Sagat in Bikaner was encroached upon and he did not succeed in getting it back.

The remarkable qualities of Sagat stood out in his dealings with his family members. Till she was alive, Sagat remained close to his mother and would remain solicitous towards her. He had neglected Kamla during his service to some extent but as her incipient schizophrenia started getting worse he went out of his way to look after her. They were never compatible in the true sense and it was always Kamla, with her sweet temperament, who suffered on account of Sagat's dominating nature and frequent absences. The death of two of her sons further exacerbated her condition. The first major tragedy to strike the Family was the death of Veervijay in a scooter accident in Aug 1975. He was the scamp of the Family but his gay and cavalier attitude made him an endearing figure. His death was a blow to Kamla who always had a soft heart towards him. Sagat's two elder sons were progressing well in the Army and Digvijay, being the senior in rank, agreed to get married, as he put it to 'keep his wayward ways under check.' Sagat went about looking for a bride in his methodical manner. Never one to follow the traditional route of comparing astrological charts, which he spurned, he was more interested in the girl's background and character. After studying several proposals he focussed on Damyanti, the daughter of the Thakur of Bhainsola, near Ujjain. Damyanti had studied at the Maharani Gayatri Devi Girls Public School at Jaipur and Sagat got ample opportunity to verify her

---

18 The Author during his visit to the Village interacted with several of Sagat's kinfolks and other villagers. They were unanimous in saying that Sagat had improved the quality of life in the Village immeasurably, resulting in a large number of youth getting gainful employment. They all felt very proud of his achievements.

antecedents. Digvijay blithely agreed and they got engaged in end Feb 1976. Barely ten days elapsed when tragedy struck. Digvijay was serving with his battalion on the Line of Control near Punch, when the jeep he was travelling in lost control and fell into a canyon, killing him. The Family was plunged into grief. Closest to his Father in nature and abilities, Digvijay was the apple of his parent's eyes. He was Ranvijay's best friend and in his death the Family never really recovered. For Kamla, this double blow was nearly overpowering, while Sagat seemed beaten to his knees.

It took time for them to recover but it is here that Sagat and his Family's character qualities truly shine. He realised that orthodox elements amongst the Rajput community and relatives from both the families would brand Damyanti unlucky. Her parents' chance of finding a suitable groom for her would be blighted. Sagat approached her father and humbly requested him if he would consent to the marriage of his daughter to Ranvijay. True to his nature, Ranvijay had no objection. The union was agreed upon. It was Sagat's natural disposition to please the people he liked and he went out of his way to win Damyanti's heart on behalf of the Family. He found out her preferences and showered her with gifts. On one occasion he even sent a guitar with a book of poems for her with a man all the way to Ujjain. He also corresponded with her regularly. This may sound pretty run of the mill to many who are not aware of the nuances and orthodox rituals required in carrying out marriages within communities where astrological charts are considered sacrosanct and girls are treated as commodities for barter. As Sagat had cut the Gordian knot of such tortuous negotiations during his marriage, he was indifferent to orthodox grumblings and willingly got Damyanti engaged to Ranvijay. The marriage took place in Feb 1977, just eleven months after Digvijay's death. Damyanti came into their lives when the Family was passing through a dark period. Adaptable, impressionable and bubbly by nature, she had a positive impact on them. Kamla took to her immediately and they both revelled in each other's company. Ranvijay, like most eldest sons, had a distant and formal relationship with his father but the marriage brought them closer to each other. The arrival of two granddaughters in Nov 78 and Oct 80 made Sagat and Kamla into doting grandparents. Sagat took Damyanti under his wing and taught her his frugal ways. As she recollects, 'every work for him was either a mission or a project which he planned for and prepared a budget. He remained careful with his money and no expenditure was ever on the spur of the moment.'[19]

As the years went by Sagat became more and more dependent on Damyanti, especially when Kamla's schizophrenia would aggravate. He could not see her suffer and Damyanti would willingly look after her. It was his grand daughters in whom he revelled and they worshipped him. They considered him more of a friend than a grandfather and became very close to him. He taught them to stand on their feet and while he remained a pillar of support he left them alone to find their own bearings. As they recollect, he taught by example and instilled confidence in them to face any situation. He always insisted on a plan to be made before they ventured into anything. He had an excellent sense of humour when he was around them and that's what made him into a good teacher. He insisted they learn to drive and would go around with them to discover anything new which came up in Jaipur.

In Feb 1985, Chandravijay, to whom he was very close, got married to Kum Kum, the daughter of Maharaj Sajjan Singh of Chhota-Udepur. Sagat was very proud of the union and happy for them, especially when they had a son and a daughter. However, by now the years were taking their toll and some alienation occurred between them. Since he did not want his children to have any disagreement with each other, he built a separate multi story bungalow for Chandravijay.

Kamla died in Nov 1996. Her death was a sad blow to the family. While the children adored her, Damyanti and she had become very close. For Sagat, she was a part of his life since he

---

[19] 'He was very particular about how a festival should be celebrated and was meticulous in its planning to the last detail'. **Damyanti in conversation.**

could remember and her passing away was a grievous blow, heightening his loneliness. Only then did the bonds between him and Ranvijay improve and later on they would converse daily on the phone, especially when Ranvijay was posted in the Rashtriya Rifles, in one of the most disturbed areas of Kashmir. The bond became closer still as Ranvijay never demanded anything from his Father and was willing to live without his family, as Sagat's dependence on Damyanti increased. Sagat's health started deteriorating shortly thereafter and Damyanti now permanently moved in with her daughters to take care of him. He, however, still enjoyed his drinks and thoroughly enjoyed the company of his granddaughters Sanyogita and Meghna and they would go out of their way to serve him.

In Jul 2001 he was admitted in the R&R Hospital in Delhi for prostrate problems and though he got discharged, he developed jaundice and got bedridden. In Sep 2001, Sagat was re-admitted in the R&R Hospital. The end was near but even till the end he neither lost his sense of humour or courtesy, even going to the extent of making an effort to get up, festooned though he was with tubes, whenever a lady visited him at the ICU. He died on 26 Sep 2001 and was cremated in Jaipur. The complete who's who of Rajasthan, including the Chief Minister and his predecessor, turned up for the funeral. For reasons incomprehensible, the Para Brigade, the organisation closest to his heart and a stone throw away at Agra, sent no representative. There were very few dry eyes as the great oak of a man was slowly consumed by the sacred fire. Independent India has not seen the like of him.

The Govt of Rajasthan and the City of Jaipur honoured his memory by naming a prominent road after him. A post script was provided to his life story, when Ranvijay and Damyanti were invited by the Bangladesh Govt in Mar 2013 and his achievements were praised fulsomely by the President, Prime Minister and the Bangladesh veterans of the 1971 War. In his own country he may have been forgotten but for those whose lives he changed, he remains enshrined in their memory.

CHAPTER TEN

THE LEGACY OF SAGAT: GENERALSHIP

Soldiers require training, whereas generals require an education

- Paraphrased from 'The Generals' by Thomas Ricks

More than four decades have elapsed since the 1971 War. The Indian armed forces continue to operate in a dynamic environment where threats and challenges continue to mutate and evolve. Since the basic principles of warfare remain universal, one may ask if there is any relevance of Sagat's legacy to generalship today.[1]

Wars are conducted at four levels. The political level is normally the domain of the national leadership. The military gets progressively involved at the strategic, theatre/ operational and tactical levels, the last being solely its purview. The political strategy in furtherance of the national interests has to consider various geo-political, social and economic implications before a nation goes to war. At this stage the strategy is decided by the country's leadership with the military standpoint being closely factored in. A successful military strategy will require the military chief working in close coordination with the political leadership and the war council.[2] This strategy will always be nuanced by compromises at the political level as it's rarely that a

---

1 Gen Rupert Smith has said, 'War no longer exists. Confrontations, conflicts and combat undoubtedly exist all over the world.' P2. **The Utility of Force: The Art of War in the Modern World.** Penguin, UK, 2006. He argues that a paradigm shift in our thinking is required if generalship is to become relevant in the 21st Century.

2 '....... The relationship between the political and strategic levels must always be close, to the point of engaging in a continuous discussion which does not stop until the overall aim or purpose is achieved.' Smith. Ibid. In India the War Council can be equated with the Cabinet Committee on Security.

nation's resources are adequate to meet all the combined threats. The theatre is the level below. This is confined to a geographical region. For example, in the case of India, the Eastern Command is a distinct theatre of operations. The theatre commander has to dovetail the political and military strategy in his context before he works out an overall plan that orchestrates his forces to achieve the objective set out for his command. The theatre or operational level is the link between the strategy devised and the tactical battles required to be fought to achieve the overall aim. Thus during 1971, Mrs Gandhi set the stage at the political level by arguing India's case at the international fora. She also concluded a defensive treaty with the Soviet Union. This constrained any adventurism, which may have been contemplated by US and China until it was too late. The Army Chief, in coordination with his service counterparts, the bureaucracy and the political leadership worked out the military strategy. He had the rare gumption of putting his foot down on the implementation of this strategy. The Eastern Army Commander thereafter had to work out the overall military plan for conduct of operations in his theatre. His corps and field commanders then got their hands dirty and fought the tactical battles to achieve the strategic aim.

A historical survey of the Indian strategic process shows that things have not always worked out that smoothly. A cautious, short sighted and occasionally shallow consideration of the National Interest has had a tendency of constraining strategy and restraining bold tactical action. As one writer has put it, 'politics is the enemy of strategy'.[3] There have been many occasions where junior leadership and blunders of our opponents have saved the day for us.[4] From 1947 onwards an analysis will show that our military operations, hamstrung by a cautious strategy, have not generated the dynamism in the battlefield, which creates a momentum for victory. Because

---

3 P.97. **Lessons in Disaster by Gordon M Goldstein** (Times Book; New York, 2008). As quoted in **Bob Woodward, Obama's Wars.** Simon & Schuster; UK, 2010. P. 129.

4 'The young officer is sitting in the cusp where his desire to can and will is being stopped by must not lose.' Mehta. Op cit.

a large part of our borders continue to be flexibly defined, the need to protect them has created a defensive linear mindset which further inhibits any audacity in vision. When not an inch of territory must be lost, mobility in ones thought process gets severely limited. Even a man like Sam, when given command sof 4 Corps, post 1962, was most hesitant in provoking the Chinese.[5] This frame of mind remained when he was COAS, adversely impacting operations in Bangladesh.[6] While commenting on the Army's misadventure in Sri Lanka, one general called the operations 'pre-determined, straight jacketed, predictive and reactive.'[7] Stephen Cohen has brought out that over the years the failure of bureaucracy, deleterious politics and marginalized military has compromised any effective long term strategic planning.[8]

Sagat's relevance lies in the fact that within this detrimental environment he succeeded. While he was a master of tactical operations at the highest level, he simultaneously understood the operational art and the requirements of theatre level strategy. Like so many in this book have testified, he was always a few steps ahead of the others. He had that unique 'ability to envision the end state and orchestrate time and resources to meet that end state.'[9] He is also the only corps commander, independent India has produced, whose accomplishments have sustained international scrutiny.

There are certain qualities in Sagat's personality which made him constantly rise above the shackles which constrained original

---

5 P 430, Palit. Op cit.

6 The advance of 101 Communication Zone from the north was denied the necessary momentum as Sam was unwilling to pull out one of the brigades facing the Chinese. The Chief of Staff Eastern Command, endorsed by none other than the Director of Military Operations, had strongly recommended this reinforcement.

7 **Lt Gen SC Sardeshpande** in his book **Assignment Jaffna.** Lancers, New Delhi, 1992. The General resigned after the Conflict was terminated.

8 P 90. **India: Emerging Power by Stephen P Cohen.** Oxford University Press; New Delhi; Second Impression, 2003. The **Economist** in its issue of 30 Mar 2013 has expressed the same views, though it holds the military equally culpable.

9 **Personal correspondence of Brig UK Dhar to the Author.**

thinking. The Goa Operations, a walkover in many ways, saw him refuse to remain on the peripheries and lead his brigade to a successful victory. He was aware of the tactical realities on the ground, knew the ability of his own troops, led from the front and was supremely confident of himself. The last quality made him bold at all times. As the BGS of 11 Corps, he quickly realised the portents of the coming conflict and tried to improve the Corp's operational readiness. In Sikkim, he understood that the Indian Army was incapable of a physical riposte against any Chinese aggressiveness as it had no wherewithal to do so. Ground, if lost was lost forever, as the border had not been delineated. He thus insisted on dominating the watershed, inspiring his troops to face the Chinese with confidence and respond to any effort to occupy Indian territory.[10] It was Sam's astute judgement of his character that he put Sagat in charge of operations in the Mizo Hills, where he succeeded in controlling the insurgency to manageable levels. However, it was in command of 4 Corps that Sagat really came into his own. During the planning process itself he realised the flaw in the theatre plans and set his sights on Dacca.[11] He established a logistical infrastructure in one of the remotest corners of India; stage managed his Corps and when the time came launched it in a brilliantly executed manoeuvre through some of the most difficult terrain. He was knocking on the gates of Dacca, an objective not given to him, within a fortnight.

When the Maharaja of Bikaner presented Sagat with the biography of General Robert E Lee, it seems he was perspicacious in understanding Sagat's character. Lee, despite being on the losing side, is considered the pre-eminent general of the American Civil War. In addition to his splendid bearing and invariable courtesy, he stood out for his fair dealing and willingness to share hardship.

---

10 During this period India forever lost control of the Jelep La Pass, which was held by a neighbouring division.

11 **Maj (retd) Chandrakant Singh, formerly of 4 GUARDS,** in a personal communication to the Author has claimed that Squadron Leader Sandhu, of 110 Helicopter Unit had informed him that as far back as 19 Sep 1971, Sagat had warned him in confidence to quietly train his pilots for HB operations, especially at night.

What was conspicuous was his great courage and hands on role in the conduct of battle. His imperturbable figure, like that of his favourite general, 'Stonewall' Jackson, was always present at the point of greatest danger. Sagat obviously followed his example in many ways. Despite being shot at several times he never exhibited an awareness of jeopardy. As Marshal Maurice De Saxe has mentioned, 'The first of all qualities is courage. Without this the others are of little value since they cannot be used.'[12] All great military philosophers have repeatedly emphasised on this quality, which is essential for generalship. Sun Tzu, Clausewitz, Jomini, JFC Fuller, Churchill and a host of other modern writers have all stressed upon this greatest of all attributes. From courage is born resolution, boldness, confidence and endurance. As Senator John McCain has said, 'Courage is the enforcing virtue, the one that makes possible all the other virtues...... Without courage all virtue is fragile: admired, sought after, professed, held cheaply and surrendered without a fight.'[13] John Keegan, the doyen of military historians, has mentioned that all commanders must have the courage of 'conspicuous participation in the dangers that confront the lowliest soldier most keenly.'[14]

Once officers grow senior in rank the importance of moral courage increases exponentially, until right at the top that's all that counts. As Gandhi demonstrated repeatedly, physical courage without a moral backing is of very little use.[15] In May 2007, Lt Col Paul Yingling, while serving in Iraq, wrote a seminal article in the US Armed Forces Journal, which brought out the crass deficiency in

---

12 P 294. **My Reveries upon the Art of War by Maurice de Saxe. Edited by Brig Gen Thomas R Phillips in the Roots of Strategy.** Natraj Publishers, Dehra Dun. First Indian Edition, 2003

13 **In Search of Courage by John McCain.** Fast Company. Issue 86, USA, Sep 2004.

14 P 365. **The Mask of Command by John Keegan.** Penguin; UK, 1988.

15 'Courage has no moral value in itself, for courage is not in itself a virtue. Vicious scoundrels...........may be brave. To describe courage as a virtue, we speak of moral courage...' Extracted from **At the Same Time by Susan Sontag. Picador, USA; Dec 1967.**

moral courage amongst American Generals.[16] Lack of moral courage slowly erodes the very structure of the military edifice so that it becomes a plaything of the bureaucrat and the politician.[17] It leads to discontinuity in policies and procedures. It effectively stymies all attempts at reform. Surrender to ignorant bureaucratic oversight in professional military matters wears away organisational values and structures. In this deteriorating climate, genuine futuristic planning gets badly affected. The armed forces are thus doomed to be organized and equipped to fight today's wars with yesterday's structures. Sagat established a reputation for moral courage, which was hard to ignore. It also became difficult to sideline him because of his professional calibre, which gained him adherents among his superiors. It was normal for him to dominate his environment, whether it was as BGS 11 Corps or while confronting his Army Commander with a change in plans during the 1971 War. Such officers being rare in the Indian Army, those who succeed tend to do so despite going against the grain. What was more important is that Sagat also created a climate of candour in his command, which encouraged his subordinates to voice an opinion without fear of being put down.

Ambition is the spur which takes a man to the greatest heights. A talented man without ambition is likely to be a poor leader. Ambition breeds energy, drive, professionalism.[18] It generates a burning determination to excel and take up a challenge. Clausewitz considered this an essential attribute. In 1977, Charles C Moskos advocated the Institutional/ Occupational Theory[19] wherein he

---

16 **A Failure in Generalship by Lt Col Paul Yingling.** Armed Forces Journal, May 2007.

17 In a talk to the students of the US Naval Academy in Apr 2010, the then Secretary of Defence, Robert M Gates repeatedly emphasized on moral courage which 'must serve the greater good.'

18 Gen Newman in his study of generalship has carefully linked ambition with professionalism and dedication. P. 244. **What Are Generals Made Of. By Maj Gen Aubrey 'Red' Newman, USA (retd).** Presidio Press; 1st Edition; Feb 1987.

19 **From Institution to Occupation: Trends in Military Organisations by Charles C Moskos.** Armed Forces and Society 4, No 1, 1977. See also **Military: More than Just a Job. Edited by Charles C Moskos and Frank R Wood.** Brassey's; USA, 1st Edition, 1988.

clearly differentiated between careerism and its negative fallouts, as opposed to traditional institutionalism. The latter is essential for the well being of the armed forces. As Moskos points out, an 'occupational' oriented military officer will only work for the organization as long as his personal goals are in sync with it; once they diverge his ambition will drive him to look after himself. As the pressure of command builds up, such people develop a 'zero error syndrome' born out of a paranoia created out of fear of failure. They tend to go into a box of self deception which colours their attitudes towards their subordinates and superiors.[20] One of the most adverse aspects of careerism is untrammelled ambition, which does not care for institutional integrity. Since career competitiveness is very high in modern armies, ambition has become a dirty word and a scapegoat for those left on the wayside. No achievement is possible without ambition. Without the taint of careerism, ambition ensures a sense of duty, responsibility and a desire for excellence. This negates the shoddy shortcuts required to claw one's way to the top.

Like all the best generals, Sagat had this intense desire to achieve. No better example can be given than the manner by which he succeeded in overcoming the handicap of coming from a vernacular background, when he joined the Army. In a short span of less than six years he reached the apex of a junior officer's military achievement by entering the Staff College at Quetta. And he was from a state force unit, which communicated in Marwari! There is no doubt that Sagat was very ambitious. He exhibited this quality from the very beginning and left no stone unturned to prove himself. As pointed out by Lt Gen Raj Anand, this ambition was always tempered by a sense of personal integrity and professionalism so that at no stage could Sagat be accused of careerism, with all its negative connotations. A key to understanding Sagat's personality can be derived from Norman Dixon who, in his book

---

See also **Getting a Grip on Careerism by Maj Michael L Mosier, USAF.** Airpower Journal. Summer 1988.

20 All aspiring senior officers are advised to read **Leadership and Self Deception by the Arbinger Institute.** Tata McGraw Hill, New Delhi. 3rd Reprint, 2008.

The Psychology of Military Incompetence clearly differentiates between an 'authoritarian' personality and an 'autocratic' one.[21] Sagat, because of his supreme confidence, was definitely autocratic but this autocracy was qualified by an extraordinary degree of approachability and lack of ego. Junior officers, who interacted with him, have all testified to his innate humility in this book. The 'authoritarian', on the other hand, is normally a careerist, highly rigid, hierarchical, sensitive, humourless, excessively concerned about his status and afraid of criticism.

Maj Gen JFC Fuller in his influential study on British generalship during the Great War stipulated that physical fitness be considered one of the three major criteria for a successful general.[22] Saxe, while laying down three important pre-requisites for a general, has mentioned good health as one of them. So has Wavell who called it 'having the robustness to stand the shocks of war'. Poor health or debility, on the other hand, can have a disastrous impact on a campaign. This is best illustrated by Napoleon's defeat at Waterloo and Gen Elphinstone's effect on the catastrophic First Afghan War. Historians have blamed a serious stomach ailment to Napoleon's poor decision making, while Elphinstone's weak and indecisive nature has been attributed to his age and poor health. Lt Gen BM Kaul commanded his Corps for a while from his bed during the 1962 War. Bahadur Shah Zafar was approaching senility when he was asked to lead the 1857 Revolt. With his large frame and craggy face Sagat was the picture of rude health. Coming from the hard, unforgiving, rural background of the desert he could withstand great strain for long periods. A very physical man when he had to be, Sagat could manage continuous stress without any effect on

---

21 **On the Psychology of Military Incompetence by Norman Dixon.** BI Publications (An Associate of Jonathan Cape). New Delhi, 1976. The story of Townshend of Kut is particularly apt as it describes an extraordinary gallant junior leader metamorphosising into an incompetent general.

22 **Generalship: Its Disease and Cure: A Study of the Personal Factor in Command by Maj Gen JFC Fuller.** Createspace Independent Publishing Platform. Reprint Edition, Sep 2010. Patton was so impressed with this book that he distributed copies of it to his colleagues and subordinates.

his health. During the 1971 War he maintained a hectic pace for months on end. The Indian borders are along some of the harshest terrain in the world and a general must be at the peak of physical and mental fitness if he is to lead troops effectively.

Frederick the Great, ruler of Prussia from 1741 to 1786, has specified the qualities required in generals in a written directive to them, which is considered a classic of war.[23] There is one quality he calls 'Coup D'Oeil', which literally means a quick glance. It is the ability to make a swift judgement based on an immediate assessment of the terrain and the situation. It is possible that some people are born with this indispensable trait but most of us have to learn through hard practice and study. People from a rural background have this quality to an extent but it is not enough and has to be acquired in the field and under tutelage. Edgar Puryear Jr, in a study of more than 150 four star generals felt that all brilliant generals had a sixth sense for the opportune moment in battle.[24] It's a priceless asset which enables one to see a situation develop and plan several moves ahead. No wonder Shamsher Mehta called Sagat the 'great chess master' and OP Kaushik saw repeatedly that he was always ahead of the game. As the situation in Brahmanbaria developed, Sagat realised its potential and changed the tenor of the Campaign. Sagat proved that written instructions were just pieces of paper once a battle was joined. Without this quality of grasping the moment based on quick assessment and a boldness of vision, a general is doomed to plod along allowing opportunities to slip through his fingers.

John Keegan wrote the Mask of Command highlighting the need for a general to mask his true feelings and present a different confident image of himself. In times of stress the troops gain strength and confidence from the indomitable attitude displayed by the commander. As he led a despairing retreat from Burma during World War 2, Field Marshal William Slim kept his fears to himself

---

23 **Instructions of Frederick the Great to his Generals, 1747.** Op cit. Phillips.

24 P.17. **Marine Corps Generalship by Edgar F Puryear Jr.** National Defence University Press. Washington DC; 2009.

and showed a resolute face to his troops. As Frederick the Great put it, the general 'should be constantly on the stage and should appear most tranquil when he is most occupied, for the whole army speculates on his looks, on his gestures, and on his moods.'[25] Newman goes so far as to say that a good general must be 'mildly schizophrenic' and have a split personality.[26] The senior one gets the greater is the need for the leader to be phlegmatic and show an imperturbable facade. If the leader gives way to his moods, is excitable, gets despondent when adversity strikes, he will infect his army with his mood swings. Barbara W Tuchman, the famous historian, in a lecture to the students of the Army War College, USA, mentioned that steadiness of temperament is essential for success in senior command.[27]

Sagat exuded confidence wherever he appeared. It seemed he knew exactly what was required to be done and his subordinates, whatever their rank, looked up to him to resolve their difficulties. Mehta remembers that people instinctively knew that here was one man who could 'address your problems.'[28] During the Battle of Dhalai, the only time during the War when people looked doubtingly at Sagat, he showed nothing but an implacable attitude, though those that knew him were aware that he was personally appalled by the high casualties the units were suffering. His actions during that period were enough to send a signal to his command and his superiors that he would not stand faintheartedness or lack of will and application amongst his officers and troops. Brigadier Shiv Yadava, who knew him well, realised then and there that the time had come for him to create some backbone in his command as Sagat would not bend. This is perhaps the only instance of Indian post Independence History that a brigade commander led troops into the attack against a conventional defence. Sagat drew a thin line between dissimulation and intelligence. Whether it was the

---

25 P. 346. Phillips. Op cit.

26 P. 270. Newman. Op cit.

27 **Barbara W Tuchman. Parameters.** Army War College; 1972.

28 Mehta. Op cit.

enemy strength at Sylhet and Maynamati or whether gingering up the troops for a difficult task, he sometimes obfuscated the intelligence picture. He kept his vision for the capture of Dacca close to his chest so that his superiors only came to know, when presented with a fait accompli.

It is not enough for a general to know the basics of warfare. He has to reach a level of intellectual attainment which makes him stand head and shoulders above his peers and officers. This is only possible if he studies in breadth and depth the nuances of his profession. This may include academic subjects which outwardly may have no relevance to military life. Only then will he be able to have the vision to put things in a strategic perspective and break the chains of convention. Yingling, commenting on the disaster of the American occupation of Vietnam and Iraq, felt that visualisation of the larger dimensions of war required an 'intelligent, creative and courageous generalship,' which was only possible if senior officers held advanced degrees from civil institutions and avoided the deadening effect of conformity.[29] Tuchman felt that 'senior command in battle was the only total human activity because it required the equal exercise of the physical, intellectual and moral faculties.'[30] Jonathan Gifford, in a historical study of leadership, listed out eight skills and abilities that a leader must have. Two of them, 'Boldness of Vision' and 'Creativity' are only possible through intellectual attainment.[31] It should come as no surprise that the US Marine Corps, one of the most professional and elite organisations of the world, emphasises the importance of reading in its officers. Puryear goes so far as to say that the 'consensus of 150 four star generals of all the services is that experience and study are the keys.... those who were avid readers were superior in

---

29 Yingling. Op cit. it is no coincidence that Gen David Patraeus, who is considered the most successful soldier of the decade (despite his sexual peccadilloes), holds an advanced degree from Princeton University. It is also worth noting that 80% of the Chiefs of Defence Staff in UK have held a degree from either Oxford or Cambridge.

30 Tuchman. Op cit.

31 **History Lessons by Jonathan Gifford.** Marshal Cavendish; Singapore, 2012.

depth and perception to those who were not readers.'[32] To develop sound military judgement an officer needs to learn 'how to think rather than what to think'[33] and that can only come about by strict intellectual rigour.

Sagat was a self made man who rose above his surroundings through sheer hard work and a will to achieve. As a young officer, his willingness to learn from the Army and his superiors was evident in all his activities. Col Mohan Singh, who served with him in Iraq, even comments on this somewhat disparagingly. In Bikaner, as his brother Jeoraj points out, he scoured the State Library and read voraciously. He had an enquiring mind, which grasped the essentials of any subject quickly. He then had the ability to apply his knowledge correctly. His retentive powers enabled him to go into issues in the minutest detail. During the build up phase of the 1971 War, his grasp of the intricacies of the corps logistics kept his subordinates and units on their toes. When officers were not aware of heliborne operations he understood the potential and technical details of their conduct. He constantly challenged his engineers to come up with innovative methods to hasten his build up and advance. Though not involved in theatre level planning, his knowledge of the operational art unerringly comprehended the geo-strategic importance of Dacca.

Though there are several other qualities essential for generalship, I will mention only one more as it showed an ambiguity in Sagat's behaviour. That quality is of ruthlessness in dealing with subordinates. Sagat sacked no one though there were several weak links in the chain. Sun Tzu has emphasised on this quality going so much as to say that showing compassion is a negative quality in a true commander. To succeed he must be strict in his dealings. Newman calls it having 'steel in the soul.'[34] Keegan says, 'Coercion

---

32 Pp. 230 & 287. Puryear. Op cit.

33 P. 355. **The Generals: American Military Command from World War II to Today by Thomas E Ricks.** Penguin; New York, 2012.

34 P. 247. Newman. Op cit. 'Chin is as important as the brain.'

is an essential component of command.'[35] The ruthlessness referred to here comes out of strength of character, a quality which Jomini highlights. Machiavelli elaborates on it by saying the ruler must have the fortitude to take the tough decision. Only if ruthlessness is born out of careerism does it negate the ethos of the army. Ricks in his detailed analysis of American generalship, points out that the fortitude to sack commanders who were not up to the job disappeared after the Korean War. Mathew Ridgway was perhaps the last general in the American Army who exercised this prerogative ruthlessly. 'If you don't sack you micro manage.'[36] Ricks maintains that the nadir of US generalship was attained when an authoritarian, insecure General Ricardo Sanchez succeeded in command in Iraq. The inability to sack makes a commander forego an essential responsibility to his command, where he should expect the highest standards from his subordinates. By not sacking one is accepting the fact that second or third rate leadership is acceptable. What is worse, the senior officer is passing on the buck to his superior, who in the case of a three star general would be a politician. As Lt Gen Chiman Singh mentions, Sagat was far too compassionate a figure to be really ruthless. This reputation sits oddly on a man who insisted on Dhalai being repeatedly attacked. The fact remains that though Sagat had an implacable will to get the job done, he was strangely unwilling to relieve those who he thought did not measure up to their jobs. He thus had to tolerate plodders and personally intervene at a lower level to get things moving. Some of these officers subsequently rose to senior ranks.

As the shape of warfare changes, the Indian armed forces will continue to face a test of their abilities, both organisationally and environmentally.[37]

- The South Asian security environment remains dynamic with

---

35 Keegan. Op cit.

36 P. 13. Ricks. Op cit. For a more balanced view see **Quality of Command by Robert H Scales. Foreign Affairs; Nov/Dec 2012**

37 P. 154. Cohen. 'On the whole India has been a status quo power.' An unwillingness to rock the boat or show an iron fist has had a toxic effect on our policies.

several potential flash points of conflict. These range from Islamic extremism having the possibility of conflagrating; non delineated northern borders and the threat from a resurgent China; poor domination of the seas and finally, internal fissiparous tendencies.

- The marked reticence amongst the political authority to get the armed forces involved in the highest levels of strategic decision making has had a harmful effect on force structure and perspective planning.[38]

- The changing face of conflict has created a continuous war amongst the people[39] and limited the utility of conventional forces. Umberto Eco has stuck his neck out to say that war making has itself become outdated 'because the existence of a society based on instant information, rapid transport, and continuous intercontinental migration, allied to the nature of the new technologies of war, has made war impossible and irrational.'[40]

- The improvement in communications and computing power has changed the dimension of war. It has brought its raw vulgarity right into every ones drawing rooms. By 2019, as per Moore's Law, a $1000 computer would have greater intelligence than the human brain. As Keegan puts it, war is like a disease which has a 'capacity to mutate, and mutates fastest in the face of efforts to control or eliminate it.'[41] Eco elaborates on this by saying that war 'is no longer a serial intelligence system' but a parallel one; like a neural

---

38 As a contrast one may compare the sheer intellectual rigour exercised by the political leadership and Pentagon in the US, when both planning for the 'Surge' in Iraq in 2007 and the troop increase of 2009 in Afghanistan. The President did not take a decision without consulting a wide range of serving and retired military officers.

39 This is the very premise of Rupert Smith's Book 'The Utility of Force.' Conventional conflict will become rare while combating extremism, insurgencies and rebellions will be a continuous process. The armed forces need to adapt to this reality.

40 P. 6 **Five Moral Pieces by Umberto Eco.** Vintage. London, 2002.

41 P. 72. **War and our World by John Keegan.** Vintage. London; Jun 2001.

network, difficult to control or predict as there would be a 'multiplication of powers in play.'[42] Ultimately war becomes circular and self devouring. Afghanistan and Iraq have seen a proliferation of civilian contractors taking over military responsibilities. It portends a grim mercenary futuristic nightmare.

The armed forces are a mirror to the society from which they spring. Indian society is in the crucible of change, requiring imaginative solutions to attract the youth. The officer class is no longer the province of the privileged few. In a democratic, capitalist society, lured by the riches of mammon, careerism is commonplace and it becomes difficult to inculcate those values that motivate men to follow their leaders in harm's way. It becomes more difficult when there is a contradiction in the enrolment pattern of soldiers and their officers. While most soldiers still come from a traditional rural background, the officers are from an urbanised, middle class milieu. In addition, the fighting arms are still deeply rooted in tradition, something which is new to the urbanised young officer whose aspirations and principles of upbringing may be different. The problems facing the armed forces senior management is how to inculcate nay enforce the values of an age gone by which looked at the military way of life as a calling rather than an occupation. Populist government policies by rulers emerging from a society which is undergoing a tremendous sociological transformation sometimes go in the teeth of principles which the military extols. However, there is very little choice. Military societies, by their very nature, are insular and have to follow a higher calling because its leaders have to motivate and command men to face grave danger and die if necessary. Surprisingly, the Indian junior leadership has time and again withstood this test and sacrificed itself leading men in forlorn hopes. Unfortunately, some of these idealistic young officers transmogrify into typical careerist, authoritarian figures, unable or unwilling to challenge either the erosion of values or dilution of ethics. As they rise to the top, it is in their nature to

---

42 P. 14. Eco. Op cit.

always imagine themselves threatened by their peers. It makes no difference to those who have perpetrated this commercialisation of society as they see no contradiction in their environment and that of the military. Thus it falls upon the armed forces to sustain their own values.

A survey by the Author amongst a cross section of senior retired and serving officers have underscored these deficiencies. A patriarchal state of mind, hierarchical and authoritarian in nature resists any challenge. This creates a 'zero error syndrome,'[43] where even an innocent exercise in initiative is taken as a challenge to authority. Sagat's life and career is a suitable guide for those who seek to bring about changes, more in sync with today's organisational ethos. The recommendations being given in the subsequent paragraphs are based on the synthesis of qualities, which Sagat embodied. They are essential for success in generalship.

There is a need to look holistically at the selection and promotion process. The role of the psychologist, which has been somewhat diluted may be reviewed in the selection of the officer candidate. He must be used as a scientific tool in first, selecting the right youngster and then, to evaluate him as he grows in rank. The fine line between careerism and institutionalism is required to be identified and rectified in the leadership before it corrodes the soul. The right type of youth may not be eager to join the armed forces, nevertheless the selection process must not be vitiated on account of careerism.

There is also a flaw in the promotion process. The armed forces are a steep pyramidal, hierarchical structure. Competitiveness, professionalism and ambition should get the cream on top. Unfortunately these words now seem to be equated with careerism. In addition, lack of moral courage has upended the promotion reviews as most officers are graded 'above average' or

---

[43] Shamsher Mehta went so far as to write a letter to all commanding officers allowing them to make mistakes as long as they were not repetitive. It made little difference. Op cit.

'outstanding.' Conversely, the fear of the confidential report makes mediocrity the norm. As an officer rises to the top rungs of the military hierarchy, his competence and competitiveness sometimes make an unhealthy mix.[44] Scales, who wrote the official history of the first Iraq War, goes so far as to suggest that the, 'winnowing process for the selection of general officers begins around the grade of major,......'[45] This process though followed in the armed forces has been compromised by the confidential reports, which have undermined this selection process. Once an officer reaches the highest ranks, it should not be age and seniority which decides his position but his competence. The large numbers of cases doing the round of courts have only proven that the armed forces are still struggling with this conundrum. As Ricks has warned, armed forces can ill afford to be either patriarchal or kind at such levels and they definitely must not abdicate their responsibility to the political and bureaucratic leadership. A survey of the corporate sector will show that executives at the level of Deputy General Manager (rough equivalent of a brigadier) display an extraordinary degree of professionalism at a comparatively younger age because the market place is an unforgiving arena and an authoritarian figure would have no place in it for long. Corporate HR practices are moving far ahead of the armed forces. It may not be a bad idea to select a cream of our officers, say at the Lt Col level and let them spend a year in the corporate sector.[46]

The military training institutions are the backbone of the culture and philosophy of the armed forces. They turn out officers competent in running units and sub units in a challenging professional environment. Beyond that they seem to be struggling in encouraging original ideas. The training institutions must create

---

44 'If you are married to the *anda, danda and jhanda* you are no use to man or beast.' Mehta. Op cit. The General is metaphorically referring to careerism, authoritarianism and the trappings of power.

45 Scales. Op cit.

46 It is possible that some of these officers may get infected by the 'occupation' virus and the lure of lucre. That risk has to be taken and while safeguards may be instituted, the best officers would always be organizationally motivated.

an academic environment or tie up with academic institutions where officers with right gifts are specially selected to 'earn an advanced degree in the art of war' or a related subject. Thereafter they should be posted to a school of instruction where they are given 'time to reflect on their profession.' Barrenness in military thought will condemn our armed forces to fighting the next war with the tools and thought processes of the previous one. Officers of Sagat's calibre need to be identified early and encouraged to develop their thinking on original lines rather than have them constantly struggle to rise above their environment. The impact of the AV Singh Committee[47] has affected the overall performance of the Army. Now a major's job is being performed by a colonel, perhaps one who has seen his best days and is looking forward to educating his children and resettling himself. This weakens the overall professional climate. The training institutions are obviously not spared. It is however essential that original thinkers and creative professionals get posted to these institutions to keep the intellectual climate churning

There is also an immediate need to improve the cerebral environment at senior level, especially as the face of war is rapidly changing. The armed forces do not discourage intellectual attainment but senior officers seem reluctant to put in the hard work required to improve their scholarly horizon. A study of military history clearly indicates that lacking clear vision, a senior officer will indulge in narrow minded thinking that would cloud his strategic ability. A certain degree of mental nimbleness and out of the box thinking is essential in view of the uncertain security environment. Without a degree of academic attainment, rationality in intellectual thinking would be missing as it seems to be happening now. Like the British Army of old we would remain doomed to prepare for a war which would have disappeared into the pages of history. People like Sagat would become rarer still. As Scales puts it, 'The challenge for

---

[47] The implementation of the AV Singh Committee Report unilaterally promoted officers in appointments which were earlier tenable by one or even two ranks below. Such 'bells and whistles' do nothing for institutional building.

the military is not tough love but rather figuring out how best to attract, retain, nurture and groom the strategic talent it needs from top to bottom.'

Sagat's generalship was in many ways heroic in nature. His actions, more than his size made him a larger than life figure. The power of his personality and his sure touch made him stand out in any company. 'His leadership was not only on the battlefield but over the minds and will of the people he commanded.'[48] There are no Spartas anymore. The armed forces of a country, because of their Spartan ethics are considered as the last bulwark against chaos and destruction. It was fortuitous rather than inevitable that Sagat commanded 4 Corps in the only decisive campaign in India's post independence history. 'Cometh the hour cometh the man.'[49] Sagat's personality and generalship; his courage and sense of duty is a fine example for those who want to follow difficult and untrodden ways. As Alfred Lord Tennyson, said of another great soldier, 'The path of duty was the way to glory.'

---

48 Cardozo. Op cit

49 P 4. **Heroes by Lucy Hughes-Hallett.** Alfred A Knopf, USA, 2004. As per the Author heroes are never paragons but they stand unique in their times.

BIBLIOGRAPHY

Primary Sources Only

Books

Anand, Dev. *Romancing with Life.* (Viking, New Delhi, 2007)

Army Training Command. *Leadership. (ARTRAC,* Shimla, 1999)

Arbinger Institute. *Leadership and Self Deception.* (Tata-Mcgraw Hill, New Delhi, 3rd Reprint, 2008)

Bhaumik, Subir. *Insurgent Crossfires.* (Lancers, New Delhi, 1996)

Bihar Warriors: The Official History of the Bihar Regt

Campbell, Joseph. *The Hero with a Thousand Faces.* (Paladin, London, 1988)

Ed. Cardozo, Maj Gen Ian. *The Indian Army: A Brief History.* (USI, New Delhi, 2005)

Chadha, Lt Col Vivek. *Low Intensity Conflict in India: An Analysis.* (Sage, New Delhi, 2005)

Cloughley, Brian. *History of the Pakistan Army: Wars and Insurrection.* (Oxford University Press, Karachi, 2nd Edition, 2002)

Cohen, Stephen. *India: Emerging Power.* (Oxford University Press, New Delhi, 2nd Impression, 2003)

Ed. Dhavala, Rajan R and Bhattacharjee,S. *Human Rights and Insurgency: The North East India.*

Dixon, Norman. *On the Psychology of Military Incompetence.* (BI Publications, New Delhi, 1976)

Eco, Umberto. *Five Moral Pieces.* (Vintage, London, 2002)

Gautum, Col PK. *Operation Bangladesh.* (Manas Publications, New Delhi, 2007)

Gifford, Jonathon. *History Lessons.* (Marshal Cavendish, Singapore, 2012)

Hanzhang, Gen Tao. *Sun Tzu: The Art of War [Translated by Yuan Shibing].* (Wordsworth, UK, 1993)

Hughes-Hallett, Lucy. *Heroes.* (Alfred A Knopf, UK, 2005)

Jacob, Lt Gen JFR. *Surrender at Dacca: Birth of a Nation.* (Manohar Publishers, New Delhi, 1997)

Kaplan, Robert D. *Warrior Politics.* (Vintage, USA, 2003)

Khasru, BZ. *Myths and Facts: Bangladesh Liberation War.* (Rupa Publications, New Delhi, 2010)

Kaul, Lt Gen BM. *The Untold Story.* (Allied Publishers, New Delhi, 1967)

Karim, Maj Gen Afsir. *The Story of the Indian Airborne Troops.* (Lancers, New Delhi, 1993)

Khera, PN. *Liberation of Goa and Other Portuguese Colonies in India, 1961.* (Historical Section, Ministry of Defence, Govt of India Press, Nasik, 1974)

Keegan, John. *Mask of Command.* (Penguin, UK, 1998)

_____*War and Our World.* (Vintage, London, 2001)

Krishna, Ashok. *Indian Armed Forces: Fifty Years of War and Peace.* (Lancers, New Delhi, 1998)

Lehl, Maj Gen Lachhman Singh. *Victory in Bangladesh.* (Natraj Publishers, Dehra Dun, 1981/ 2005)

Ed. Daniel Marstein and Carter Malkesian. *Counter Insurgency in Modern Warfare.* (Osprey Publishing Limited, Oxford, UK, 2008)

Ed. Charlas C Moskos and Frank R Wood. *Military: More than Just a Job.* (Brasseys, USA, 1988)

Nibedon, Nirmal. *Mizoram: The Dagger Brigade.* (Lancers, New Delhi, 2nd Edition, 1983)

Niazi, Lt Gen AAK. *The Betrayal of East Pakistan.* (Manohar Publishers, Delhi, 1988)

Newman, Maj Gen Aubrey 'Red'. *What are Generals Made Of.* (Presidio Press, USA, 1987)

Proudfoot, CL. *Flash of the Kukhri: History of 3 Gorkha Rifles, 1947 to 1980.* (Vision Books, New Delhi, 1984)

Palit, Maj Gen DK. *War in the High Himalayas: The Indian Army in Crisis.* (Lancers, New Delhi, 1991)

_____ . *Memories and Musings, Vol 2.* (Palit and Palit, New Delhi, 2004)

_____ . *The Lightning Campaign.* (Lancers, New Delhi, 1998)

Phillips, Brig Gen Thomas R. *Roots of Strategy.* (Natraj Publishers, Dehra Dun, 2003)

Puryear Jr, Edgar F. *Marine Corps Generalship.* (National Defence University Press, Washington DC, 2009)

Qureshi, Maj Gen Hakeem Arshad. *The 1971 Indo-Pak War: A Soldier's Narrative.* (Oxford University Press, Karachi, 3rd impression, 2004)

Ramani, Shrikant Y. *Op Vijay: The Ultimate Solution.* (Broadway Book Centre, Panjim, 2008)

Rao, Gen KV Krishna Rao. *In the Service of the Nation.* (Penguin, New Delhi, 2001)

_____ . *Prepare or Perish: a Study of National Security.* (Lancers, New Delhi, 1991)

Rehman, Hamoodar. *Report on Commission of Inquiry into the 1971 War.* (Vanguard Books, Lahore)

Ricks, Thomas. *The Generals: American Military Command from World War 2 to Today.* (Penguin, New York, 2012)

_____ . *the Gamble: General Patraeus and the Untold Story of the American Surge in Iraq, 2006-2008.* Allen Lane, UK, 2009.

Selbourne, David. *The Principle of Duty.* (Sinclair-Stevenson, UK, 1995)

Salik, Sadiq. *Witness to Surrender.* (Lancers, New Delhi, 1988)

Sodhi, Brig R S. *Operation Windfall: Emergence of Bangladesh.* (Allied Publishers, New Delhi, 1980)

Siddiqi, Brig AR. *East Pakistan: The Endgame.* (Oxford University Press, Karachi, 2nd Impression, 2005)

Singh, Brig Jagdev. *Dismemberment of Pakistan: 1971 Indo-Pak War.* (Lancers, New Delhi, 1988)

Singh, Jaswant. *Defending India.* (Macmillan India, Chennai, 1999)

Singh, Maj Gen VK. *Leadership in the Indian Army.* (Sage Publishers, Delhi, 5th Printing, 2008)

_____ . *History of the Corps of Signals, Vol 3 (unpublished)*

Singh, Maj Gen Sukhwant. *Defence of the Western Borders.* (Lancers, New Delhi, 1998)

_____ . *Liberation of Bangladesh.* (Lancers, New Delhi, 1998)

Singh, Maj Gen Joginder. *Behind the Scenes: An Analysis of India's Military Operations from 1947 to 1971.* (Lancers, New Delhi, 1993)

Singh, Lt Gen Depinder. *Field Marshal Sam Manekshaw: Soldiering with Dignity.* (Natraj Publishers, Dehra Dun, 2003)

Sinha, Brig (Dr) SP Sinha. *50 Years of Insurgency in the North East and India's Response.* (Lancers, New Delhi, 2007)

Smith, Gen Sir Rupert. *The Utility of Force: The Art of War in the Modern World.* (Penguin, UK, 2006)

Sood, Maj Gen Shubhi. *Leadership: Field Marshal Sam Manekshaw.* (SDS Publishers, New Delhi, 2006)

Toffler, Alvin and Heidi. *War and Anti-War.* (Warner, UK, 1994)

Verghese, BG. *Insurgency, Governance and Development.* (Konark Publishers, New Delhi, 2nd Revised Edition, 2004)

Verma, Maj Gen AK. *The Bridge on the River Meghna.* (KW Publishers, New Delhi, 2009)

Weddle, Peter. *Generalship: HR Leadership in a Time of War.* (Weddle's, USA, 2003)

Woodward, Bob. *Obama's Wars.* (Simon and Schuster, UK, 2010)

Zais, Major Mitchell M. *Generalship and the Art of Senior Command: Historical and Scientific Perspective.* (Thesis presented to the Command and General Staff College, Fort Leavenworth, Kansas, 1985)

http://www.bharat-rakshak.com/LAND-FORCE/army/history/1971war/PDF/1971

Articles and Documents

Foreword written by Brig AK Sanyal on 28 Feb 98 to 'Claims of Battle Honours of 3 GR during World War 2.

'Chinese Offensive Threat on Sikkim in Aug/ Sep 1965'. Brig K Lakhpat Singh (unpublished).

Copies of Newspaper cuttings of Nathula Incident given by Brig Rai Singh.

Article on the standoff at Sikkim in the Defence and Security Alert, Nov 2010 by Maj Gen VK Singh.

Detailed Report on the Nathula Incident prepared for the Regimental History of the Grenadier Regiment (unpublished) along with script of talk given to the Grenadier Regiment by Lt Col Attar Singh.

Letter written by Maj OP Kaushik, BM, 61 Mountain Brigade to Brig SDS Yadava.

Excerpt of speech given by Lt Gen Sagat Singh to officers on the Corps of Signals Day at Tezpur (courtesy Maj Gen VK Singh).

'Victory has Many Fathers, Defeat is an Orphan.' Anonymous article obtained from the Internet.

'The Babar of Tribal Lashkar. Interview in the Defence Journal by AH Amin of Maj Gen (retd) Naseerullah Khan Babar.

'The Nathula Incident. When Chinese were Given a Bloody Nose.' Maj Gen Sheru Thapliyal. Article 1855 published by The Centre for Land Warfare Studies (CLAWS) ON 27 May 2011.

Article on the operations conducted by 5 PARA in Mizo Hills.

'Liberation of Bangladesh – 1971.' Unpublished article written by Brig JS Goraya.

'Remembering Sagat Singh 1918 to 2001.' PVS Jagan Mohan. Bharat Rakshak Monitor Vol 4, Nov-Dec 2001.

'Enduring Mysteries of the 1971 War'. Maj Gen Sheru Thapliyal

Article on Achievements of Gen VK Singh during 1971 War received from the COAS Secretariat, Army HQ.

'*A Failure in Generalship*'. Lt Col Paul Yingling. Armed forces Journal, May 2007.

'*Generalship*'. Barbara W Tuchman. Parameters, 1972 http://www.wired.com/dangerroom/2012/10tom-ricks/all/ Interview with Thomas Ricks.

'*Pillars of Generalship*'. Maj John Vermillion. Parameters, Summer 1987.

'*Army's Most Critical Deficiency: Good Generals*.' Lt Gen KK Khanna. Indian Defence Review, 28 Nov 2012.

'*Fuller on Generalship.*' Wing Commander Nigel B Baldwin. Air University Review, Sep-Oct 1981.

'*Generalship in War: The Principles of Operational Command.*' Maj Gregory C Gardner. Command and General Staff College, Fort Leavenworth, Kansas, May 1987.

http://www.rajputsamaj.net/history/bikaner/bikaner-thikana.htm

'*Henderson Brooks Report.*' Neville Maxwell. Economic and Political Weekly, Apr 14-20, 2001.

http://www.defence.pk/forces/miliitary.history/9201-battle-dhalai-bangladesh-campaign-1971-a.htm

'*Flash of the Kukhri at Atgram*'. Maj Gen Ian Cardozo. 5 GR Regimental Newsletter, Apr 2009.

'*Reminiscences of a Battalion Commander.*' Maj Gen AS Chopra. Anubhav Vol 2, Feb 2010.

Talk given to the students of BRAC University, Dacca. Col Nadir Ali

'*Lesson in Close Quarter Battle from Live Experiences.*' Lt Col S Mukherjee. Infantry, Mhow, 2005.

'*Humour and Courage.*' Lt Gen Himmeth Singh. Scholar Warrior (Journal of CLAWS). Spring 2013.

'*India as a Great Power: Know your Strength.*' Economist, 30 Mar 2013.

'Susan Sontag on Courage and Resistance.' Maria Popova. Brainpickings.

org

'*Most Memorable Event in War in the Life of Maj Gen SDS Yadava.*' Handwritten note by Maj Gen SDS Yadava describing the Battle of Dhalai.

'*The Drive to Dhaka - whose idea was it?* Praveen Swami. Hindu, 22 May 2007.

Note received from 3/3 GR on Gen Sagat Singh.

Extracts from the Battalion History of 9 GUARDS.

'*Reminiscences of Battle of Maynamati.*' Col Shyam Singh.

'*Proud Moments of RAJRIF at the Maynamati Ridge.* Lt Gen OP Kaushik.

'*In Search of Courage.*' John McCain. Fast Company, Issue 86, Sep 2004.

Script of Speech to the students of the US Naval Academy by US Secretary of Defence Robert M Gates. Apr 2010.

'*Quality of Command.*' Robert H Scales. Foreign Affairs, Nov/Dec 2012.

Personal Correspondence with the Author

Ali, Air Cmdre (retd) Mirza

Balagopal, Col (retd) RN

Bedi, Col (retd) Ravi

Chanda, Mrs Soma

DeSouza, Maj Gen (retd) Eustace

Dewan, Col (retd) Satish

Dhar, Brig (retd) UK

Jamwal, Maj Gen (retd) KJS

Kaul, Brig (retd) Rattan

Kler, Maj Gen (retd) HS

Mukherjee, Maj Gen (retd) Dipak

Panthaki, Brig (retd) Behram

Rajpal, Col (retd) Rohit

Sabharwal, Brig (retd) LM

Sihota, Lt Gen (retd) GS

Singh, Maj (retd) Avtar

Singh, Maj (retd) Chandrakant

Singh, Lt Gen (retd) Chiman

Singh, Col (retd) Gad

Singh, Shri Jeoraj

Singh, Col (retd) Shyam

Verma, Maj Gen (retd) AK

Interviews (Audio/Video)

Recordings of interviews by late Col Pyare Lal, Director USI. Done between 1973 to 1975

Lt Gen Sagat Singh

Air Cmdre (later Air Marshal) Chandan Singh

Brig (later Lt Gen) Himmeth Singh

Video Recording of Interview between Brig R N Mishra and Maj Chandrakant Singh

Interviews conducted by the Author

Anand, Lt Gen (retd) Raj on 16 Sep 2009 at New Delhi.

Bakshi, Brig (retd) MMS on 04 Nov 2009 at Vadodara.

Cardozo, Maj Gen (retd) Ian on 28 Sep 2009 at Dehra Dun.

Chatterjee, Col (retd) RR on 22 Sep 2009 at New Delhi.

Dhankar, Sub (retd) Lajja Ram on 01 Mar 2009 at Jaipur.

Gupta, Lt Gen (retd) Susheel on 24 Feb 2009 at Jaipur.

Karim, Maj Gen (retd) Afsir on 17 Sep 2009 at NOIDA.

BIBLIOGRAPHY

Kaushik, Lt Gen OP on 25 Sep 2009 at Dehra Dun.

Kaushik, Col (retd) Subhash on 03 Jan 2011 at Secunderabad.

Khandelwal, Shri TD on 01 Jun 2008 at Jaipur .

Lahiri, Lt Col (later Lt Gen) MK. Informal chat with Author and other officers at Lohitpur in 1970.

Lal, Shri Bajrang, IPS (retd) on 02 Jun 2009 at Jaipur.

Mehta, Lt Gen (retd) Shamsher on30 Sep 2009 at New Delhi.

Negi, Lt Gen (retd) GS on 27 Sep 2009 at Dehra Dun.

Rana, Hav (retd) Pas Bahadur on 29 Sep 2009 at Dehra Dun.

Ranawat, Brig (retd), RS On 16 Feb 2011 at Udaipur

Rao, Gen KV Krishna on 03 Jan 2011 at Secunderabad.

Rathore, Sanyogita & Meghna on 01 Jun 2009 at Jaipur.

Sabharwal, Brig (retd) LM 29 Sep 2009 at Dehra Dun.

Sabharwal, Maj Gen (retd) OP on 26 Sep 2009 at Dehra Dun.

Sihota, Lt Gen (retd) GS on 19 Sep 2009 at Chandigarh.

Sinh, Lt Col (retd) Duleep on 16 Mar 2009 at Rajpipla.

Sinh, Mrs Shanta Duleep on 16 Mar 2009 at Rajpipla.

Singh, Dr Ajit on 17 Jul 2010 at Jaipur

Singh, Lt Col (retd) Attar on 21 Sep 2009 at New Delhi

Singh, Mrs Damyanti on 01 Jun 2009 at Jaipur

Singh, Brig (retd) Jagmal on 29 May 2009 at Bikaner.

Singh, Shri Jeoraj on 29 May 2009 at Bikaner

Singh, Col (retd) Mohan 29 May 2009 near Ratangarh.

Singh, Col (retd) Nawal on 30 May 2009 at Bikaner.

Singh, Brig (retd) Rai 18 & 21 Sep 2009 at Gurgaon & New Delhi.

Singh, Col (retd) Ranvijay on 27 May 2009 at Jaipur.

Singh, Col (retd) Surajmal on 30 May 2009 at Bikaner

Singh, Maj Gen (retd) VK on 23 Sep 2009 at New Delhi

Verma, Maj Gen (retd) TS on 27 Sep 2009 at Dehra Dun.

Verma, Mrs TS on 27 Sep 2009 at Dehra Dun.

Village Relatives and folks on 01 Jan 2009 at Kusum Desar

Appendix A

ORGANISATION TREE
IV CORPS

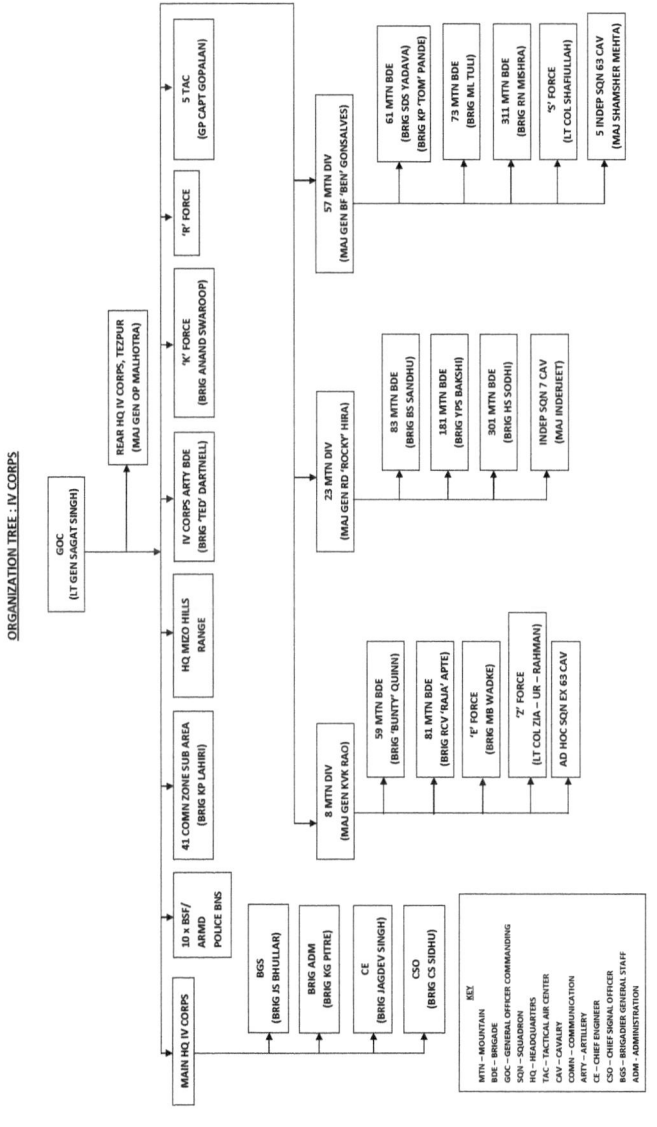

Appendix B

MAIN CHARACTERS AND UNITS MENTIONED IN CHAPTERS ON

4 CORPS OPERATIONS

INDIA

Army HQ

Gen SHFJ Manekshaw	COAS
Brig KK Singh	DMO
Brig IS Gill	DMO

Eastern Command

Lt Gen JS 'Jaggi' Aurora	Army Commander
Maj Gen JFR Jacob	Chief of Staff
Group Captain Chandan Singh	Deputed by Eastern Air Command to conduct heliborne operations for 4 Corps

4 Corps

Lt Gen Sagat Singh	GOC 4 Corps
Brig KG Pitre	Brig in Charge Administration
Brig GS Sidhu	Chief Signal Officer
Brig Jagdev Singh	Chief Engineer
Brig Ted Dartnell	Commander Corps Artillery
Brig Anand Swarup	Commander 'K' Force

8 Mountain Division

Maj Gen KV Krishna Rao	GOC 8 Mountain Division

Brig CA 'Bunty' Quinn	Commander 59 Mountain Brigade
Lt Col AB Harolikar	CO 4/5 GR
Lt Col Raghubir Singh	CO 9 Guards
	6 Rajput
Brig RV 'Raja' Apte	Commander 81 Mountain Brigade
	3 Punjab
	4 Kumaon
	10 Mahar
Brig MB Wadke	Cdr 'E' Force
Lt Col Rao	CO 5/5 GR

23 Mountain Division

Maj Gen RD 'Rocky' Hira	GOC 23 Mountain Division
Brig BS Sandhu	Commander 83 Mountain Brigade
Lt Col AS Chopra	CO 3 Dogra
	2 Rajput
	8 Bihar
Brig YPS Bakshi	Commander 181 Mountain Brigade
	14 Kumaon
	6 Jat
	9 Kumaon
Brig HS Sodhi	Commander 301 Mountain Brigade
Lt Col Sankaran Nair	CO 1/11 GR
Lt Col LM Sabharwal	CO 14 Jat

Lt Col TS Pall	CO 3 Kumaon
Maj Inderjeet	Indep Squadron 7 Cavalry

57 Mountain Division

Maj Gen BF 'Ben' Gonsalves	GOC 57 Mountain Division
Brig SDS Yadava	Commander 61 Mountain Brigade
Brig KP 'Tom' Pande	Commander 2 Artillery Brigade; later Commander 61 Mountain Brigade
Lt Col S Devesan/ Lt Col AS Brar	CO 7 Rajrif
Lt Col KS Dalal	CO 2 Jat
Lt Col SC Sardeshpande	CO 12 Kumaon
Brig ML Tuli	Commander 73 Mountain Brigade
Lt Col VS Channa	CO 14 Guards
	19 Rajrif
	19 Punjab
Brig RN Mishra	Commander 311 Mountain Brigade
Lt Col Himmeth Singh	CO 4 Guards
Lt Col PC Sawhney	CO 10 Bihar
Lt Col AK Verma	CO 18 Rajput
Maj Shamsher Mehta	Indep Squadron 63 Cavalry

101 Communication Zone Area

Maj Gen GS Gill & later Maj Gen Gandharv Nagra	GOC 101 Communication Zone

Brig HS Kler	Commander 95 Mountain Brigade
	167 Mountain Brigade
Brig Sant Singh	Commander FJ Sector
Lt Col GS Pannu	CO 2 Para

PAKISTAN

Lt Gen AAK 'Tiger' Niazi	Army Commander, Eastern Command, Pakistan & Chief Martial Law Administrator
Brig Baqar Siddiqui	COS
Brig Ataullah	Commander 97 (Independent) Pak Brigade
	2 SSG
	24 FF
	48 Baluch (?)
Brig Taskeen-ud-Deen	Commander 91 (adhoc) Brigade
Maj Gen Kazi Abdul Majid	GOC 14 Pak Division
Brig Sa'adullah Khan	Commander 27 Pak Brigade
	12 FF
	33 Baluch
	21 POK
Brig Salimullah	Commander 202 Pak Brigade
	31 Punjab
	12 POK (2 companies)
	91 Mujahid
Brig Iftikhar Rana	Commander 313 Pak Brigade

Lt Col Ahmed Mukhtar Khan	CO 30 FF
	22 Baluch
Maj Gen M Rahim Khan	GOC 39 Pak Division
Brig Aslam Niazi	Commander 53 Pak Brigade
	15 Punjab
Lt Col Nayeem	39 Baluch
Brig Atif	Commander 117 Pak Brigade
Lt Col Akbar Baig	CO 25 FF
Lt Col Ashfaq Syed	CO 23 Punjab

BANGLADESH

Col MAG Osmani	C-in-C Bangladesh Armed Forces
Maj Khalid Musharraf	CO 4 EBR
Lt Col KM Shafiullah	CO 2 EBR later Sierra Force
Lt Col Zia-ur-Rahman	CO 8 EBR later of 1 EB Brigade

Note :- Only those personalities and organisations which have been mentioned in the chapters have been included for ease of understanding.

Index

Symbols

1 Armoured Division 49, 70

1 Assam Rifles 87

1 Para 55, 56, 57, 60, 61, 64, 65

2/3 GR xxvi, 33, 37, 39, 76, 99, 234, 236, 238

2 Corps 68, 116, 118, 126, 127, 160

2 Grenadiers 80, 81, 83

2 Para 2, 8, 46, 50, 51, 52, 55, 56, 57, 61, 64, 225, 226, 284

2 Rajput 159, 205, 282

2 Sikh LI 52, 55, 58, 59, 61, 63, 64, 65

3/3 GR viii, 31, 36, 37, 38, 40, 99, 275

3 Dogra 159, 282

3 Punjab 167, 216, 222, 282

4/5 GR xxi, 155, 156, 184, 185, 192, 195, 197, 202, 282

4 Guards 3, 8, 173, 174, 175, 176, 199, 200, 206, 210, 211, 221, 283

4 Kumaon 167, 282

7/11 GR 84

7 Cavalry 53, 58, 63, 161, 181, 283

8 Cavalry 53, 58

8 Mountain Division 5, 111, 116, 120, 124, 140, 163, 164, 166, 183, 192, 193, 194, 228, 281

9 Guards 128, 155, 156, 183, 185, 208, 282

9 Infantry Division 116

10 Bihar 173, 174, 175, 176, 177, 189, 200, 218, 225, 283

10 Mahar 167, 282

11 Corps 71, 73, 252, 254

12 Kumaon 144, 173, 198, 206, 217, 220, 283

17 Assam Rifles 74, 75

17 Infantry Division 49

17 Mountain Division 49, 50, 73, 129

17 Para Field Regiment 70

18 Rajput 81, 83, 173, 174, 175, 177, 200, 208, 210, 216, 218, 283

19 Rajrif 172, 173, 174, 223, 283

20 Rajput 49, 54

23 Mountain Division 2, 116, 125, 126, 158, 159, 164, 282

27 Mountain Division 74, 75

57 Mountain Division 2, 3, 5, 124, 139, 140, 160, 163, 283

61 Mountain Brigade 140, 163, 273

63 Brigade 54, 55, 57, 61, 65, 84

311 Brigade 168, 172, 173, 175, 199, 206, 217, 218, 223

A

AAK Niazi ix, 4, 6, 7, 8, 9, 10, 11, 106, 107, 108, 109, 110, 111, 112, 123, 134, 135, 136, 141, 154, 158, 159, 160, 162, 164, 167, 179, 180, 182, 184, 186, 187, 188, 191, 193, 203, 204, 212, 222, 224, 225, 226, 230, 232, 233, 270, 284, 285

Abhimanyu Vohra 34, 37

Air Marshal Chandan Singh ix, xix, 3, 6, 138, 193, 194, 195, 196, 197, 206, 207, 209, 210, 211, 218, 219, 220, 221, 276, 281

Akhaura ix, 122, 126, 129, 139, 140, 163, 167, 168, 171, 173, 174, 175, 176, 177, 186, 189, 190, 192, 199, 201

Ashuganj 122, 132, 171, 192, 193, 199, 200, 208, 209, 210, 216, 218

Assonara 55, 58, 59

Atgram- Zakigunj Bulge 155

Awami League 100, 103, 227

B

Banastirim River 65

Barak 85, 121, 155

Battle of Akhaura ix, 140, 168, 173, 177, 192

Battle of Dhalai viii, xxi, 137, 147, 153, 154, 258, 275

Battle of Gangasagar 173

  Naik Albert Ekka- was awarded PVC in this battle 173

Belonia Bulge 111, 132, 158, 159, 160, 162, 164, 179, 188

Bicholim 53, 55, 56, 60

Bikaner Ganga Risala 17, 18, 19, 20, 26

Bikaner State Forces 11, 17, 19, 22, 29

Bikaner Ganga Risala 17

B K Nehru ix, 90

BP Chaliha 86

Brahmanbaria 111, 122, 123, 132, 163, 164, 168, 171, 172, 173, 184, 199, 200, 206, 207, 208, 209, 210, 216, 218, 225, 257

Brigadier JW Hinchcliffe 24

Brigadier Raja Apte 1

Brig GS Sidhu 5, 221, 281

Brig Jagdev Singh 2, 3, 4, 121, 123, 127, 128, 132, 135, 139, 173, 181, 186, 187, 192, 207, 216, 227, 228, 230, 231, 272, 281

Brig Jagmal Singh xx, 31, 242

Brig KG Pitre 5, 124, 281

Brig PK Lahiri 124

Brig R N Mishra ix, 140, 173, 174, 176, 177, 199, 200, 207, 208, 210, 223, 276, 283

INDEX

C

Candepar River 57

Chandpur 112, 122, 123, 126, 158, 159, 160, 164, 165, 179, 180, 181, 187, 192, 203, 204, 205, 206, 212, 215, 217, 219

Changgu 73, 74, 77

Chittagong Hill Tracts 87, 94, 104, 130, 166, 227

Chogyal ix, 76, 78

Chola Pass 74

Chumbi Valley 82

Col Pyare Lal xix, 6, 8, 103, 126, 128, 129, 130, 135, 137, 139, 193, 276

Comilla 1, 5, 6, 109, 111, 112, 123, 126, 129, 139, 164, 166, 171, 179, 180, 181, 187, 189, 192, 197, 198, 201, 205, 219, 221, 231, 232, 234

D

Damyanti xix, 243, 245, 246, 247, 248, 277

Daudkhandi 121, 122, 126, 163, 186, 189, 192, 193, 198, 205, 206, 217, 219, 220, 224, 227

Dhalai viii, ix, xxi, 137, 138, 139, 140, 141, 142, 143, 144, 147, 148, 149, 150, 151, 152, 153, 154, 155, 164, 169, 183, 200, 213, 258, 261, 275

Dharmanagar 120, 124, 125, 163

Digvijay 31, 40, 76, 99, 234, 236, 238, 243, 245, 246

Dodamarg 55, 56, 58, 62

E

East Pakistan Civil Armed Force xxiv, 108

F

Fort Aguada 63

G

General KV Krishna Rao ix, xx, 5, 40, 113, 116, 117, 118, 133, 137, 138, 155, 160, 165, 167, 168, 178, 183, 184, 185, 192, 193, 194, 195, 202, 203, 222, 227, 228, 231, 271, 281

General Yahya Khan 100, 105, 127, 212

Gen Hari Singh Bhati 20

Gen PN Thapar 54

Gen SHFJ Manekshaw xv, 8, 36, 70, 71, 74, 79, 82, 84, 87, 89, 90, 93, 102, 112, 113, 114, 115, 116, 117, 118, 119, 126, 137, 166, 232, 234, 237, 251, 252, 272, 281

Giagong Plateau 75

Governor BK Nehru ix, 90, 91

H

Hoor Agitation 20

HQ 33 Corps 116

I

IV Corps 97, 124, 163, 191, 279

J

Jaisalmer Risala 26
  Indian Camel Corps 26
Jane Himmeth Singh xix
Jelep La 74, 75, 252
John Keegan 257

K

Kailashahar 167, 192, 193, 194, 195, 222
Kaladan 85
Kamalpur 137, 139, 140, 142, 146, 148, 149, 151
Kapna Pahar 184, 185, 186
Karni Mata 15
Kulwant Singh Pannu 2, 57, 284
Kushiyara River 156, 167, 185, 216
Kusumdesar viii, 13, 16, 243
Kyangnosla 74

L

Laldenga 86, 87, 91, 94
Lalmai 1, 2, 104, 121, 122, 123, 134, 164, 171, 179, 180, 181, 198, 204, 205, 206, 217, 219, 220
Lalmai Hills 1, 2, 134, 180
Lieutenant General HK Sibal 97
LM Sabharwal xxi, 197, 201, 219, 224, 234, 235, 282

Lt Col Duleep Sinh 30, 71
Lt Gen AAK Niazi ix, 106, 233
Lt Gen BM Kaul 45, 114, 256
Lt Gen Himmeth Singh xix, 8, 173, 174, 176, 199, 207, 211, 223, 274, 276, 283
Lt Gen HK Sibal 23, 97
Lt Gen JN Chaudhury 39, 46
Lt Gen JS Aurora xv, xx, 4, 6, 7, 8, 9, 10, 40, 79, 102, 113, 114, 116, 117, 118, 119, 124, 125, 126, 130, 131, 142, 154, 161, 162, 164, 175, 180, 181, 198, 199, 200, 201, 202, 226, 232, 237, 238, 281
Lt Gen K Chiman Singh xx, 31, 41, 261
Lt Gen KM Cariappa 30
Lt Gen ML Thapan 116
Lt Gen OP Kaushik 72, 142, 154, 189, 204, 275
Lt Gen PG Kamath xxii
Lt Gen PP Kumaramanglam xii, 42, 46
Lt Gen Sagat Singh i, iii, viii, xi, xii, xiii, xiv, xv, xvi, xvii, xix, xx, xxi, 1, 2, 3, 4, 5, 6, 7, 8, 10, 11, 16, 17, 18, 19, 20, 21, 22, 23, 24, 25, 26, 27, 28, 29, 30, 31, 32, 33, 34, 35, 36, 37, 39, 40, 41, 42, 43, 45, 46, 48, 49, 50, 51, 52, 53, 54, 55, 56, 57, 58, 59, 60, 61, 62, 63, 64, 65, 66, 67, 68, 69, 70, 71, 72, 73, 74, 75, 76, 77, 79, 80, 81, 82, 83, 84, 90, 91, 92, 93, 94, 97, 98, 99, 100, 103, 105, 110, 115, 116,

Index

117, 118, 119, 120, 124, 125, 126, 127, 128, 129, 130, 131, 132, 133, 135, 136, 137, 139, 142, 143, 146, 147, 148, 149, 150, 151, 152, 153, 154, 158, 159, 160, 161, 162, 163, 164, 165, 166, 167, 168, 171, 172, 173, 175, 177, 178, 179, 180, 181, 182, 183, 184, 186, 187, 188, 189, 190, 191, 192, 193, 194, 195, 198, 199, 200, 201, 202, 203, 204, 205, 206, 208, 209, 210, 212, 213, 215, 216, 217, 218, 219, 220, 221, 222, 223, 224, 225, 226, 227, 228, 229, 230, 231, 232, 234, 235, 236, 237, 238, 239, 240, 241, 242, 243, 245, 246, 247, 248, 249, 251, 252, 253, 254, 255, 256, 257, 258, 260, 261, 264, 266, 267, 273, 275, 276, 281

Lt Gen Sir Edward Quinan 20

Lt Gen Sir Harold Briggs 88

Lt Gen TN Raina 68, 116

Lungleh 85, 87

Lungthu Ridge 74

Lushai Hills 86

M

Maharaja Sadul Singh 24, 25, 26, 29, 30

Maj Ashok Tara 230

Maj Gen Gandharv Nagra ix, 117, 233, 283

Maj Gen MM Khanna 50

Maj Gen RN Batra 62

Maj Gen Tara Singh Bal 30

Maj Gen Tirath Singh Verma xx, 33

Maj Gen VK Singh xxi, 54, 77, 84, 221, 273

Maj Kaptan Singh Rana 37

Major Bhag Singh 20

Major General Afsir Karim 46

Major General BF 'Ben' Gonsalves ix, 5, 138, 139, 141, 145, 147, 165, 178, 207, 283

Major General Hakeem Qureshi 101

Major General Shaukat Riza 111

Malayan Races Liberation Army 88

Mandovi River 59, 64

Maynamati 1, 2, 123, 163, 164, 165, 179, 180, 186, 187, 188, 189, 192, 197, 198, 259, 275

McGregor Medal 99

McMahon Line 97

Meghna River xv, 3, 118, 121, 126, 127, 160, 220

Mishmi Tribes 98

Mizo Hills ix, 84, 85, 87, 89, 90, 91, 92, 97, 127, 130, 252, 273

Mukti Bahini xxv, 10, 101, 102, 103, 107, 108, 122, 124, 128, 131, 132, 134, 136, 137, 139, 153, 159, 217, 226, 228, 230, 231

Mymensingh 104, 109, 111, 112, 117, 122, 224

N

Nathu La ix, 75, 76, 77, 79, 80, 81, 82, 83, 84

NATO Alliance 49

North Sikkim 74, 75

O

OP JERICHO 86

OP VIJAY 52

P

Para Brigade xii, xiii, 42, 43, 45, 46, 47, 49, 50, 51, 53, 54, 58, 61, 62, 64, 65, 66, 67, 68, 70, 236, 248

Pernem - Mapuca Road 59

Pirkanthi Day 35

R

Ram Gopal Saraf 243

Ram Manohar Lohia 44

Ranawat Ransher Singh xxi, 128, 156, 157, 158, 185, 186, 277

Ranvijay xix, 30, 32, 37, 40, 42, 43, 77, 99, 238, 246, 248, 277

Razakars xxvi, 11, 108, 134, 141, 159, 226

S

Salasar 243

Sanquelim 55, 56

Sawantwadi 51, 52, 54, 55

Sebula 79, 80

Sheikh Mujib-ur-Rahman 100

Sherathang 81

Silchar 85, 89, 129, 130

Siliguri corridor xiii

Sitakund Range 222

Subedar Lajja Ram Dhankar 241

Surma River 155

Sylhet xxi, 1, 5, 104, 109, 111, 118, 121, 122, 123, 126, 127, 132, 137, 163, 166, 167, 168, 171, 183, 184, 186, 193, 194, 195, 196, 197, 199, 202, 203, 204, 212, 216, 222, 227, 259

T

Thegu Ridge 74

THE LIBERATION OF GOA 44

Titas River 174

Tom Pande ix, 138, 140, 147, 148, 170

U

Usgao Bridge 53, 57

V

Vairangte 91

Y

Yatung 83

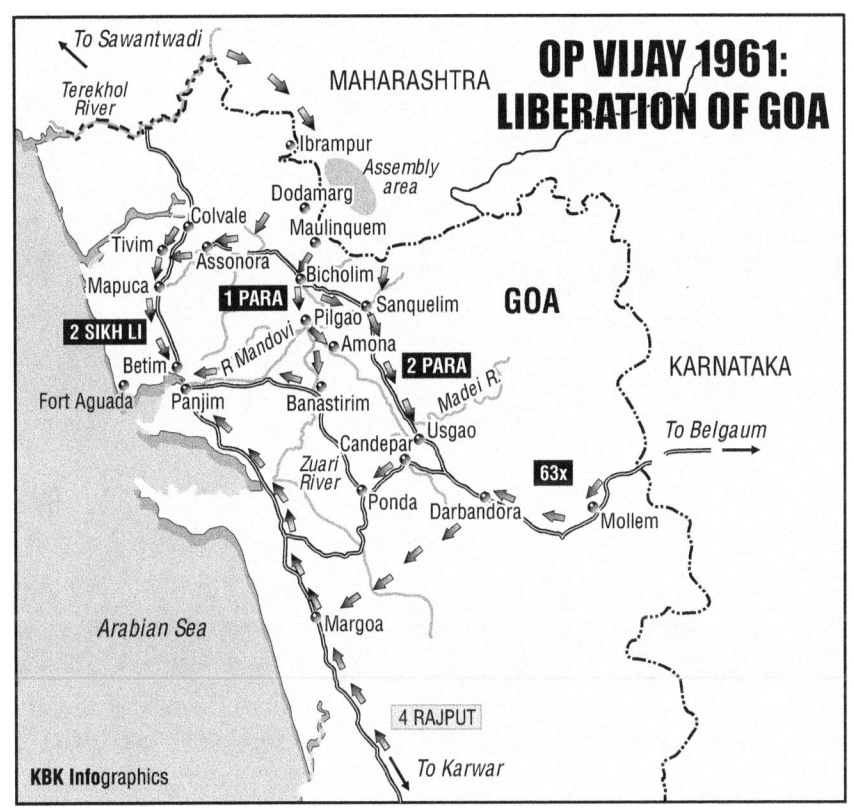

Map 1

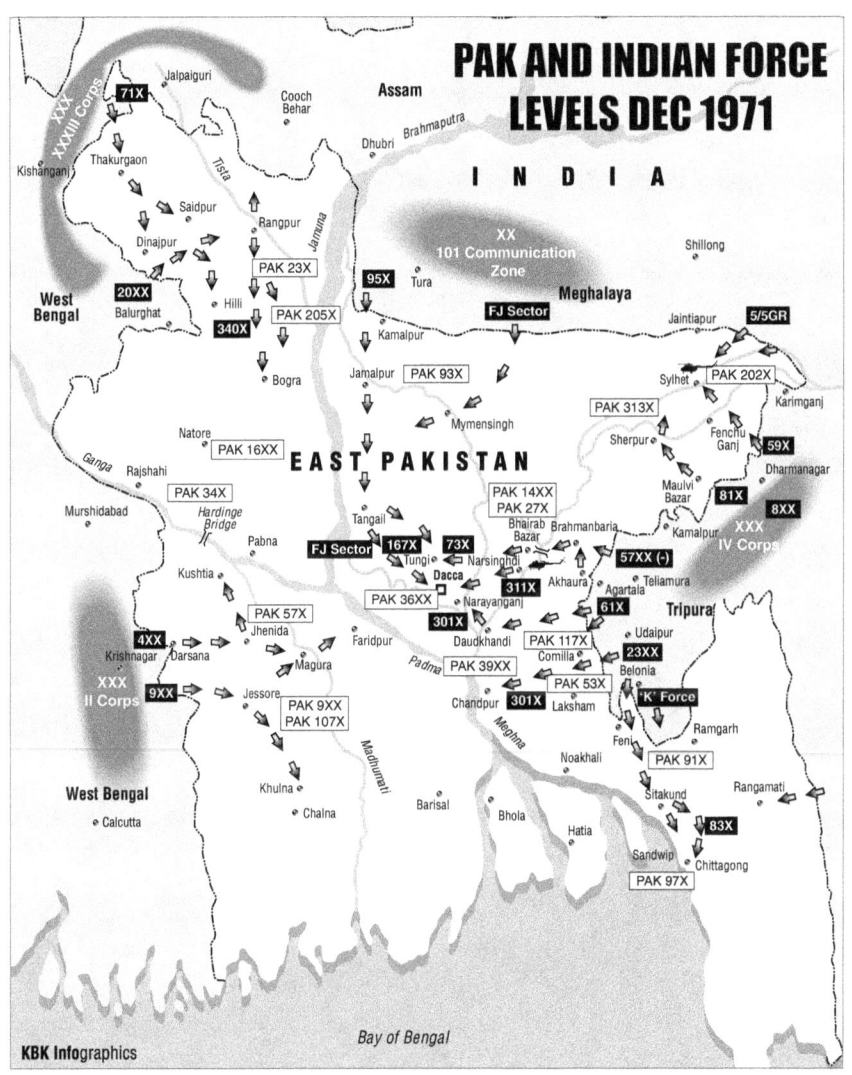

Map 2

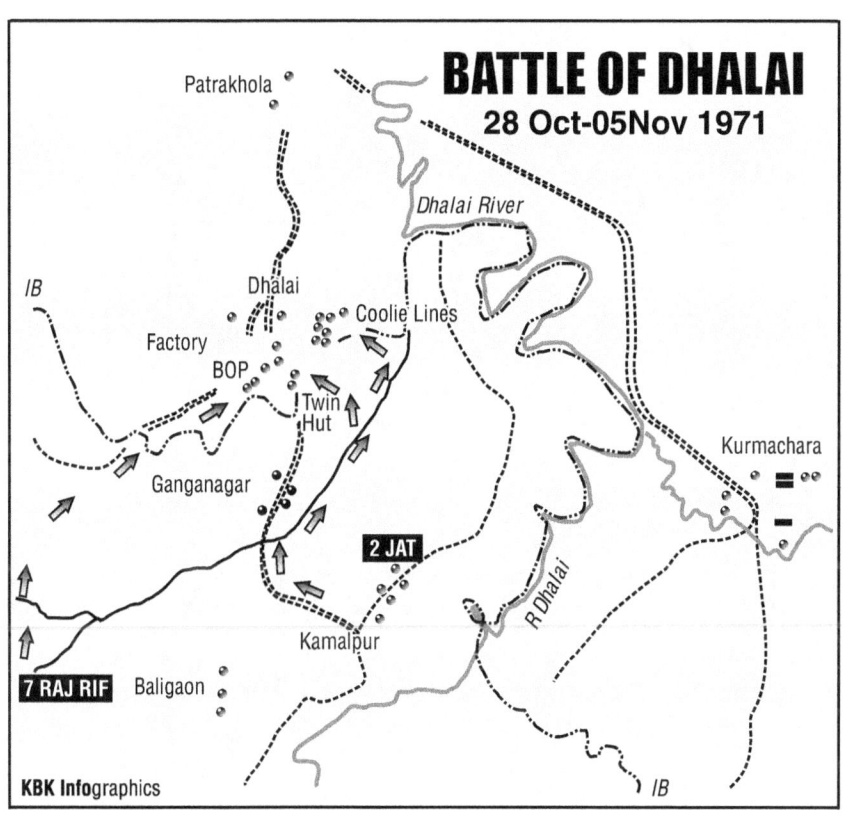

Map 3

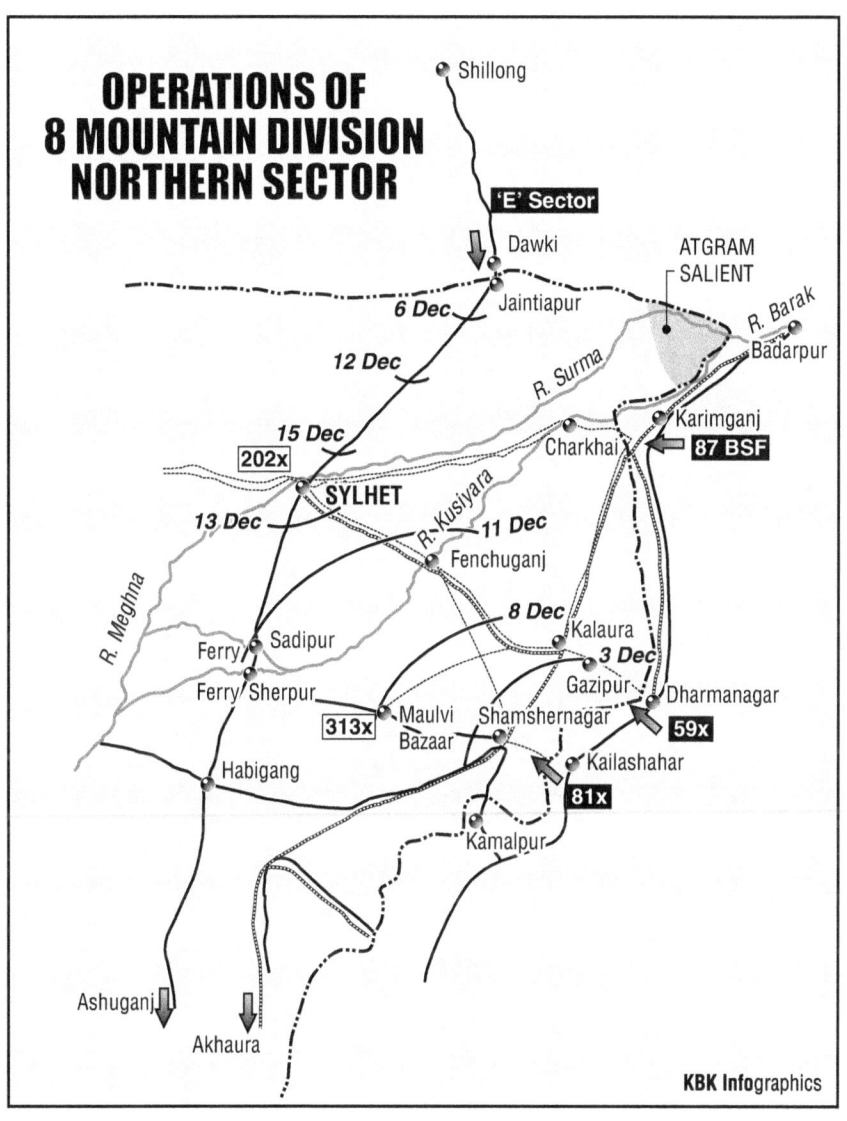

Map 4

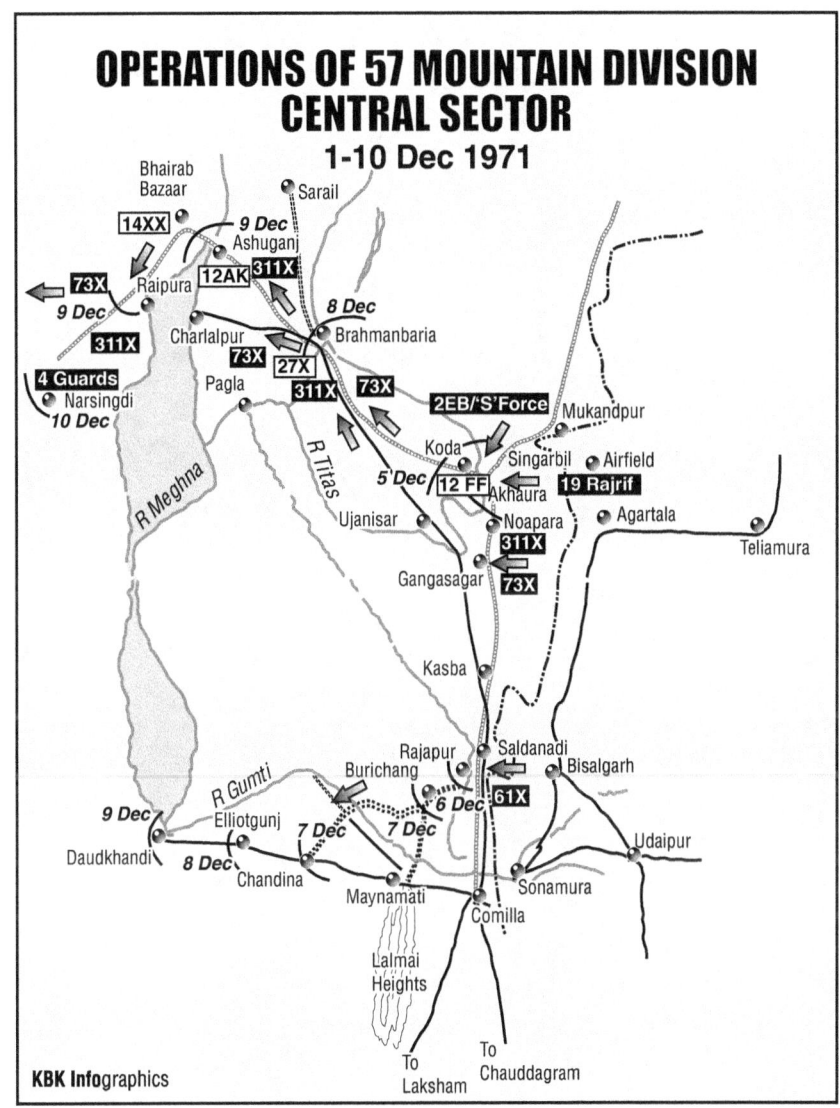

Map 5

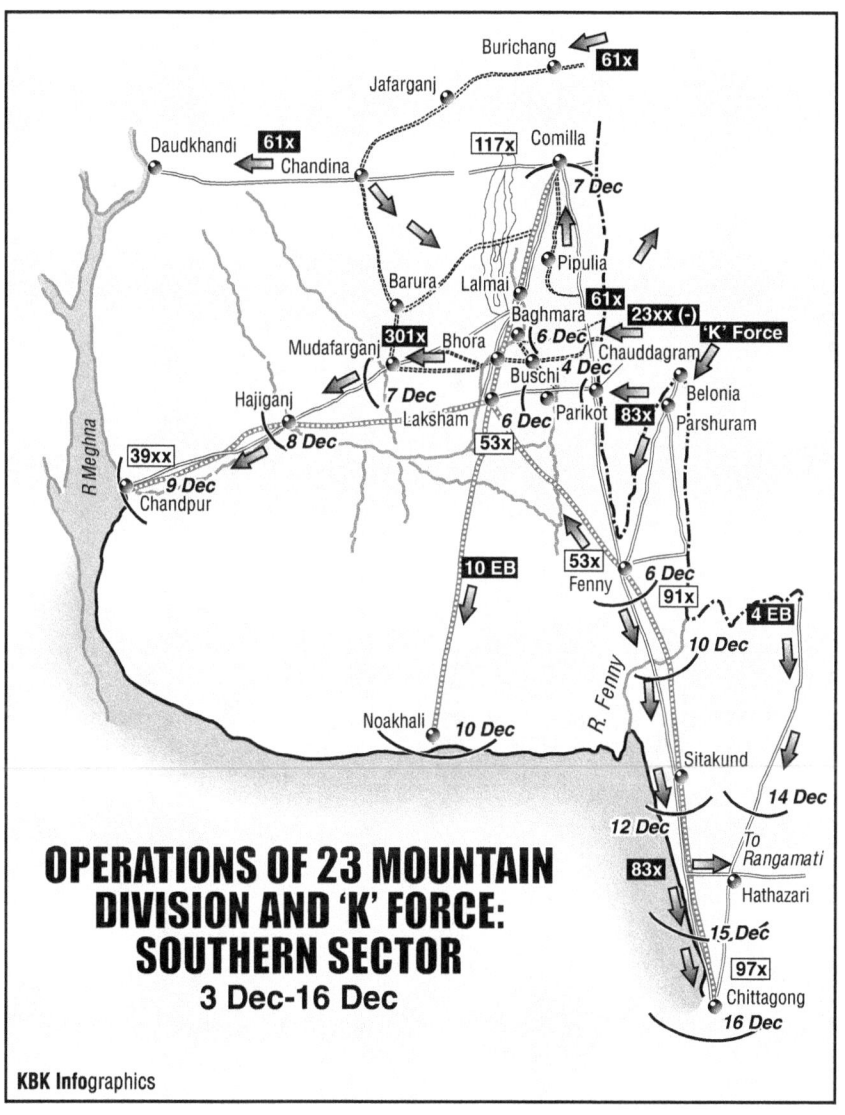

Map 6

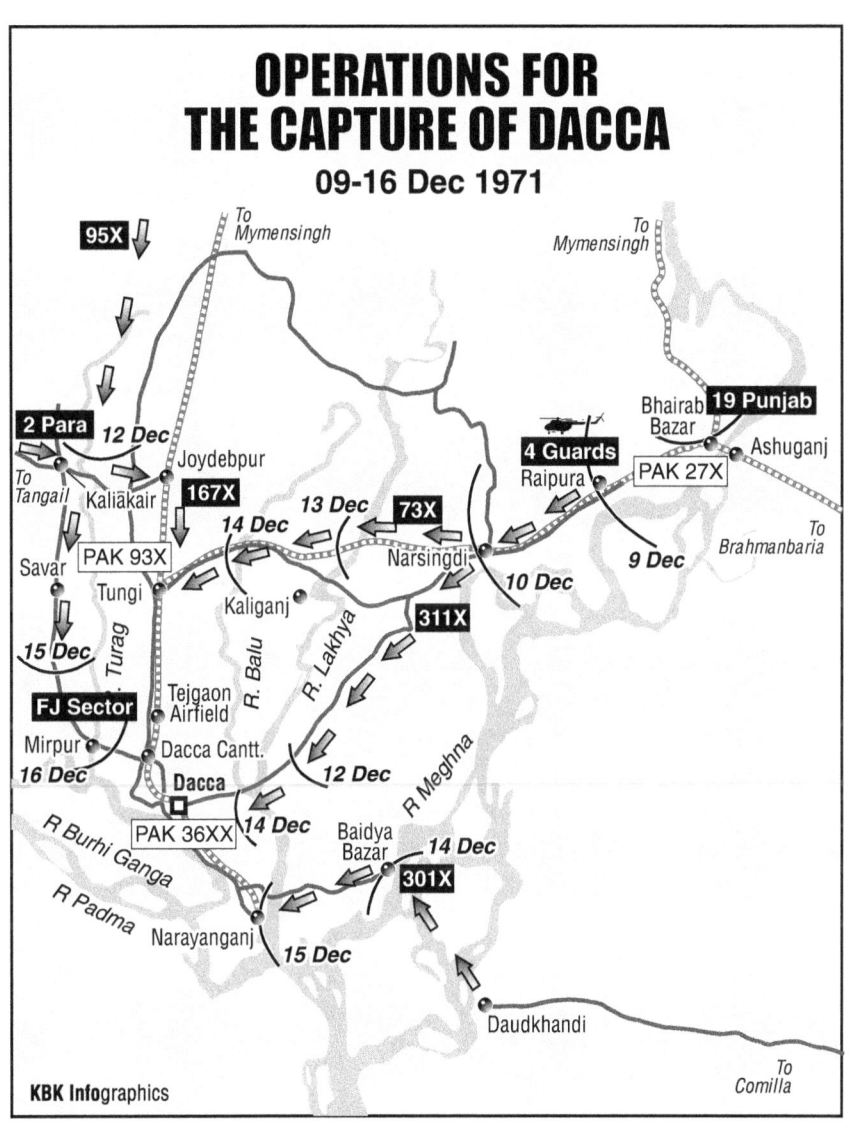

Map 7

www.ingramcontent.com/pod-product-compliance
Lightning Source LLC
Chambersburg PA
CBHW050334230426
43663CB00010B/1858